W9-AWW-148

HAMLET

WILLIAM SHAKESPEARE

Shakespeare's text

on the left;

a modern rendering

on the right.

Prestwick House

P.O. Box 658 • Clayton, DE 19938
Tel: 1.800.932.4593
Web site: www.prestwickhouse.com

ISBN 978-1-58049-518-9

Copyright ©2003 by Prestwick House, Inc.

Revised, 2011

2

Table of Contents

Dramatis Personae

Claudius, King of Denmark
Hamlet, son to the late King, and nephew to Claudius
Polonius, Lord Chamberlain, advisor to Claudius
Horatio, friend of Hamlet
Laertes, son of Polonius
Voltimand, courtier
Cornelius, courtier
Rosencrantz, courtier
Guildenstern, courtier
Osric, courtier
A Gentleman, courtier
A Priest
Marcellus, an officer
Bernardo, an officer
Francisco, a soldier
Reynaldo, servant to Polonius
Players
Two Clowns, gravediggers
Fortinbras, Prince of Norway
A Norwegian Captain.
English Ambassadors
Getrude, Queen of Denmark, mother of Hamlet
Ophelia, daughter of Polonius
Ghost of Hamlet's Father

Lords, Ladies, Officers, Soldiers, Sailors, Messengers, Attendants

ACT I

Scene 1

Elsinore. A platform before the Castle.

[Enter two Sentinels first, Francisco, who paces up and down at his post; then Bernardo, who approaches him.]

BERNARDO: Who's there?

FRANCISCO: Nay, answer me. Stand and unfold yourself.

BERNARDO: Long live the King!

FRANCISCO: Bernardo?

5 BERNARDO: He.

FRANCISCO: You come most carefully upon your hour.

BERNARDO: 'Tis now struck twelve. Get thee to bed, Francisco.

FRANCISCO: For this relief much thanks. 'Tis bitter cold,
    And I am sick at heart.

10 BERNARDO: Have you had quiet guard?

FRANCISCO: Not a mouse stirring.

ACT I

Scene 1

Elsinore. A platform before the castle.

[Two sentinels meet. Francisco stands guard. Benardo enters]

BERNARDO: *Who's there?*

FRANCISCO: *No, you answer me! Stop and show yourself!*

BERNARDO: *Long live the King!*

FRANCISCO: *Bernardo?*

BERNARDO: *Yes!*

FRANCISCO: *You're right on time.*

BERNARDO: *It has just turned twelve. Go to bed, Francisco!*

FRANCISCO: *Thank you for relieving me. It is bitter cold, and I am in low spirits.*

BERNARDO: *Has everything been quiet tonight?*

FRANCISCO: *Not even a mouse has stirred.*

BERNARDO: Well, good night.
    If you do meet Horatio and Marcellus,
    The rivals of my watch, bid them make haste.

15 FRANCISCO: I think I hear them. Stand, ho! Who is there?

[Enter Horatio and Marcellus.]

HORATIO: Friends to this ground.

MARCELLUS: And liegemen to the Dane.

FRANCISCO: Give you good night.

MARCELLUS: O, farewell, honest soldier.
20   Who hath relieved you?

FRANCISCO: Bernardo hath my place.
    Give you good night.   *[Exit.]*

MARCELLUS: Holla, Bernardo!

BERNARDO: Say,
25   What, is Horatio there?

HORATIO: A piece of him.

BERNARDO: Welcome, Horatio. Welcome, good Marcellus.

MARCELLUS: What, has this thing appear'd again to-night?

BERNARDO: I have seen nothing.

30 MARCELLUS: Horatio says 'tis but our fantasy,
    And will not let belief take hold of him
    Touching this dreaded sight, twice seen of us.
    Therefore I have entreated him along,
    With us to watch the minutes of this night,

BERNARDO: *Well, good night. If you meet Horatio and Marcellus, my fellow guardsmen, tell them to hurry.*

FRANCISCO: *I think I hear them. Stop! Who is there?*

[Horatio and Marcellus enter]

HORATIO: *Friends of this castle.*

MARCELLUS: *And loyal subjects of the King of Denmark.*

FRANCISCO: *May God give you a good night.*

MARCELLUS: *Goodbye, honest soldier. Who has relieved you?*

FRANCISCO: *Bernardo has taken my place. I wish you a good night.*
                              [Francisco exits]

MARCELLUS: *Hello, Bernardo!*

BERNARDO: *Is Horatio here?*

HORATIO: [Stretching out his hand] *Part of him.*

BERNARDO: *Welcome, Horatio. Welcome, good Marcellus.*

MARCELLUS: *Has this thing appeared again tonight?*

BERNARDO: *I haven't seen anything.*

MARCELLUS: *Horatio says it is only our imagination, and he will not believe in this dreadful sight that we have seen twice. Therefore, I have asked him to join us on our watch tonight, so that, if this apparition comes again, he will verify what we have seen and speak to it.*

35   That if again this apparition come
    He may approve our eyes and speak to it.

HORATIO: Tush, tush, 'twill not appear.

BERNARDO: Sit down awhile,
    And let us once again assail your ears,
40   That are so fortified against our story,
    What we two nights have seen.

HORATIO: Well, sit we down,
    And let us hear Bernardo speak of this.

BERNARDO: Last night of all,
45   When yond same star that's westward from the pole
    Had made his course to illume that part of heaven
    Where now it burns, Marcellus and myself,
    The bell then beating one—

[Enter Ghost]

MARCELLUS: Peace! break thee off! Look where it comes again!

50 BERNARDO: In the same figure, like the King that's dead.

MARCELLUS: Thou art a scholar; speak to it, Horatio.

BERNARDO: Looks it not like the King? Mark it, Horatio.

HORATIO: Most like. It harrows me with fear and wonder.

BERNARDO: It would be spoke to.

55 MARCELLUS: Question it, Horatio.

HORATIO: What art thou that usurp'st this time of night,
    Together with that fair and warlike form
    In which the majesty of buried Denmark
    Did sometimes march? By heaven, I charge thee, speak!

10

HORATIO: *Enough of that. It will not appear.*

BERNARDO: *Sit down for a moment and allow us once again to explain to you what we have seen these last two nights, even though you don't believe it.*

HORATIO: *Well, let's sit down and hear Bernardo talk about this.*

BERNARDO: *Last night, when the star that's west of the North star had moved to that part of the sky where it now shines, Marcellus and myself—the bell was just striking one—*

[A Ghost enters]

MARCELLUS: *Silence! Be quiet! Look! Here it comes again!*

BERNARDO: *It looks like the dead King.*

MARCELLUS: *You are a scholar; speak to it, Horatio!*

BERNARDO: *Does it not look like the King? Look, Horatio!*

HORATIO: *Very much so. It fills me with fear and amazement.*

BERNARDO: *It wants to be addressed.*

MARCELLUS: *Question it, Horatio!*

HORATIO: [To Ghost] *What are you, that steals this time of night, displaying that handsome armor the late King of Denmark used to wear? By heaven, I command you, speak!*

60   **MARCELLUS:** It is offended.

BERNARDO: See, it stalks away!

HORATIO: Stay! speak, speak! I charge thee, speak!
                                [Exit Ghost.]

MARCELLUS: 'Tis gone, and will not answer.

BERNARDO: How now, Horatio? You tremble and look pale.
65   Is not this something more than fantasy?
          What think you on't?

HORATIO: Before my God, I might not this believe
          Without the sensible and true avouch
          Of mine own eyes.

70   **MARCELLUS:**   Is it not like the King?

HORATIO: As thou art to thyself.
          Such was the very armour he had on
          When he the ambitious Norway combated.
          So frown'd he once when, in an angry parle,
75   He smote the sledded Polacks on the ice.
          'Tis strange.

MARCELLUS: Thus twice before, and jump at this dead hour,
          With martial stalk hath he gone by our watch.

HORATIO: In what particular thought to work I know not;
80   But, in the gross and scope of my opinion,
          This bodes some strange eruption to our state.

MARCELLUS: Good now, sit down, and tell me, he that knows,
          Why this same strict and most observant watch
          So nightly toils the subject of the land,
85   And why such daily cast of brazen cannon,
          And foreign mart for implements of war,

MARCELLUS: *It is offended.*

BERNARDO: *Look, it's walking away!*

HORATIO: *Stay! Speak, speak! I demand that you speak!*
                                        [Ghost exits]

MARCELLUS: *It is gone and will not answer.*

BERNARDO: *Well, Horatio, you're trembling and look pale. Isn't this more than a fantasy? What do you think now?*

HORATIO: *By God, I would not believe this had I not seen it with my own eyes.*

MARCELLUS: *Doesn't it look like the King?*

HORATIO: *Just as you look like yourself. This was the armor he wore when he fought against the ambitious King of Norway. One time, he frowned exactly like that, when he defeated the Polish army crossing the icy lake on their sleds. It is strange.*

MARCELLUS: *Twice before, and exactly at this dark, nightly hour, has he walked past our watch like a soldier.*

HORATIO: *I am not sure what to make of this. But, based on what I know, I believe that this predicts disorder within our country.*

MARCELLUS: *Sit down now and tell me, whoever knows, why this strict nightly watch has been set, which troubles the subjects within the kingdom? Why are cannons manufactured daily and why do we trade with foreign markets for war machinery? Why are shipmakers forced to work every single day of the week, including Sunday?*

Why such impress of shipwrights, whose sore task
Does not divide the Sunday from the week.
What might be toward, that this sweaty haste
90 Doth make the night joint-labourer with the day?
Who is't that can inform me?

HORATIO: That can I;
At least the whisper goes so. Our last King,
Whose image even but now appear'd to us,
95 Was, as you know, by Fortinbras of Norway,
Thereto prick'd on by a most emulate pride,
Dared to the combat; in which our valiant Hamlet—
For so this side of our known world esteem'd him—
Did slay this Fortinbras; who by a seal'd compact,
100 Well ratified by law and heraldry,
Did forfeit, with his life, all those his lands
Which he stood seized of, to the conqueror;
Against the which, a moiety competent
Was gaged by our King; which had return'd
105 To the inheritance of Fortinbras,
Had he been vanquisher, as, by the same covenant
And carriage of the article design'd,
His fell to Hamlet. Now, sir, young Fortinbras,
Of unimproved metal hot and full,
110 Hath in the skirts of Norway here and there,
Shark'd up a list of lawless resolutes,
For food and diet to some enterprise
That hath a stomach in't; which is no other—
As it doth well appear unto our state—
115 But to recover of us, by strong hand
And terms compulsatory, those foresaid lands
So by his father lost. And this, I take it,
Is the main motive of our preparations,
The source of this our watch and the chief head
120 Of this post-haste and romage in the land.

What might be going to happen that requires working day and night? Who can tell me?

HORATIO: *I can do that. This is what people say: Our last king, whose ghostly image has just appeared to us, was, as you know, challenged to a fight by Fortinbras of Norway, whose jealous pride urged him on. Our noble King Hamlet, as he is known in this part of the world, killed Fortinbras. According to the terms and rules governing combat, Fortinbras, with his life, forfeited all the lands he possessed to his conqueror. Our King had pledged to give an equivalent portion to Fortinbras, had he been the winner, just as Fortinbras' portion fell to Hamlet, in accordance with the contract they had agreed upon. Now, sir, his son, the inexperienced but headstrong young Fortinbras, has gathered up a gang of outlaws from the outer Norwegian territories, who are hungry for a dangerous adventure. This adventure, it seems, is nothing less than an attempt to recover from us, by military force, the lands his father lost. And this, I believe, is the main reason for our preparations, our nightly watch, and the explanation for all the activity and turmoil throughout the country.*

BERNARDO: I think it be no other but e'en so.
    Well may it sort that this portentous figure
    Comes armed through our watch, so like the King
    That was and is the question of these wars.

125   HORATIO: A mote it is to trouble the mind's eye.
    In the most high and palmy state of Rome,
    A little ere the mightiest Julius fell,
    The graves stood tenantless, and the sheeted dead
    Did squeak and gibber in the Roman streets;
130   As stars with trains of fire and dews of blood,
    Disasters in the sun; and the moist star,
    Upon whose influence Neptune's empire stands
    Was sick almost to doomsday with eclipse.
    And even the like precurse of feared events,
135   As harbingers preceding still the fates
    And prologue to the omen coming on,
    Have heaven and earth together demonstrated
    Unto our climature and countrymen.
[Enter Ghost again.]
    But soft! behold! Lo, where it comes again!
140   I'll cross it, though it blast me. Stay illusion!
    If thou hast any sound, or use of voice,
    Speak to me;
    If there be any good thing to be done,
    That may to thee do ease and grace to me,
145   Speak to me;
    If thou art privy to thy country's fate,
    Which, happily, foreknowing may avoid,
    O, speak!
    Or if thou hast uphoarded in thy life
150   Extorted treasure in the womb of earth,
    For which, they say, you spirits oft walk in death,
    Speak of it! stay, and speak! *[The cock crows.]* Stop it,
    Marcellus!

MARCELLUS: Shall I strike at it with my partisan?

16

BERNARDO: *I think that must be the case. It seems fitting that this ominous figure walks past our watch, armed, looking so much like the King who is the reason for this war.*

HORATIO: *One speck of dust troublest the mind's eye. During the glorious days of Rome, just before the mighty Julius Caesar was killed, the graves stood vacant and dead corpses in rags shrieked and chattered in the streets of Rome. Stars with strings of fire and blood appeared as ominous signs from the sun; the moon, which controls the seas, was sick and almost in complete darkness. Heaven and earth have predicted that what happens in the sky usually precedes upcoming dreadful events that occur in our country and to our countrymen.*

[Ghost enters]

But quiet—look! Here it comes again! I'll confront it even though it might strike me. Don't leave, illusion! If you can make any sound or use your voice, speak to me! If there is any good deed that can be done that might ease your pain and bring me grace, speak to me! If you know what fate might befall your country, it could be avoided if we know what it is. Speak! If you have hoarded stolen treasures in the ground during your life, a deed which, so they say, often forces spirits to walk the earth after death, speak about it! Stay and speak! [The cock crows] *Stop it, Marcellus!*

MARCELLUS: *Shall I strike at it with my spear?*

155 HORATIO: Do, if it will not stand.

BERNARDO: 'Tis here!

HORATIO: 'Tis here!

MARCELLUS: 'Tis gone!   [Exit Ghost.]
          We do it wrong, being so majestical,
160   To offer it the show of violence;
          For it is, as the air, invulnerable,
          And our vain blows malicious mockery.

BERNARDO: It was about to speak, when the cock crew.

HORATIO: And then it started, like a guilty thing
165   Upon a fearful summons. I have heard
          The cock, that is the trumpet to the morn,
          Doth with his lofty and shrill-sounding throat
          Awake the god of day, and at his warning,
          Whether in sea or fire, in earth or air,
170   The extravagant and erring spirit hies
          To his confine; and of the truth herein
          This present object made probation.

MARCELLUS: It faded on the crowing of the cock.
          Some say that ever, 'gainst that season comes
175   Wherein our Saviour's birth is celebrated,
          The bird of dawning singeth all night long;
          And then, they say, no spirit dare stir abroad,
          The nights are wholesome, then no planets strike,
          No fairy takes, nor witch hath power to charm,
180   So hallow'd and so gracious is the time.

HORATIO: So have I heard and do in part believe it.
          But look, the morn, in russet mantle clad,
          Walks o'er the dew of yon high eastward hill.
          Break we our watch up; and by my advice
185   Let us impart what we have seen tonight

HORATIO: *Yes, if it will not stop.*

BERNARDO: *It is here!*

HORATIO: *It is here!*

MARCELLUS: *It is gone!*   [Ghost exits]
It is wrong of us to threaten this majestic figure with violence. It is invulnerable like air, and our vain attempts are merely evil.

BERNARDO: *It was about to speak when the cock crowed.*

HORATIO: *Then it was startled, like someone who's guilty and hears a dreaded warning. I have heard that the cock, being the morning's trumpet, wakes the god of daytime with its shrill cry. Upon hearing this warning, the wandering spirits, whether they belong to the sea or fire, to the earth or air, hasten back to their graves. The appearance of this ghost proves that what I have related is true.*

MARCELLUS: *It vanished when the cock crowed. Some people say that just before the Christmas season, the cock crows all night long. At that time, they say that no spirit dares to wander. The nights are undisturbed, stars are in balance, fairies don't enchant and witches cannot cast evil spells. This is how holy and blessed the season is.*

HORATIO: *I have heard this and partly believe it. But look, the reddish morning is dawning over the dewy eastern hills. Let's end our nightly watch. I suggest that we tell young Hamlet what we have seen tonight. I'd bet my life that this ghost, although it won't speak*

Unto young Hamlet; for, upon my life,
This spirit, dumb to us, will speak to him.
Do you consent we shall acquaint him with it,
As needful in our loves, fitting our duty?

190 MARCELLUS: Let's do't, I pray: and I this morning know
Where we shall find him most conveniently.

[Exeunt.]

Scene 2

A room of state in the Castle.

Flourish. [Enter Claudius, King of Denmark, Gertrude the Queen, Hamlet, Polonius, Laertes and his sister Ophelia, Voltimand, Cornelius, Lords Attendant.]

KING: Though yet of Hamlet our dear brother's death
The memory be green, and that it us befitted
To bear our hearts in grief and our whole kingdom
To be contracted in one brow of woe,
5 Yet so far hath discretion fought with nature
That we with wisest sorrow think on him
Together with remembrance of ourselves.
Therefore our sometime sister, now our queen,
The imperial jointress to this warlike state,
10 Have we, as 'twere with a defeated joy,
With an auspicious, and a dropping eye,
With mirth in funeral, and with dirge in marriage,
In equal scale weighing delight and dole,
Taken to wife. Nor have we herein barr'd
15 Your better wisdoms, which have freely gone
With this affair along. For all, our thanks.
Now follows, that you know, young Fortinbras,
Holding a weak supposal of our worth,

20

to us, will speak to him. Do you agree that we should tell him about it, as our friendship and duty toward him commands?

MARCELLUS: *Let's do it, I say. I know where we will easily find him this morning.*

[They exit]

Scene 2

A room in the castle of the King of Denmark.

[A trumpet sounds. Claudius, the King of Denmark, Gertrude, the Queen, Hamlet, son of the late King and Gertrude, Polonius, Laertes, Voltimand, Cornelius, Lords, and Attendants enter]

KING: *Though the memory of our dear brother Hamlet's death is still fresh, and though it was appropriate for us to face our grief and to share our sorrow with the entire kingdom, our reason must balance our natural sorrow, and we must mourn sensibly, by thinking of our own needs while remembering him. Therefore, I have taken my former sister-in-law, who is now my queen and equal ruler in this warlike situation, as my wife. However, our joy was compromised, our union happy, yet tearful, bringing hope to the funeral, and sadness to our marriage, as we balanced our feelings of delight and sorrow. We have not ignored your good advice in these matters, which you have given openly and without reservation. We thank you for everything. Now I must inform you that young Fortinbras, either because he holds our country in contempt or because he believes that we are in a state of disorder due to the death of our brother, the late king, pursuing his dreams of regaining his lands, has not failed to trouble me with messages, demanding the return of the lands his father legally lost to our most valiant brother. Enough about him. As far as we are concerned, the reason*

Or thinking by our late dear brother's death
20 Our state to be disjoint and out of frame,
Colleagued with this dream of his advantage,
He hath not fail'd to pester us with message,
Importing the surrender of those lands
Lost by his father, with all bonds of law,
25 To our most valiant brother. So much for him.
Now for ourself, and for this time of meeting.
Thus much the business is: we have here writ
To Norway, uncle of young Fortinbras—
Who, impotent and bed-rid, scarcely hears
30 Of this his nephew's purpose—to suppress
His further gait herein, in that the levies,
The lists, and full proportions, are all made
Out of his subject; and one here dispatch
You, good Cornelius, and you, Voltimand,
35 For bearers of this greeting to old Norway,
Giving to you no further personal power
To business with the King, more than the scope
Of these dilated articles allow. [Gives a paper.]
Farewell, and let your haste commend your duty.

40 CORNELIUS, VOLTIMAND: In that and all things will we show our duty.

KING: We doubt it nothing. Heartily farewell.
                              [Exeunt Voltimand and Cornelius.]
And now, Laertes, what's the news with you?
You told us of some suit. What is't, Laertes?
You cannot speak of reason to the Dane,
45 And lose your voice. What wouldst thou beg, Laertes,
That shall not be my offer, not thy asking?
The head is not more native to the heart,
The hand more instrumental to the mouth,
Than is the throne of Denmark to thy father.
50 What wouldst thou have, Laertes?

LAERTES: Dread my lord,
Your leave and favour to return to France;

for this meeting is the following business: We have written to the King of Norway, the uncle of young Fortinbras, who is feeble and bedridden and hardly knows anything of his nephew's intentions. I asked him to stop Fortinbras' further proceedings, since all taxes, troops, and payments come from his former subjects. I am sending you, Cornelius, and you, Voltimand, to deliver this letter to the old King of Norway, giving you no further personal power to do business with the King beyond the instructions of this document. [Handing them a document] *Good-bye. Move quickly, as your duty demands.*

CORNELIUS, VOLTIMAND: *In that, as in all things, will we show our duty.*

KING: *We have no doubts. Our fondest farewell!*
                    [Voltimand and Cornelius exit]
And now, Laertes, what is your news? You mentioned a request. What is it, Laertes? You can never speak reasonably to me, the King of Denmark, and waste your voice. What would you ask, Laertes, that I would not offer, even without your asking? A head is no more closely related to the heart, a hand no more useful to the mouth, than the throne of Denmark is to your father. What do you ask, Laertes?

LAERTES: *My noble lord, your gracious permission to return to France. I came willingly to Denmark to show my duty at your coronation,*

From whence though willingly I came to Denmark,
To show my duty in your coronation,
55 Yet now, I must confess, that duty done,
My thoughts and wishes bend again toward France
And bow them to your gracious leave and pardon.

KING: Have you your father's leave? What says Polonius?

POLONIUS: He hath, my lord, wrung from me my slow leave
60 By laboursome petition, and at last
Upon his will I seal'd my hard consent.
I do beseech you, give him leave to go.

KING: Take thy fair hour, Laertes. Time be thine,
And thy best graces spend it at thy will!
65 But now, my cousin Hamlet, and my son,—

HAMLET: *[Aside]* A little more than kin, and less than kind!

KING: How is it that the clouds still hang on you?

HAMLET: Not so, my lord: I am too much i' the sun.

QUEEN: Good Hamlet, cast thy nighted color off,
70 And let thine eye look like a friend on Denmark.
Do not for ever with thy vailed lids
Seek for thy noble father in the dust.
Thou know'st 'tis common. All that lives must die,
Passing through nature to eternity.

75 HAMLET: Ay, madam, it is common.

QUEEN: If it be,
Why seems it so particular with thee?

but, now, I must confess, my duty being done, that my thoughts and wishes turn again toward France, and I ask for your permission to depart.

KING: *Do you have your father's permission? What does Polonius say about this?*

POLONIUS: *My lord, he has received my reluctant permission through constant begging. In the end, I agreed to support his wishes. I entreat you, please give him permission to leave.*

KING: *Enjoy your youthful years, Laertes; time is at your disposal, and you should make the best use of it. But now, Hamlet, my nephew, and my son—*

HAMLET: *[Aside] I am more than a kin, and less than friendly.*

KING: *Why is your mind still clouded with sadness?*

HAMLET: *It is not, my lord; I am too much in the sun.*

QUEEN: *Dear Hamlet, cast off this dark mood and look at the new King as a friend. You cannot always look with downcast eyes for traces of your noble father in the dust. You understand that it's common knowledge that everything that lives must die, passing through life on the way to eternity.*

HAMLET: *Yes, madam, it is common knowledge.*

QUEEN: *If that is true, why do you, in particular, seem so upset?*

HAMLET: Seems, madam? Nay, it is. I know not seems.
    'Tis not alone my inky cloak, good mother,
80   Nor customary suits of solemn black,
    Nor windy suspiration of forced breath,
    No, nor the fruitful river in the eye,
    Nor the dejected havior of the visage,
    Together with all forms, modes, shapes of grief,
85   That can denote me truly. These indeed seem,
    For they are actions that a man might play;
    But I have that within which passeth show,
    These but the trappings and the suits of woe.

KING: 'Tis sweet and commendable in your nature, Hamlet,
90   To give these mourning duties to your father;
    But you must know, your father lost a father;
    That father lost, lost his, and the survivor bound
    In filial obligation for some term
    To do obsequious sorrow. But to persever
95   In obstinate condolement is a course
    Of impious stubbornness; 'tis unmanly grief;
    It shows a will most incorrect to heaven,
    A heart unfortified, a mind impatient,
    An understanding simple and unschool'd;
100   For what we know must be, and is as common
    As any the most vulgar thing to sense,
    Why should we, in our peevish opposition,
    Take it to heart? Fie! 'tis a fault to heaven,
    A fault against the dead, a fault to nature,
105   To reason most absurd, whose common theme
    Is death of fathers, and who still hath cried,
    From the first corse till he that died today,
    This must be so. We pray you throw to earth
    This unprevailing woe, and think of us
110   As of a father; for let the world take note
    You are the most immediate to our throne,
    And with no less nobility of love
    Than that which dearest father bears his son
    Do I impart toward you. For your intent

26

HAMLET: "Seem," madam? No, I am! I do not know how to "seem" upset. It is not merely my dark mood, good mother, nor traditional mourning clothes, nor forced sighs, nor my abundant tears, nor the sad expression of my face, together with all forms, types, and shades of grief, that can fully define me. These things do indeed "seem," because they are outward signs any man could display. But I feel something inside that goes beyond those outward display and pretense of mourning.

KING: It's a sweet and admirable part of your nature, Hamlet, to grieve dutifully for your father. But you must know that your father lost a father, too. That father, in turn, lost his father, and the surviving son must mourn for some time to show his duty and sadness. But to persevere in continuous mourning is an act of sinful stubbornness. It's a childish grief that shows willful disobedience to heaven, a weak heart, a disorganized mind, and an ignorant and uneducated intellect. If we know that some things must happen because they're an inevitable part of nature, why should we foolishly resist them and take them to heart? Shame! It's an offense against heaven, an offense to the dead, an offense against nature and a contradiction of reason. The death of a father is a common part of nature, and nature has announced—from the first who died to one who died today: "This is the way things must be!" We beg you to stop this futile misery and think of us as you would a father. Let the world know: you are the immediate heir to the throne, and I give no less love to you than the most loving father would give to a son. As far as your intentions of returning to school in Wittenberg are concerned, it goes against our wishes. We ask you to change your mind and stay here in the happiness and comfort or our company as the most important member of our royal court, our relation, and our son.

115   In going back to school in Wittenberg,
             It is most retrograde to our desire;
             And we beseech you, bend you to remain
             Here in the cheer and comfort of our eye,
             Our chiefest courtier, cousin, and our son.

120   QUEEN: Let not thy mother lose her prayers, Hamlet.
             I pray thee, stay with us, go not to Wittenberg.

HAMLET: I shall in all my best obey you, madam.

KING: Why, 'tis a loving and a fair reply.
             Be as ourself in Denmark. Madam, come.
125   This gentle and unforced accord of Hamlet
             Sits smiling to my heart; in grace whereof,
             No jocund health that Denmark drinks today
             But the great cannon to the clouds shall tell,
             And the King's rouse the heaven shall bruit again,
130   Re-speaking earthly thunder. Come away.
                          [Flourish. Exeunt all but Hamlet.]

HAMLET: O, that this too too sullied flesh would melt,
             Thaw and resolve itself into a dew,
             Or that the Everlasting had not fix'd
             His canon 'gainst self-slaughter! O God! God!
135   How weary, stale, flat and unprofitable
             Seem to me all the uses of this world!
             Fie on't! ah, fie! 'Tis an unweeded garden
             That grows to seed; things rank and gross in nature
             Possess it merely. That it should come to this!
140   But two months dead! Nay, not so much, not two;
             So excellent a king, that was, to this,
             Hyperion to a satyr; so loving to my mother
             That he might not beteem the winds of heaven
             Visit her face too roughly. Heaven and earth!
145   Must I remember? Why, she would hang on him
             As if increase of appetite had grown
             By what it fed on; and yet, within a month—

QUEEN: *Don't let your mother's prayers go unanswered, Hamlet. Please stay with us; do not go to Wittenberg.*

HAMLET: *I will try my best to obey you, madam.*

KING: *Why, that is a loving and fair reply. Act as we would in Denmark. Come, madam. Hamlet's loving and unforced consent delights me. In honor of that decision, every joyful drink Denmark has today shall be followed by a great cannon fired toward the clouds, and the heavens will re-announce the King's enjoyment, sounding like earthly thunder. Come, let's go.*

[A trumpet sounds. All but Hamlet exit]

HAMLET: *If my blemished flesh could only melt, thaw, and dissolve into water! If only God's laws did not prohibit suicide. Oh, God, God! How all worldly customs seem weary, dry, dull, and pointless to me! Shame on it. Shame! It's an unweeded garden grown to maturity; only disgusting and horrid things live there. That it should come to this! Only two months dead—no, not even that long, not even two—such an excellent king, who was a sun god compared to this monster. He was so loving to my mother that he would not allow the heavenly winds to blow into her face too roughly. Heaven and earth, do I have to remember this? She would cling to him as if the nourishment he gave her made her hungrier for more. And yet, within a month's time—I mustn't think about it— Women are weak! One short month since she had worn the shoes she wore my poor father's body, weeping endlessly, like Niobe did over her children. Why she, even she—Oh, God! Any beast that lacks to the power to reason would have mourned longer! But she married my uncle, my father's brother, who is no more like my*

Let me not think on't! Frailty, thy name is woman–
A little month, or ere those shoes were old
150   With which she follow'd my poor father's body
Like Niobe, all tears—why she, even she—
O God! a beast that wants discourse of reason
Would have mourn'd longer—married with my uncle,
My father's brother, but no more like my father
155   Than I to Hercules. Within a month,
Ere yet the salt of most unrighteous tears
Had left the flushing in her galled eyes,
She married. O, most wicked speed, to post
With such dexterity to incestuous sheets!
160   It is not, nor it cannot come to, good.
But break, my heart, for I must hold my tongue!

[Enter Horatio, Marcellus, and Bernardo.]

HORATIO: Hail to your lordship!

HAMLET: I am glad to see you well.
    Horatio—or I do forget myself.

165   HORATIO: The same, my lord, and your poor servant ever.

HAMLET: Sir, my good friend; I'll change that name with you.
    And what make you from Wittenberg, Horatio?—
    Marcellus?

MARCELLUS: My good lord!

170   HAMLET: I am very glad to see you.— *[To Bernardo]* Good even,
    sir.—
    But what, in faith, make you from Wittenberg?

HORATIO: A truant disposition, good my lord.

HAMLET: I would not hear your enemy say so,
175   Nor shall you do my ear that violence

father than I am like Hercules! Within a month, before those insincere tears stopped pouring from her watery eyes, she married. Oh, the awful haste with which she jumped so skillfully into an incestuous bed! It is not good and cannot come to any good. But my heart must break because I must be silent.

[Horatio, Marcellus, and Bernardo enter]

Horatio: Greetings, your lordship!

Hamlet: I am glad to see you well. Horatio, if I remember right.

Horatio: It is I, my lord, always your humble servant.

Hamlet: Sir, my good friend—I am the same to you. But why are you not in Wittenberg, Horatio? [Recognizing Marcellus] and Marcellus!

Marcellus: My good lord!

Hamlet: I am very glad to see you. [To Bernardo] Good evening, sir. But what made you leave Wittenberg?

Horatio: An inclination to be idle, my good lord.

Hamlet: I would not allow your enemy to speak like this. And you will not force my ears to hear you speak this way about yourself. I know

To make it truster of your own report
Against yourself. I know you are no truant.
But what is your affair in Elsinore?
We'll teach you to drink deep ere you depart.

180 HORATIO: My lord, I came to see your father's funeral.

HAMLET: I prithee do not mock me, fellow student.
      I think it was to see my mother's wedding.

HORATIO: Indeed, my lord, it followed hard upon.

HAMLET: Thrift, thrift, Horatio. The funeral baked meats
185   Did coldly furnish forth the marriage tables.
      Would I had met my dearest foe in heaven
      Or ever I had seen that day, Horatio!
      My father—methinks I see my father.

HORATIO: O, where, my lord?

190 HAMLET: In my mind's eye, Horatio.

HORATIO: I saw him once. He was a goodly king.

HAMLET: He was a man, take him for all in all;
      I shall not look upon his like again.

HORATIO: My lord, I think I saw him yesternight.

195 HAMLET: Saw? Who?

HORATIO: My lord, the King your father.

HAMLET: The King my father?

HORATIO: Season your admiration for a while
      With an attent ear, till I may deliver
200   Upon the witness of these gentlemen,
      This marvel to you.

you are no idler. But what is your business in Elsinore? We'll teach you to drink deeply before you depart!

HORATIO: *My lord, I came to attend your father's funeral.*

HAMLET: *Please do not mock me, my fellow student. I think it was to attend my mother's wedding.*

HORATIO: *Indeed, my lord, it happened soon after.*

HAMLET: *Thriftiness, Horatio. The funeral's leftover meats were served cold at the wedding feast. I wish I had met my most hated enemy in heaven rather than seen that day, Horatio. My father—I think, I see my father.*

HORATIO: *Oh, where, my lord?*

HAMLET: *In my mind, Horatio.*

HORATIO: *I saw him once; he was a true king.*

HAMLET: *He was a man, taken altogether. I will never encounter anyone quite like him again.*

HORATIO: *My lord, I think I saw him last night.*

HAMLET: *Saw? Who?*

HORATIO: *The King, your father, my lord.*

HAMLET: *The King, my father?*

HORATIO: *Hold your amazement for a while and listen, so I can tell you this wondrous story, which these gentlemen also witnessed.*

HAMLET: For God's love let me hear!

HORATIO: Two nights together had these gentlemen
    Marcellus and Bernardo, on their watch
205   In the dead vast and middle of the night,
    Been thus encountered. A figure like your father,
    Armed at point exactly, cap-à-pie,
    Appears before them, and with solemn march
    Goes slow and stately by them. Thrice he walk'd
210   By their oppress'd and fear-surprised eyes,
    Within his truncheon's length; whilst they distill'd
    Almost to jelly with the act of fear,
    Stand dumb and speak not to him. This to me
    In dreadful secrecy impart they did,
215   And I with them the third night kept the watch;
    Where, as they had deliver'd, both in time,
    Form of the thing, each word made true and good,
    The apparition comes. I knew your father.
    These hands are not more like.

220 HAMLET: But where was this?

MARCELLUS: My lord, upon the platform where we watch'd.

HAMLET: Did you not speak to it?

HORATIO: My lord, I did;
    But answer made it none. Yet once methought
225   It lifted up his head and did address
    Itself to motion, like as it would speak;
    But, even then, the morning cock crew loud,
    And at the sound it shrunk in haste away
    And vanish'd from our sight.

230 HAMLET: 'Tis very strange.

HORATIO: As I do live, my honour'd lord, 'tis true;
    And we did think it writ down in our duty
    To let you know of it.

HAMLET: *For the love of God, let me hear!*

HORATIO: *For two nights in a row, these gentlemen, Marcellus and Bernardo, have encountered the following during their watch in the middle of the night: A figure resembling your father, armed correctly from head to toe, appeared before them and marched solemnly past them. He walked past their amazed and fear-stricken eyes three times, at staff-length, while they, numbed by fear, stood and dared not speak to him. They shared their story with me in frightful secrecy, and I joined their watch on the third night. Exactly as they had told me, the apparition appeared—at the same time and looking word-for-word as they had described it. I knew your father. My hands are as similar to one another as the apparition is to your father.*

HAMLET: *But where was this?*

MARCELLUS: *On the platform where we stood guard, my lord.*

HAMLET: *Didn't you speak to it?*

HORATIO: *I did, my lord, but it did not answer. At one point, I thought that it lifted its head and began to make a gesture, as if it were going to speak. But just at that moment, the morning cock crowed loudly, and when it heard that sound, it stole away quickly and vanished from our sight.*

HAMLET: *This is very strange.*

HORATIO: *I swear by my life, my lord, that it's true. And we considered it our duty to let you know about it.*

HAMLET: Indeed, indeed, sirs. But this troubles me.
235   Hold you the watch tonight?

MARCELLUS AND BERNARDO: We do, my lord.

HAMLET: Arm'd, say you?

MARCELLUS AND BERNARDO: Arm'd, my lord.

HAMLET: From top to toe?

240   MARCELLUS AND BERNARDO: My lord, from head to foot.

HAMLET: Then saw you not his face?

HORATIO: O, yes, my lord! He wore his beaver up.

HAMLET: What, look'd he frowningly?

HORATIO: A countenance more in sorrow than in anger.

245   HAMLET: Pale, or red?

HORATIO: Nay, very pale.

HAMLET: And fix'd his eyes upon you?

HORATIO: Most constantly.

HAMLET: I would I had been there.

250   HORATIO: It would have much amazed you.

HAMLET: Very like, very like. Stay'd it long?

HORATIO: While one with moderate haste might tell a hundred.

MARCELLUS AND BERNARDO: Longer, longer.

HAMLET: *Indeed, indeed, gentlemen. But this worries me. Are you on guard duty tonight?*

MARCELLUS AND BERNARDO: *We are, my lord.*

HAMLET: *Armed, you said?*

MARCELLUS AND BERNARDO: *Armed, my lord.*

HAMLET: *From head to toe?*

MARCELLUS AND BERNARDO: *From head to foot, my lord.*

HAMLET: *Then you did not see his face?*

HORATIO: *O, yes, my lord! He wore his visor up.*

HAMLET: *Was he frowning?*

HORATIO: *His expression was more in sorrow than anger.*

HAMLET: *Pale or red?*

HORATIO: *Very pale, indeed.*

HAMLET: *And he was staring at you?*

HORATIO: *Constantly.*

HAMLET: *I wish I had been there.*

HORATIO: *It would have amazed you.*

HAMLET: *Most likely, most likely. Did it stay for long?*

HORATIO: *Maybe as long as it takes to count to one hundred.*

MARCELLUS AND BERNARDO: *Longer, longer!*

HORATIO: Not when I saw't.

255   HAMLET: His beard was grizzled, no?

HORATIO: It was as I have seen it in his life,
     A sable silvered.

HAMLET: I will watch tonight.
     Perchance 'twill walk again.

260   HORATIO: I warrant it will.

HAMLET: If it assume my noble father's person,
     I'll speak to it, though hell itself should gape
     And bid me hold my peace. I pray you all,
     If you have hitherto conceal'd this sight,
265   Let it be tenable in your silence still;
     And whatsoever else shall hap tonight,
     Give it an understanding, but no tongue.
     I will requite your loves. So, fare you well.
     Upon the platform, 'twixt eleven and twelve,
270   I'll visit you.

ALL: Our duty to your honour.

HAMLET: Your loves, as mine to you. ⌐ . well.
                       [Exeunt a but Hamlet.]
     My father's spirit in arms! All is not well.
     I doubt some foul play. Would the night were come.
275   Till then sit still, my soul. Foul deeds will rise,
     Though all the earth o'erwhelm them, to men's eyes.
                         [Exit.]

HORATIO: *Not when I saw it.*

HAMLET: *His beard was grayish, was it?*

HORATIO: *It was the way I have seen it in his lifetime, black and silver.*

HAMLET: *I will watch tonight; perhaps it will come again.*

HORATIO: *I assure you it will.*

HAMLET: *If it looks like my noble father, I'll speak to it, even if hell itself should opene up and command me to be quiet. I ask you all, if you kept this sight a secret until now, keep quiet for a while longer. And whatever else will happen tonight, watch it closely, but do not talk about it. I will compensate you for your friendship. Goodbye. I will meet you on the platform between eleven and twelve o'clock.*

ALL: *Our duty is to your honor.*

HAMLET: *And mine to you; farewell.*

[All but Hamlet exit]

The ghost of my father—armed! All is not well. I suspect some foul play. I wish it were nighttime already. Until then, be quiet, my soul! Foul deeds will eventually be revealed to men, though they may be hidden by the entire earth.

[Hamlet exits]

Scene 3

A room in the house of Polonius.

[Enter Laertes and Ophelia.]

LAERTES: My necessaries are embark'd. Farewell.
    And, sister, as the winds give benefit
    And convoy is assistant, do not sleep,
    But let me hear from you.

5   OPHELIA: Do you doubt that?

LAERTES: For Hamlet, and the trifling of his favours,
    Hold it a fashion, and a toy in blood;
    A violet in the youth of primy nature,
    Forward, not permanent, sweet, not lasting;
10   The perfume and suppliance of a minute;
    No more.

OPHELIA: No more but so?

LAERTES: Think it no more.
    For nature, crescent, does not grow alone
15   In thews and bulk; but as this temple waxes,
    The inward service of the mind and soul
    Grows wide withal. Perhaps he loves you now,
    And now no soil nor cautel doth besmirch
    The virtue of his will; but you must fear,
20   His greatness weigh'd, his will is not his own;
    For he himself is subject to his birth.
    He may not, as unvalued persons do,
    Carve for himself; for on his choice depends
    The safety and health of this whole state,
25   And therefore must his choice be circumscribed
    Unto the voice and yielding of that body
    Whereof he is the head. Then if he says he loves you,

Scene 3

A room in the house of Polonius.

[Laertes and his sister Ophelia enter]

LAERTES: *My important things are on board. Farewell, and, sister, because means of transportation are available, do not rest until you have written a letter to me.*

OPHELIA: *Do you doubt it?*

LAERTES: *As for Hamlet and his regard for you, consider his actions the common behavior of a young man, the idle fancy of youthful passion, a mere bud in the spring of his flourishing youth. Premature, not permanent, charming, but not lasting; a sweet yet temporary pastime. No more.*

OPHELIA: *No more than that?*

LAERTES: *Don't take it for anything else. Maturity does not only affect muscles and strength; as the body develops, the perceptions of the mind and soul grow as well. Perhaps he loves you now and no evil thoughts infiltrate his virtuous passion. But you must consider his princely rank and understand that he cannot make his decisions based on himself alone. He must obey his royal responsibilities. Unlike persons of lower rank, he cannot pursue his own wishes, because his decisions affect the safety and well-being of his entire country. Therefore, his decisions must be guided and approved by the country he rules. So, if he says he loves you, you should be wise enough to believe only these words which he, acting in accordance with his rank, can turn into actions; he cannot forego the general approval of the entire state of Denmark. Consider how it could compromise your honor if you naively believed his declarations of love, gave away your heart, or sacrificed your virginity to his*

It fits your wisdom so far to believe it
As he in his particular act and place
30   May give his saying deed; which is no further
Than the main voice of Denmark goes withal.
Then weigh what loss your honour may sustain
If with too credent ear you list his songs,
Or lose your heart, or your chaste treasure open
35   To his unmast'red importunity.
Fear it, Ophelia, fear it, my dear sister,
And keep you in the rear of your affection,
Out of the shot and danger of desire.
The chariest maid is prodigal enough
40   If she unmask her beauty to the moon.
Virtue itself 'scapes not calumnious strokes.
The canker galls the infants of the spring
Too oft before their buttons be disclosed,
And in the morn and liquid dew of youth
45   Contagious blastments are most imminent.
Be wary then; best safety lies in fear.
Youth to itself rebels, though none else near.

OPHELIA: I shall the effect of this good lesson keep
As watchman to my heart. But, good my brother,
50   Do not, as some ungracious pastors do,
Show me the steep and thorny way to heaven,
Whilst, like a puff'd and reckless libertine,
Himself the primrose path of dalliance treads
And recks not his own rede.

55 LAERTES: O, fear me not!
I stay too long. But here my father comes.
[Enter Polonius.]
A double blessing is a double grace;
Occasion smiles upon a second leave.

POLONIUS: Yet here, Laertes? Aboard, aboard, for shame!
60   The wind sits in the shoulder of your sail,
And you are stay'd for. There, my blessing with thee.

uncontrolled pleas. Fear it, Ophelia, fear it, my dear sister, and control your affection in order to stay far away from the dangers of desire. The most chaste maiden becomes reckless if she reveals her beauty, even to the moon. Virtue itself does not prevent vile comments. Too often, worms destroy the flowers of spring before the buds can fully open. In the freshness and purity of youth, corrupting diseases strike most frequently. Be careful, then; fear will keep you safe. Young people seek trouble, even when nobody else is around.

OPHELIA: I will take the essence of your valuable lesson as my heart's guardian. But, my good brother, don't show me the steep and difficult way to heaven, like some insincere pastors do, while you yourself pursue a life of easy pleasure, like a bloated, reckless lecher, who does not listen to his own advice

LAERTES: Don't worry about me. I've now stayed here too long. Here comes my father.
[Polonius enters]
    To give a farewell blessing twice brings twice the joy. I will have an opportunity to take my leave a second time.

POLONIUS: Still here, Laertes? Aboard, aboard, shame on you! The winds favor your voyage, and everyone is waiting for you. There, may all my blessings go with you. Remember these few lessons. Don't

And these few precepts in thy memory
Look thou character. Give thy thoughts no tongue,
Nor any unproportion'd thought his act.
65   Be thou familiar, but by no means vulgar.
Those friends thou hast, and their adoption tried,
Grapple them to thy soul with hoops of steel;
But do not dull thy palm with entertainment
Of each new-hatch'd, unfledged comrade. Beware
70   Of entrance to a quarrel; but being in,
Bear't that the opposed may beware of thee.
Give every man thy ear, but few thy voice;
Take each man's censure, but reserve thy judgment.
Costly thy habit as thy purse can buy,
75   But not express'd in fancy; rich, not gaudy;
For the apparel oft proclaims the man,
And they in France of the best rank and station
Are of a most select and generous chief in that.
Neither a borrower nor a lender be;
80   For loan oft loses both itself and friend,
And borrowing dulls the edge of husbandry.
This above all: to thine own self be true,
And it must follow, as the night the day,
Thou canst not then be false to any man.
85   Farewell. My blessing season this in thee!

LAERTES: Most humbly do I take my leave, my lord.

POLONIUS: The time invites you. Go, your servants tend.

LAERTES: Farewell, Ophelia, and remember well
    What I have said to you.

90   OPHELIA: 'Tis in my memory lock'd,
    And you yourself shall keep the key of it.

LAERTES: Farewell.   [Exit.]

POLONIUS: What is't, Ophelia, he hath said to you?

express your thoughts, nor act out any rash thoughts. Be sociable, but don't associate with common people. Keep these friends who have proven their dedication to you chained close to your heart, but don't invite and indulge every immature, unproven person. Avoid conflicts, but if you have to fight, make sure that your enemy fears you. Listen to everyone, but don't say much. Listen to every man's opinion, but make your own decision. Wear the most expensive outfits you can afford, although they should not be extravagant— valuable, not flashy, because you can judge a man by the clothes he wears. People of the highest ranks and positions in France pay the closest attention to fashion. Don't borrow or lend money. A loan destroys friendships, and borrowing makes you less thrifty. Above all, be true to yourself. It will then follow, as certain as night follows the day, that you cannot do anyone wrong. Goodbye. May my blessing reinforce these lessons.

LAERTES: *I leave humbly, my lord.*

POLONIUS: *The time is short. Go, your servants are waiting.*

LAERTES: *Goodbye, Ophelia, and remember well what I have said to you.*

OPHELIA: *It is locked in my memory, and you yourself shall keep the key.*

LAERTES: *Goodbye.*   [Laertes exits]

POLONIUS: *What has he said to you, Ophelia?*

45

OPHELIA: So please you, something touching the Lord Hamlet.

95 POLONIUS: Marry, well bethought!
  'Tis told me, he hath very oft of late
  Given private time to you, and you yourself
  Have of your audience been most free and bounteous.
  If it be so— as so 'tis put on me,
100   And that in way of caution—I must tell you,
  You do not understand yourself so clearly
  As it behooves my daughter and your honour.
  What is between you? Give me up the truth.

OPHELIA: He hath, my lord, of late made many tenders
105   Of his affection to me.

POLONIUS: Affection? Pooh! You speak like a green girl,
  Unsifted in such perilous circumstance.
  Do you believe his tenders, as you call them?

OPHELIA: I do not know, my lord, what I should think.

110 POLONIUS: Marry, I'll teach you. Think yourself a baby,
  That you have ta'en these tenders for true pay,
  Which are not sterling. Tender yourself more dearly,
  Or—not to crack the wind of the poor phrase,
  Running it thus—you'll tender me a fool.

115 OPHELIA: My lord, he hath importuned me with love
  In honourable fashion.

POLONIUS: Ay, fashion you may call it. Go to, go to!

OPHELIA: And hath given countenance to his speech, my lord,
  With almost all the holy vows of heaven.

120 POLONIUS: Ay, springes to catch woodcocks. I do know,
  When the blood burns, how prodigal the soul
  Lends the tongue vows. These blazes, daughter,

OPHELIA: *If you want to know, something concerning Lord Hamlet.*

POLONIUS: *He did well, indeed. I have heard that Hamlet has lately spent a lot of private time with you and that you have given him the pleasure of your company generously and often. If that is the case, as I have been warned, I must tell you that you are not acting according to your position as my daughter and your honor. What is happening between you? Tell me the truth!*

OPHELIA: *My lord, he has lately declared affections for me.*

POLONIUS: *Affection? Ha! You speak like an immature girl, inexperienced in such risky circumstances. Do you believe his "affections," as you call them?*

OPHELIA: *My lord, I do not know what I should think.*

POLONIUS: *Well, I will teach you. Think of yourself as a baby who takes these counterfeit offers at true value, when they were not valuable. Value yourself more highly, or, though this repetition may be a stretch, you will "value" me like a fool.*

OPHELIA: *My lord, he has stated his love for me in an honorable fashion.*

POLONIUS: *Yes, you may call it a fashion. Come! Come!*

OPHELIA: *And he declared his beliefs with almost all the holy vows of heaven, my lord.*

POLONIUS: *Yes, traps to catch gullible birds! I know how easily vows are spoken, when passion burns in the blood. My daughter, these blazes produce more light than heat and extinguish their prom-*

Giving more light than heat, extinct in both
Even in their promise, as it is a-making,
125   You must not take for fire. From this time
Be something scanter of your maiden presence.
Set your entreatments at a higher rate
Than a command to parley. For Lord Hamlet,
Believe so much in him, that he is young,
130   And with a larger tether may he walk
Than may be given you. In few, Ophelia,
Do not believe his vows; for they are brokers,
Not of that dye which their investments show,
But mere implorators of unholy suits,
135   Breathing like sanctified and pious bawds,
The better to beguile. This is for all:
I would not, in plain terms, from this time forth
Have you so slander any moment leisure
As to give words or talk with the Lord Hamlet.
140   Look to't, I charge you. Come your ways.

OPHELIA: I shall obey, my lord.

[Exeunt.]

Scene 4

Elsinore. The platform before the Castle.

[Enter Hamlet, Horatio, and Marcellus.]

HAMLET: The air bites shrewdly; it is very cold.

HORATIO: It is a nipping and an eager air.

HAMLET: What hour now?

HORATIO: I think it lacks of twelve.

ises a moment after they flare up; but don't mistake them for fire. From now on, grant your maidenly companionship rarely. Do not agree to meet with him only because he asks you to. As far as Lord Hamlet is concerned, understand that he is young and that he has more leeway than you do. In short, Ophelia, do not believe his vows because they are manipulative, expressing not what they mean, but are a desire for sinful behavior. His words sound holy and pious in order to convince you. This is what I mean in plain speech: from this moment on, I forbid you to waste your time in conversation with Lord Hamlet. Do as I say, I command you. Come along.

OPHELIA: I will obey, my lord.

[They exit]

Scene 4

The platform before the castle.

[Hamlet, Horatio, and Marcellus enter]

HAMLET: The wind bites wickedly; it is very cold.

HORATIO: The wind is bitter and sharp.

HAMLET: What time is it?

HORATIO: I think it is before twelve.

5   MARCELLUS: No, it is struck.

HORATIO: Indeed? I heard it not. It then draws near the season
      Wherein the spirit held his wont to walk.
      [A flourish of trumpets, and ordnance go off.]
      What doth this mean, my lord?

HAMLET: The King doth wake tonight and takes his rouse,
10   Keeps wassail, and the swaggering upspring reels,
      And as he drains his draughts of Rhenish down,
      The kettle-drum and trumpet thus bray out
      The triumph of his pledge.

15   HORATIO: Is it a custom?

HAMLET: Ay, marry, is't;
      But to my mind, though I am native here
      And to the manner born, it is a custom
      More honour'd in the breach than the observance.
20   This heavy-headed revel, east and west,
      Makes us traduced and tax'd of other nations;
      They clepe us drunkards and with swinish phrase
      Soil our addition; and indeed it takes
      From our achievements, though perform'd at height,
25   The pith and marrow of our attribute.
      So, oft it chances in particular men,
      That for some vicious mole of nature in them,
      As in their birth—wherein they are not guilty,
      Since nature cannot choose his origin—
30   By the o'ergrowth of some complexion,
      Oft breaking down the pales and forts of reason,
      Or by some habit that too much o'erleavens
      The form of plausive manners, that these men—
      Carrying, I say, the stamp of one defect,
35   Being nature's livery, or fortune's star—
      Their virtues else—be they as pure as grace,
      As infinite as man may undergo—
      Shall in the general censure take corruption

MARCELLUS: *No, it has struck twelve.*

HORATIO: *Really? I did not hear it. It's getting close to the time when the ghost normally appears.*
[A trumpet sounds and two guns go off inside]
What does this mean, my lord?

HAMLET: *The King stays up late tonight and parties. He drinks excessively and entertains wild dances. As he rapidly gulps full glasses of Rhine wine, kettledrums and trumpets celebrate his toasts.*

HORATIO: *Is it a custom?*

HAMLET: *Yes, indeed. But in my mind, even though I am a native in Denmark and understand it, it is a custom more honorable when broken than observed. These lavish festivities defame us everywhere and earn us the disapproval of other nations, who call us drunkards and ruin our reputation with their name-calling. Indeed, these excesses diminish our achievements, although they are outstanding, and, thus, compromise the core and essence of our reputation. It often happens that certain individuals, either because of one small imperfection from birth (which is not their fault, because they cannot choose their ancestral origins), or due to an excessive personality trait that destroys the boundaries of reason, or through a habit that corrupts a friendly attitude—that these men, who, as I have said, are marked by a defect—whether they were born with it or received it through some act of fate—will be harshly criticized by public opinion for their fault, even if they are otherwise infinitely virtuous and absolutely pure. One bit of evil outweighs all the good and ruins a man's reputation.*

From that particular fault. The dram of evil
40 Doth all the noble substance of a doubt
To his own scandal.

[Enter Ghost.]

HORATIO: Look, my lord, it comes!

HAMLET: Angels and ministers of grace defend us!
Be thou a spirit of health or goblin damn'd,
Bring with thee airs from heaven or blasts from hell,
45 Be thy intents wicked or charitable,
Thou comest in such a questionable shape
That I will speak to thee. I'll call thee Hamlet,
King, father, royal Dane. O, answer me!
Let me not burst in ignorance, but tell
50 Why thy canonized bones, hearsed in death,
Have burst their cerements, why the sepulchre
Wherein we saw thee quietly inurn'd,
Hath oped his ponderous and marble jaws
To cast thee up again. What may this mean
55 That thou, dead corse, again, in complete steel,
Revisits thus the glimpses of the moon,
Making night hideous, and we fools of nature
So horridly to shake our disposition
With thoughts beyond the reaches of our souls?
60 Say, why is this? Wherefore? What should we do?
[Ghost beckons Hamlet.]

HORATIO: It beckons you to go away with it,
As if it some impartment did desire
To you alone.

MARCELLUS: Look with what courteous action
65 It waves you to a more removed ground.
But do not go with it!

HORATIO: No, by no means.

52

[Ghost enters]

HORATIO: *Look, my lord; it comes!*

HAMLET: *May the angels and ministers of God defend us! Whether you are a good spirit or an evil goblin, whether you bring heavenly airs or hellish blasts, whether your intentions are evil or good, the shape you have assumed demands questioning, and I will speak to you. I'll call you Hamlet, King, father, royal Dane! Oh, answer me! Don't let me explode in ignorance, but tell me why your blessed bones, laid to rest in a coffin, have torn out of their shrouds; why your tomb, in which we laid you to rest in peace, opened its massive marble doors to cast you out again. What does this mean that you, a dead corpse, now dressed again in full armor, revisit us by moonlight and make the night seem so frightful to living beings that we trouble ourselves with thoughts about what lies beyond the limits of our souls. Tell us why? What for? What should we do?*
[Ghost beckons Hamlet]

HORATIO: *It signals you to go away with it, as if it wants to speak to you alone.*

MARCELLUS: *Look how gracefully it waves you to follow him to a more distant place. But do not go with it!*

HORATIO: *No, by no means!*

HAMLET: It will not speak; then will I follow it.

HORATIO: Do not, my lord!

70 HAMLET: Why, what should be the fear?
    I do not set my life at a pin's fee;
    And for my soul, what can it do to that,
    Being a thing immortal as itself?
    It waves me forth again. I'll follow it.

75 HORATIO: What if it tempt you toward the flood, my lord,
    Or to the dreadful summit of the cliff
    That beetles o'er his base into the sea,
    And there assume some other horrible form,
    Which might deprive your sovereignty of reason
80 And draw you into madness? Think of it.
    The very place puts toys of desperation,
    Without more motive, into every brain
    That looks so many fathoms to the sea
    And hears it roar beneath.

85 HAMLET: It waves me still.
    Go on; I'll follow thee.

MARCELLUS: You shall not go, my lord.

HAMLET: Hold off your hands!

HORATIO: Be ruled. You shall not go.

90 HAMLET: My fate cries out,
    And makes each petty artery in this body
    As hardy as the Nemean lion's nerve.
    [Ghost beckons.]
    Still am I call'd. Unhand me, gentlemen.
    By heaven, I'll make a ghost of him that lets me.
95 I say, away! Go on. I'll follow thee.
                        [Exeunt Ghost and Hamlet.]

HAMLET: *It will not speak, so I'll follow it.*

HORATIO: *Do not, my lord!*

HAMLET: *Why, what should I fear? My life is not worth the price of a pin to me, and what can it do to my soul, which is immortal like the ghost itself? It is waving to me again; I'll follow it.*

HORATIO: *What if it tempts you to walk into the sea, my lord, or to the dreadful top of the cliff that overlooks the ocean, and then assumes some other horrible form that will rob you off your reason and drive you into madness? Think about it. That place could tempt any man to perform a pointless, desperate act when he looks down far out to the sea and hears it roaring below.*

HAMLETS: *It waves to me, still. Go on! I'll follow you soon.*

MARCELLUS: *You mustn't go, my lord!*

HAMLET: *Let go of me!*

HORATIO: *Listen to us! You mustn't go!*

HAMLET: *My fate is calling me and gives the strength of the Nemean lion nerves to every one of my weak arteries. It is still calling me. Let me go, gentlemen! By heaven, I swear I will make a ghost out of anyone who tries to hinder me. I say, let me be! Go on! I'll follow you!*

[Ghost and Hamlet exit]

HORATIO: He waxes desperate with imagination.

MARCELLUS: Let's follow. 'Tis not fit thus to obey him.

HORATIO: Have after. To what issue will this come?

MARCELLUS: Something is rotten in the state of Denmark.

100   HORATIO: Heaven will direct it.

MARCELLUS: Nay, let's follow him.

                                      [Exeunt.]

Scene 5

The Castle. Another part of the fortifications.

[Enter Ghost and Hamlet.]

HAMLET: Whither wilt thou lead me? Speak! I'll go no further.

GHOST: Mark me.

HAMLET: I will.

GHOST: My hour is almost come,
5   When I to sulphurous and tormenting flames
     Must render up myself.

HAMLET: Alas, poor ghost!

GHOST: Pity me not, but lend thy serious hearing
     To what I shall unfold.

10   HAMLET: Speak; I am bound to hear.

HORATIO: *He grows increasingly desperate through his thought.*

MARCELLUS: *Let's follow him! It is not right to obey him.*

HORATIO: *Follow him! What will come of this?*

MARCELLUS: *Something is rotten in the state of Denmark.*

HORATIO: *Heaven will decide it.*

MARCELLUS: *No, let's follow him!*

[They exit]

Scene 5

Another part of the castle's platform.

[Ghost and Hamlet enter]

HAMLET: *Where are you taking me? Speak! I won't go any further.*

GHOST: *Listen to me!*

HAMLET: *I will.*

GHOST: *The time is near when I must return to infernal and tormenting flames.*

HAMLET: *Alas, poor ghost!*

GHOST: *Do not pity me, but listen closely to what I will tell you.*

HAMLET: *Speak. I am ready to listen.*

GHOST: So art thou to revenge, when thou shalt hear.

HAMLET: What!

GHOST: I am thy father's spirit,
      Doom'd for a certain term to walk the night,
15   And for the day confined to fast in fires,
      Till the foul crimes done in my days of nature
      Are burnt and purged away. But that I am forbid
      To tell the secrets of my prison-house,
      I could a tale unfold whose lightest word
20   Would harrow up thy soul, freeze thy young blood,
      Make thy two eyes, like stars, start from their spheres,
      Thy knotted and combined locks to part,
      And each particular hair to stand an end
      Like quills upon the fretful porpentine.
25   But this eternal blazon must not be
      To ears of flesh and blood. List, list, O, list!
      If thou didst ever thy dear father love—

HAMLET: O God!

GHOST: Revenge his foul and most unnatural murder.

30 HAMLET: Murder?

GHOST: Murder most foul, as in the best it is;
      But this most foul, strange, and unnatural.

HAMLET: Haste me to know't, that I, with wings as swift
      As meditation or the thoughts of love,
35   May sweep to my revenge.

GHOST: I find thee apt;
      And duller shouldst thou be than the fat weed
      That roots itself in ease on Lethe wharf,
      Wouldst thou not stir in this. Now, Hamlet, hear.
40   'Tis given out that, sleeping in mine orchard,

GHOST: *You will be ready for revenge when you hear this.*

HAMLET: *What?*

GHOST: *I am your father's spirit, doomed for a certain period of time to walk at night and to starve in the fires of purgatory during the day, until the evil sins committed during my lifetime have been burned away and purified. If I were not forbidden to tell the secret of my imprisonment, I could relate a tale to you that—with every little word—would terrify your soul, freeze your young blood, make your eyes swell in their sockets like stars, make your tangled hair straighten, and each one of them stand on end, like quills on the most-feared porcupine. But this description of the afterlife is not for human ears. Listen, listen, oh, listen! If you ever loved your dear father—*

HAMLET: *Oh, God!*

GHOST: *Revenge his foul and most unnatural murder!*

HAMLET: *Murder?*

GHOST: *Murder most evil, as it always is! But this one was foul, extraordinary, and unnatural.*

HAMLET: *Tell me quickly what happened, so that I can sweep to my revenge quicker than thoughts and emotions can fly!*

GHOST: *I know that you are smart, but you would be duller than the lazy weeds rooted in the riverbank of Lethe if this did not stir you into action. Now, Hamlet, listen. It's been said that, while I was sleeping in my garden, a snake bit me. The entire state of Denmark has been deceived and harmed by this false account of my death. But*

A serpent stung me. So the whole ear of Denmark
Is by a forged process of my death
Rankly abused. But know, thou noble youth,
The serpent that did sting thy father's life
45   Now wears his crown.

HAMLET: O my prophetic soul! My uncle!

GHOST: Ay, that incestuous, that adulterate beast,
       With witchcraft of his wit, with traitorous gifts—
       O wicked wit and gifts, that have the power
50   So to seduce!—won to his shameful lust
       The will of my most seeming-virtuous queen.
       O Hamlet, what a falling off was there!
       From me, whose love was of that dignity
       That it went hand in hand even with the vow
55   I made to her in marriage, and to decline
       Upon a wretch, whose natural gifts were poor
       To those of mine.
       But virtue, as it never will be moved,
       Though lewdness court it in a shape of heaven,
60   So lust, though to a radiant angel link'd,
       Will sate itself in a celestial bed
       And prey on garbage.
       But soft! methinks I scent the morning air.
       Brief let me be. Sleeping within my orchard,
65   My custom always of the afternoon,
       Upon my secure hour thy uncle stole,
       With juice of cursed hebona in a vial,
       And in the porches of my ears did pour
       The leperous distilment, whose effect
70   Holds such an enmity with blood of man
       That, swift as quicksilver, it courses through
       The natural gates and alleys of the body,
       And, with a sudden vigour, it doth posset
       And curd, like eager droppings into milk,
75   The thin and wholesome blood. So did it mine;
       And a most instant tetter bark'd about,

understand, noble youth, that the snake that took your father's life, now wears his crown.

HAMLET: *Oh, I knew it in my heart! My uncle?*

GHOST: *Yes, that incestuous, that adulterous beast, with witchcraft and the skills of a traitor—oh, evil wits and skills have the power to seduce!—won over my seemingly virtuous queen for the fulfillment of his shameful lust. Oh, Hamlet, what a fall from grace to forget me, whose love was full of dignity and had never diminished since I made my marital vows—to stoop to this wretched man whose qualities are poor compared to mine! But just as virtue cannot be tempted—even when desire assumes an angelic form—so lust— even if it appears as a radiant angel—will seek satisfaction in a holy bed and devour garbage. But quiet! I think I smell the morning air. Let me be brief. While sleeping in my orchard, as was my habit in the afternoon, your uncle invaded my carefree hour carrying a container filled with a cursed poison. He poured the diseased liquid into my ears. The effects are so detrimental to human blood, that it spreads fast as mercury through the veins and suddenly and actively curdles the thin and healthy blood like drops of acid into milk. This is what happened to me. Instantly, a skin disease erupted, like leprosy, and covered my smooth body with a vile and disgusting crust. Thus, while I was sleeping, I was, in an instant, deprived of my life, my crown, and my queen by my brother, killed as a sinner, without a chance to receive a holy blessing, spiritual preparations, or my last rites, without reckoning, sent to my final judgment with all my sins upon my head.*

Most lazar-like, with vile and loathsome crust
All my smooth body.
Thus was I, sleeping, by a brother's hand
80   Of life, of crown, of queen, at once dispatch'd;
Cut off even in the blossoms of my sin,
Unhouseled, disappointed, unaneled,
No reckoning made, but sent to my account
With all my imperfections on my head.

85 HAMLET: O, horrible! O, horrible! most horrible!

GHOST: If thou hast nature in thee, bear it not.
Let not the royal bed of Denmark be
A couch for luxury and damned incest.
But, howsoever thou pursuest this act,
90   Taint not thy mind, nor let thy soul contrive
Against thy mother aught. Leave her to heaven,
And to those thorns that in her bosom lodge
To prick and sting her. Fare thee well at once.
The glow-worm shows the matin to be near
95   And 'gins to pale his uneffectual fire.
Adieu, adieu, adieu! Remember me.   *[Exit.]*

HAMLET: O all you host of heaven! O earth! What else?
And shall I couple hell? O, fie! Hold, hold, my heart!
And you, my sinews, grow not instant old,
100   But bear me stiffly up. Remember thee?
Ay, thou poor ghost, while memory holds a seat
In this distracted globe. Remember thee?
Yea, from the table of my memory
I'll wipe away all trivial fond records,
105   All saws of books, all forms, all pressures past,
That youth and observation copied there;
And thy commandment all alone shall live
Within the book and volume of my brain,
Unmix'd with baser matter. Yes, by heaven!
110   O most pernicious woman!
O villain, villain, smiling, damned villain!

HAMLET: *Oh, horrible! Oh, horrible! Most horrible!*

GHOST: *If you have any humanity in you, do not allow this. Don't let the royal bed of Denmark be a couch for lust and damnable incest. But whatever you are going to do, do not contaminate your mind or allow your soul to plot against your mother. Leave her to heaven and to the thorns of her conscience that pierce and sting her heart. Quickly, goodbye! The glowworm announces the approaching morning and begins to lose its dim glow. Adieu, adieu, adieu! Remember me!*

[Ghost exits]

HAMLET: *Oh, all you messengers of heaven! Oh, earth! What else? Shall I marry with hell? Oh, shame! Hold, my heart, do not break! And you, my muscles, do not grow instantly old, but firmly bear my weight. Remember you! Yes, you poor ghost, as long as any memory remains within my confused mind. Remember you? Yes, I will erase all trivial foolish memories, all sayings from books, all images and past impressions created by youth and observation, and your command alone will occupy my brain, untouched by more trivial matters. Yes, by heaven! Oh, most wicked woman! Oh, villain, villain, smiling, damned villain! My notebook—it is advisable that I write it down—that one can smile and smile, and be a villain. At least I know that it can be this way in Denmark. [Writing] So, uncle, there you are. Now to my oath. It is, 'Adieu, adieu, Remember me!' I have sworn it.*

My tables—meet it is I set it down
That one may smile, and smile, and be a villain;
At least I am sure it may be so in Denmark.
[Writes.]
115 So, uncle, there you are. Now to my word:
It is 'Adieu, adieu! Remember me.'
I have sworn't.

HORATIO: *[Without.]* My lord, my lord!

[Enter Horatio and Marcellus.]

MARCELLUS: Lord Hamlet!

120 HORATIO: Heaven secure him!

HAMLET: So be it!

MARCELLUS: Illo, ho, ho, my lord!

HAMLET: Hillo, ho, ho, boy! Come, bird, come.

MARCELLUS: How is't, my noble lord?

125 HORATIO: What news, my lord?

MARCELLUS: O, wonderful!

HORATIO: Good my lord, tell it.

HAMLET: No; you will reveal it.

HORATIO: Not I, my lord, by heaven!

130 MARCELLUS: Nor I, my lord.

HAMLET: How say you, then; would heart of man once think it?
But you'll be secret?

HORATIO AND MARCELLUS: [Offstage] *My lord, my lord!*

[Horatio and Marcellus enter]

MARCELLUS: *Lord Hamlet!*

HORATIO: *May God protect him!*

HAMLET: *So be it!*

MARCELLUS: *Hello! Ho, ho, my lord!*

HAMLET: *Hello! Ho, ho, boy! Come, you bird, come.*

MARCELLUS: *How are you, my noble lord?*

HORATIO: *What news do you have, my lord?*

HAMLET: *Oh, amazing news!*

HORATIO: *Good, my lord, tell it!*

HAMLET: *No, you would reveal it.*

HORATIO: *By heaven, my lord, I swear I will not.*

MARCELLUS: *Nor will I, my lord.*

HAMLET: *What do you say, then? Would any man ever think that—but you'll keep the secret?*

Marcellus and Bernardo: Ay, by heaven, my lord.

Hamlet: There's ne'er a villain dwelling in all Denmark
135   But he's an arrant knave.

Horatio: There needs no ghost, my lord, come from the grave
       To tell us this.

Hamlet: Why, right! You are in the right!
       And so, without more circumstance at all,
140   I hold it fit that we shake hands and part;
       You, as your business and desire shall point you—
       For every man hath business and desire,
       Such as it is; and for my own poor part,
       Look you, I'll go pray.

145   **Horatio:** These are but wild and whirling words, my lord.

Hamlet: I am sorry they offend you, heartily;
       Yes, faith, heartily.

Horatio: There's no offence, my lord.

Hamlet: Yes, by Saint Patrick, but there is, Horatio,
150   And much offence too. Touching this vision here,
       It is an honest ghost, that let me tell you.
       For your desire to know what is between us,
       O'ermaster't as you may. And now, good friends,
       As you are friends, scholars, and soldiers,
155   Give me one poor request.

Horatio: What is't, my lord? We will.

Hamlet: Never make known what you have seen to-night.

Marcellus and Bernardo: My lord, we will not.

Hamlet: Nay, but swear't.

HORATIO AND MARCELLUS: Yes, we swear by heaven, my lord.

HAMLET: There's no villain in all of Denmark who's not a complete rogue.

HORATIO: We need no ghost coming from the grave to tell us this, my lord.

HAMLET: Well, you are certainly right. And so, without further ceremony, I think it best if we shake hands and part. You go to wherever your business or pleasure may lead you—because every man has business and pleasure, such as it is—and I, for my own poor part, see, I will go and pray.

HORATIO: These are strange and confusing words, my lord.

HAMLET: I am very sorry that they offend you. Yes, indeed, very sorry.

HORATIO: There's no offense, my lord.

HAMLET: Yes, by Saint Patrick, there is, Horatio, a great offense indeed. With regard to this vision, I can tell you that it is a truthful ghost. As far as your desire to know what happened between us is concerned, try to control it as best as you can. And now, dear friends, as you are friends, scholars, and soldiers, grant me one small request.

HORATIO: What is it, my lord? We will do it!

HAMLET: Never tell anyone what you have seen tonight.

MARCELLUS AND BERNARDO: My lord, we will not.

HAMLET: No, swear to it.

160 HORATIO: In faith,
     My lord, not I.

MARCELLUS: Nor I, my lord, in faith.

HAMLET: Upon my sword.

MARCELLUS: We have sworn, my lord, already.

165 HAMLET: Indeed, upon my sword, indeed.

GHOST: *[Ghost cries under the stage.]* Swear.

HAMLET: Ah, ha boy, say'st thou so? Art thou there, truepenny?
     Come on! You hear this fellow in the cellarage.
     Consent to swear.

170 HORATIO: Propose the oath, my lord.

HAMLET: Never to speak of this that you have seen.
     Swear by my sword.

GHOST: *[Beneath.]* Swear.

HAMLET: Hic et ubique? Then we'll shift our ground.
175   Come hither, gentlemen,
     And lay your hands again upon my sword.
     Never to speak of this that you have heard:
     Swear by my sword.

GHOST: *[Beneath.]* Swear.

180 HAMLET: Well said, old mole! Canst work i' the earth so fast?
     A worthy pioner! Once more remove, good friends.

HORATIO: O day and night, but this is wondrous strange!

HORATIO: *Really, my lord, I won't say anything.*

MARCELLUS: *Neither will I, my lord, I swear.*

HAMLET: *Swear upon my sword!*

MARCELLUS: *We have already sworn it, my lord.*

HAMLET: *Yes, but now swear on my sword.*

GHOST: [Heard offstage] *Swear!*

HAMLET: *Ah, ha, boy, do you say so, too? Are you there, my trusted fellow? Come on! You hear this fellow in the cellar. Agree to swear!*

HORATIO: *Propose the oath, my lord.*

HAMLET: *Never to speak about what you have see; swear by my sword!*

GHOST: [From beneath] *Swear!*

HAMLET: *Here and everywhere? Then we'll move to a new spot. Come here, gentlemen, and lay your hands on my sword again. Swear by my sword never to speak of what you have heard.*

GHOST: [Beneath] *Swear!*

HAMLET: *Well said, old mole. Can you work your way through the earth so fast? A worthy digger! Let's move to yet another spot, my friends.*

HORATIO: *Oh, day and night, this is wondrous and strange!*

HAMLET: And therefore as a stranger give it welcome.
There are more things in heaven and earth, Horatio,
185 Than are dreamt of in your philosophy.
But come!
Here, as before, never, so help you mercy,
How strange or odd soe'er I bear myself—
As I perchance hereafter shall think meet
190 To put an antic disposition on—
That you, at such times seeing me, never shall,
With arms encumber'd thus, or this head-shake,
Or by pronouncing of some doubtful phrase,
As "Well, well, we know," or "We could, an if we would,"
195 Or "If we list to speak" or "There be, an if they might,"
Or such ambiguous giving out, to note
That you know aught of me; this is not to do,
So grace and mercy at your most need help you,
Swear.

200 GHOST: [Beneath.] Swear.

HAMLET: Rest, rest, perturbed spirit! [They swear.] So, gentlemen,
With all my love I do commend me to you;
And what so poor a man as Hamlet is
May do to express his love and friending to you,
205 God willing, shall not lack. Let us go in together;
And still your fingers on your lips, I pray.
The time is out of joint. O cursed spite,
That ever I was born to set it right!
Nay, come, let's go together.
                    [Exeunt]

HAMLET: *And, therefore, as a stranger, welcome it. There are more things in heaven and earth, Horatio, than your beliefs can explain. But come! Here, as before, swear that you will never—so help you God—no matter how strange or odd I may appear or act—since, from now on, I might act like a madman—that whenever you see me like this, you will never—by folding your arms like this, or shaking your head like this, or muttering doubtful phrases such as, "well, well, we know," or "we could if we wanted to," or "if we cared to say something," or "somebody knows," or any other ambiguous hints—indicate that you understand what I am doing. Swear this, so God may help you when you need Him most.*

GHOST: [Beneath] *Swear!*

HAMLET: *Rest, rest, troubled spirit!* [They swear] *So, gentlemen, with all my love, I wish you goodbye. Whatever a poor man like Hamlet can do to express his love and friendship to you, it shall be done, God willing. Let's leave together. And always keep your lips sealed, I beg you! These times are chaotic. Oh, damn the fact that I was born to set things straight! No, come, let's go together.*
                                                          [They exit]

ACT II

Scene 1

Elsinore. A room in the house of Polonius.

[Enter Polonius and Reynaldo.]

POLONIUS: Give him this money and these notes, Reynaldo.

REYNALDO: I will, my lord.

POLONIUS: You shall do marvellous wisely, good Reynaldo,
    Before you visit him, to make inquire
5   Of his behaviour.

REYNALDO: My lord, I did intend it.

POLONIUS: Marry, well said, very well said. Look you, sir,
    Inquire me first what Danskers are in Paris,
    And how, and who, what means, and where they keep,
10   What company, at what expense; and finding
    By this encompassment and drift of question
    That they do know my son, come you more nearer
    Than your particular demands will touch it.
    Take you, as 'twere, some distant knowledge of him,
15   As thus, 'I know his father and his friends,
    And in part him.' Do you mark this, Reynaldo?

REYNALDO: Ay, very well, my lord.

ACT II

Scene 1

A room in the house of Polonius.

[Polonius and Reynaldo enter]

POLONIUS: *Give him this money and these notes, Reynaldo.*

REYNALDO: *I will, my lord.*

POLONIUS: *You will be well advised, good Reynaldo, to ask about his behavior before you visit him.*

REYNALDO: *My lord, I intended to.*

POLONIUS: *Indeed, well said, very well said. Look, sir, find out first which Danes are in Paris, how they got there, who they are, what they want, where they lodge, what company they keep, and how much they spend. If, by asking these questions, you find out that they know my son, you will get closer to the truth than you could by asking direct questions. Act as if you know him remotely, saying, for example, "I know his father and his friends and him, too, to a certain extent." Do you understand this, Reynaldo?*

REYNALDO: *Yes, very well, my lord.*

POLONIUS: 'And in part him, but,' you may say, 'not well.
　　　But if't be he I mean, he's very wild,
20　　Addicted so and so'; and there put on him
　　　What forgeries you please—marry, none so rank
　　　As may dishonour him, take heed of that—
　　　But, sir, such wanton, wild and usual slips
　　　As are companions noted and most known
25　　To youth and liberty.

REYNALDO:　　　　　　　　　　As gaming, my lord?

POLONIUS: Ay, or drinking, fencing, swearing, quarrelling,
　　　Drabbing. You may go so far.

REYNALDO: My lord, that would dishonour him.

30　POLONIUS: Faith, no; as you may season it in the charge.
　　　You must not put another scandal on him,
　　　That he is open to incontinency.
　　　That's not my meaning; but breathe his faults so quaintly
　　　That they may seem the taints of liberty,
35　　The flash and outbreak of a fiery mind,
　　　A savageness in unreclaimed blood,
　　　Of general assault.

REYNALDO:　　　　　　　　　But, my good lord—

POLONIUS: Wherefore should you do this?

40　REYNALDO:　　　　　　　　　　Ay, my lord,
　　　I would know that.

POLONIUS: Marry, sir, here's my drift,
　　　And I believe it is a fetch of warrant.
　　　You laying these slight sullies on my son
45　　As 'twere a thing a little soil'd i' the working,
　　　Mark you,
　　　Your party in converse, him you would sound,

POLONIUS: Say that you "know him to a certain extent." You could say, "not well. But if he's the one I'm thinking about, he's very wild, addicted to such-and-such." You can accuse him of anything you can think of. Of course, nothing so repulsive that it would be dishonorable to him; make sure of that! Only the sportive, wild, and common blunders that naturally come with youth age and liberty.

REYNALDO: Like gambling, my lord?

POLONIUS: Yes, or drinking, fencing, swearing, quarrelling, following loose women—you may go this far.

REYNALDO: My lord, that would dishonor him.

POLONIUS: No, really, because you can adjust the vices as you see fit—you shouldn't bring a scandal on him, by saying that he is habitually whoring, for example. That is not what I want. Speak of his faults in such a skillful way that they seem like behavior caused by a sense of liberty, like the bursting fires of a young mind, the wild traits of immaturity, to which all young men are liable.

REYNALDO: But, my good lord—

POLONIUS: Why should you do this?

REYNALDO: Yes, my lord, I would like to know that.

POLONIUS: Indeed, sir, here's my plan, and I believe it is ingenious. If you connect these minor blemishes with my son—as if he was a little soiled—while you are in a conversation, whatever person you talk to—if he knows the young man to be guilty of the aforementioned crimes—will definitely agree with you and say things like "good

Having ever seen in the prenominate crimes
The youth you breathe of guilty, be assured
50   He closes with you in this consequence:
'Good sir,' or so, or 'friend,' or 'gentleman'
According to the phrase or the addition
Of man and country

REYNALDO: Very good, my lord.

55   POLONIUS: And then, sir, does he this—he does—what was I about to
say?
By the mass, I was about to say something! Where did I leave?

REYNALDO: At 'closes in the consequence,' at 'friend or so,' and gentleman.'

60   POLONIUS: At 'closes in the consequence,' ay, marry!
He closes with you thus: 'I know the gentleman.
I saw him yesterday,' or 't'other day,'
Or then, or then, with such, or such; 'and, as you say,
There was a gaming,' 'there o'ertook in's rouse,'
65   'There falling out at tennis'; or perchance,
'I saw him enter such a house of sale,'
Videlicet, a brothel, or so forth.
See you now;
Your bait of falsehood takes this carp of truth;
70   And thus do we of wisdom and of reach,
With windlasses and with assays of bias,
By indirections find directions out.
So, by my former lecture and advice,
Shall you my son. You have me, have you not?

75   REYNALDO: My lord, I have.

POLONIUS: God be wi' ye. Fare ye well!

REYNALDO: Good my lord! *[Going.]*

sir," or "friend," or "gentleman," or whatever the style of address is of this man and his country.

REYNALDO: *Very good, my lord.*

POLONIUS: *And then, sir, he will do this—he will—what was I about to say? By God, I was about to say something. Where did I leave off?*

REYNALDO: *At "will definitely agree with you," at "friend or so," and "gentleman."*

POLONIUS: *Yes, at "will definitely agree with you." Yes, indeed. He will end like this: "I know the gentleman, I saw him yesterday," or "the other day," then or then, doing such-and-such, "and, as you say, he was gambling," "drunk," "quarreling at the tennis court," or, perhaps, "I saw him enter a house of business," namely, a whorehouse, or so forth. Do you now see? Your use of falsehoods will uncover the truth. This is how men who possess wisdom and ability—through indirect methods directly find out how things are going. If you consider my instructions and advice, you will find out the truth about my son. You understand me, don't you?*

REYNALDO: *I do, my lord.*

POLONIUS: *Goodbye. Farewell.*

REYNALDO: *Yes, my lord.*

POLONIUS: Observe his inclination in yourself.

REYNALDO: I shall, my lord.

80   POLONIUS: And let him play his music.

REYNALDO: Well, my lord.

POLONIUS: Farewell!
                      [Exit Reynaldo.]
[Enter Ophelia.]
    How now, Ophelia, what's the matter?

OPHELIA: O, my lord, my lord, I have been so affrighted!

85   POLONIUS: With what, i' the name of God?

OPHELIA: My lord, as I was sewing in my closet,
    Lord Hamlet, with his doublet all unbraced,
    No hat upon his head, his stockings fouled,
    Ungartered, and down-gyved to his ankle;
90   Pale as his shirt, his knees knocking each other,
    And with a look so piteous in purport
    As if he had been loosed out of hell
    To speak of horrors, he comes before me.

POLONIUS: Mad for thy love?

95   OPHELIA: My lord, I do not know,
    But truly I do fear it.

POLONIUS: What said he?

OPHELIA: He took me by the wrist and held me hard;
    Then goes he to the length of all his arm,
100   And, with his other hand thus o'er his brow,
    He falls to such perusal of my face
    As he would draw it. Long stay'd he so.

POLONIUS: *Observe him closely yourself!*

REYNALDO: *I will, my lord.*

POLONIUS: *And make sure he practices his music.*

REYNALDO: *Yes, my lord.*

POLONIUS: *Goodbye!*

[Reynaldo exits]

[Ophelia enters]
 How are you, Ophelia? What's the matter?

OPHELIA: *Oh, my lord, my lord, I have been so frightened!*

POLONIUS: *Why, in the name of God?*

OPHELIA: *My lord, as I was sewing in my chamber, Lord Hamlet entered my room with his shirt unbuttoned, without a hat, with dirty stockings without garters, white as his shirt, his knees shaking, and with a terrified look on his face as if he had escaped hell to describe its horrors.*

POLONIUS: *Mad for your love?*

OPHELIA: *My lord, I do not know, but I'm truly afraid that's the case.*

POLONIUS: *What did he say?*

OPHELIA: *He took me by the wrist and held me firmly. Then he held me at arm's length and, with his other hand over his brow, he began to study my face as if he was going to draw it. He stayed like this for a long time. At last, as he was shaking my arm a little and nodding three times, his sigh was so deep and intense that it seemed as his*

79

At last, a little shaking of mine arm,
And thrice his head thus waving up and down,
105   He raised a sigh so piteous and profound
As it did seem to shatter all his bulk
And end his being. That done, he lets me go,
And with his head over his shoulder turn'd
He seem'd to find his way without his eyes;
110   For out o' doors he went without their help,
And to the last bended their light on me.

POLONIUS: Come, go with me. I will go seek the King.
This is the very ecstasy of love,
Whose violent property fordoes itself
115   And leads the will to desperate undertakings
As oft as any passion under heaven
That does afflict our natures. I am sorry.
What, have you given him any hard words of late?

OPHELIA: No, my good lord; but, as you did command,
120   I did repel his letters and denied
His access to me.

POLONIUS: That hath made him mad.
I am sorry that with better heed and judgment
I had not quoted him. I fear'd he did but trifle
125   And meant to wrack thee; but beshrew my jealousy!
By heaven, it is as proper to our age
To cast beyond ourselves in our opinions
As it is common for the younger sort
To lack discretion. Come, go we to the King.
130   This must be known; which, being kept close, might move
More grief to hide than hate to utter love.

[Exeunt.]

80

entire body seemed to shake and end his life. Having done that, he let me go, and, looking back at me over his shoulder, he seemed to find his way without the help of his eyes. He went out the door without looking in front of himself and stared at me until the very last moment.

POLONIUS: *Come, come with me. I will find the king. This is the most extreme form of love, which, in its violent nature, leads to destruction and drives the will to take desperate measures, the way any passion's known to affect men's souls. I am sorry. Have you spoken harshly to him recently?*

OPHELIA: *No, my good lord; but, as you commanded me, I did not accept his letters and denied him access to me.*

POLONIUS: *That has made him mad. I am sorry that I did not observe him more closely. I was afraid that he was merely playing with you and planned to ruin your reputation. Woe to my suspicious mind! By heaven, it is as characteristic of men of my age to overestimate our own opinions as it is for the young ones to lack discretion. Come, let's go to the king. He must be notified of this incident which, could cause more trouble if we keep it a secret than it would cause resentment if we revealed it.*

[They exit]

Scene 2

Elsinore. A room in the Castle.

Flourish. [Enter King, Queen, Rosencrantz and Guildenstern, and attendants.]

KING: Welcome, dear Rosencrantz and Guildenstern.
Moreover that we much did long to see you,
The need we have to use you did provoke
Our hasty sending. Something have you heard
5 Of Hamlet's transformation—so call it,
Sith nor the exterior nor the inward man
Resembles that it was. What it should be,
More than his father's death, that thus hath put him
So much from the understanding of himself,
10 I cannot dream of. I entreat you both
That, being of so young days brought up with him,
And sith so neighbour'd to his youth and haviour,
That you vouchsafe your rest here in our court
Some little time; so by your companies
15 To draw him on to pleasures, and to gather
So much as from occasion you may glean,
Whether aught to us unknown afflicts him thus
That open'd lies within our remedy.

QUEEN: Good gentlemen, he hath much talk'd of you,
20 And sure I am two men there are not living
To whom he more adheres. If it will please you
To show us so much gentry and good will
As to expend your time with us awhile
For the supply and profit of our hope,
25 Your visitation shall receive such thanks
As fits a king's remembrance.

ROSENCRANTZ: Both your Majesties
Might, by the sovereign power you have of us,

Scene 2

A room in the castle.

[A trumpet sounds. King, Queen, Rosencrantz, Guildenstern, and Attendants enter]

KING: *Welcome, dear Rosencrantz and Guildenstern! Besides the fact that we really wanted to see you, we sent for you with great haste, because we need your services. You have heard a little about Hamlet's transformation. I call it that, because he does not resemble his former self, physically or mentally. I cannot begin to imagine what it is, apart from his father's death, that has changed him so much. I am asking you both, since you have been brought up with him from a young age, and since you are so close to him in age and personality, that you agree to remain here at our court for a while, so that he will pay attention to life's pleasures again in your company and so that you can find out—as much as any opportunity may allow you—if something we do not know about torments him and whether we could solve the problem.*

QUEEN: *Good gentlemen, he has talked a lot about you, and I am sure there are no two men he is more attached to than to you. If you would be so kind to show your good will and do us the favor of spending your time here with us for a while in order to support and advance our hopes, we will reward your visit in a most royal manner.*

ROSENCRANTZ: *Both your Majesties, due to your power as sovereigns, can order us to fulfill you revered wishes instead of asking for our support.*

Put your dread pleasures more into command
30   Than to entreaty.

GUILDENSTERN: But we both obey,
        And here give up ourselves, in the full bent,
        To lay our service freely at your feet,
        To be commanded.

35   KING: Thanks, Rosencrantz and gentle Guildenstern.

QUEEN: Thanks, Guildenstern and gentle Rosencrantz.
        And I beseech you instantly to visit
        My too much changed son. Go, some of you,
        And bring these gentlemen where Hamlet is.

40   GUILDENSTERN: Heavens make our presence and our practices
        Pleasant and helpful to him!

QUEEN: Ay, amen!

        [Exeunt Rosencrantz and Guildenstern, with some Attendants.]

[Enter Polonius.]

POLONIUS: The ambassadors from Norway, my good lord,
        Are joyfully return'd.

45   KING: Thou still hast been the father of good news.

POLONIUS: Have I, my lord? Assure you, my good liege,
        I hold my duty as I hold my soul,
        Both to my God and to my gracious King.
        And I do think, or else this brain of mine
50   Hunts not the trail of policy so sure
        As it hath used to do, that I have found
        The very cause of Hamlet's lunacy.

KING: O, speak of that! That do I long to hear.

GUILDENSTERN: But we both obey you and give ourselves up entirely. We offer our services freely to your command.

KING: Thanks, Rosencrantz and gentle Guildenstern.

QUEEN: Thanks, Guildenstern and gentle Rosencrantz. And I ask you to visit my strangely changed son immediately. Go, one of you attendants, and lead these gentlemen to Hamlet.

GUILDENSTERN: May God assure that our presence and our assistance will be welcome and helpful!

QUEEN: Yes, amen!

[Rosencrantz, Guildenstern, and some Attendants exit]

[Polonius enters]

POLONIUS: My good lord, the ambassadors from Norway have safely returned.

KING: You have always been the bearer of good news.

POLONIUS: Have I, my lord? I assure you, my sovereign, that my sense of duty and my soul are dedicated to God and to my gracious king. And I do believe, unless my brain has ceased to function as well as it used to, that I have found the precise cause of Hamlet's madness.

KING: Oh, tell me that! I long to hear what it is!

POLONIUS: Give first admittance to the ambassadors.
55   My news shall be the fruit to that great feast.

KING: Thyself do grace to them, and bring them in.
                        [Exit Polonius.]
        He tells me, my dear Gertrude, he hath found
        The head and source of all your son's distemper.

QUEEN: I doubt it is no other but the main,
60   His father's death and our o'erhasty marriage.

KING: Well, we shall sift him.

[Enter Polonius, Voltimand, and Cornelius.]
                  Welcome, my good friends.
        Say, Voltimand, what from our brother Norway?

VOLTIMAND: Most fair return of greetings and desires.
65   Upon our first, he sent out to suppress
        His nephew's levies; which to him appear'd
        To be a preparation 'gainst the Polack,
        But better look'd into, he truly found
        It was against your Highness; whereat griev'd,
70   That so his sickness, age, and impotence
        Was falsely borne in hand, sends out arrests
        On Fortinbras; which he, in brief, obeys,
        Receives rebuke from Norway, and, in fine,
        Makes vow before his uncle never more
75   To give the assay of arms against your Majesty.
        Whereon old Norway, overcome with joy,
        Gives him three thousand crowns in annual fee
        And his commission to employ those soldiers,
        So levied as before, against the Polack;
80   With an entreaty, herein further shown,
        [Gives a paper.]
        That it might please you to give quiet pass
        Through your dominions for this enterprise,
        On such regards of safety and allowance
        As therein are set down.

POLONIUS: First, admit the ambassadors. My news will be the dessert that follows that great feast.

KING: Do the honors yourself and bring them inside. [Polonius exits] He tells me, my dear Gertrude, that he has found the source of your son's illness.

QUEEN: I believe the main cause is his father's death and our hasty marriage.

KING: Well, we will examine him.

[Polonius enters with Voltimand and Cornelius] Welcome, my good friends. Explain, Voltimand, what news do you bring from our fellow King of Norway?

VOLTIMAND: An agreeable response to your greetings and wishes. When we first presented our concerns, he sent orders to his nephew ordering him to cease raising an army, which Norway had believed was part of war preparations against Poland, but when he investigated the issue further, he found that the war preparations were, indeed, directed against you, your Highness. He was very sad that his sickness, old age, and lack of power had thus been taken advantage of and sent orders to restrict Fortinbras. In brief, Fortinbras obeyed these orders, accepted the King of Norway's disapproval, and, in the end, swore in front of his uncle that he will never again order an attack against your Majesty. The old King of Norway, overjoyed, promised him an annual allowance of three thousand crowns, and gave him permission to reassemble the troops and move against the King of Poland. He requests from you in writing [Handing over a paper] that you will allow his troops to pass through your dominions safely, according to the terms and condition expressed in this letter.

85 KING: It likes us well;
   And at our more consider'd time we'll read,
   Answer, and think upon this business.
   Meantime we thank you for your well-took labour.
   Go to your rest; at night we'll feast together.
90 Most welcome home!   *[Exeunt Ambassadors.]*

  POLONIUS: This business is well ended.
   My liege, and madam, to expostulate
   What majesty should be, what duty is,
   Why day is day, night night, and time is time.
95 Were nothing but to waste night, day, and time.
   Therefore, since brevity is the soul of wit
   And tediousness the limbs and outward flourishes,
   I will be brief. Your noble son is mad.
   Mad call I it; for, to define true madness,
100 What is't but to be nothing else but mad?
   But let that go.

  QUEEN: More matter, with less art.

  POLONIUS: Madam, I swear I use no art at all.
   That he is mad, 'tis true: 'tis true 'tis pity;
105 And pity 'tis 'tis true—a foolish figure!
   But farewell it, for I will use no art.
   Mad let us grant him then. And now remains
   That we find out the cause of this effect
   Or rather say, the cause of this defect,
110 For this effect defective comes by cause.
   Thus it remains, and the remainder thus.
   Perpend.
   I have a daughter—have while she is mine—
   Who in her duty and obedience, mark,
115 Hath given me this. Now gather, and surmise.

  [Reads] To the celestial, and my soul's idol, the most beautified
  Ophelia—

KING: *I am very pleased, and when I have time to address these issues, I will read this letter, answer it, and think about the entire matter. In the meantime, I thank you for doing a good job. Go, rest! Tonight, we'll feast together. Welcome home, indeed!*
[Voltimand and Cornelius exit]

POLONIUS: *This matter has been settled favorably. My sovereign, and dear madam, to explain what royalty should be like, what duty is, why day is day, why night is night, and why time is time would be nothing but a waste of night, day, and time. Therefore, since briefness is the essence of wisdom, and too many words are merely decorations, the arms and legs, I will be brief. Your noble son is mad. I call it mad, because the definition of madness means nothing other than to be mad. But don't worry about that.*

QUEEN: *More substance and less style.*

POLONIUS: *Madam, I swear I'm not stylizing at all. It's true that he's mad. That it's true is a pity, and it's a pity that it's true—that's a foolish figure of speech. But never mind that; I will use no more stylized language. Granted, he is mad; it remains for us to find out the cause of this effect, or I should rather say, the cause of this defect, because this effect has a defective cause. It remains like that, and what remains is this: Consider! I have a daughter—I'll have her as long as she's young—who, dutiful and obedient, has given me this. Consider this: [He reads] "To the celestial idol of my soul, the most made beautiful Ophelia"—That is a bad phrase, a vile phrase, "made beautiful," is a vile phrase. But you will hear: [He reads] "to her excellent pure heart, etc. etc."*

That's an ill phrase, a vile phrase; 'beautified' is a vile phrase.
But you shall hear.
120   *[Reads.]* In her excellent white bosom, these, &c.

QUEEN: Came this from Hamlet to her?

POLONIUS: Good madam, stay awhile. I will be faithful.
       [Reads.]   Doubt thou the stars are fire;
                  Doubt that the sun doth move;
125   Doubt truth to be a liar;
                  But never doubt I love.
    O dear Ophelia, I am ill at these numbers; I have not art to reckon
my groans. But that I love thee best, O most best, believe it. Adieu.
             Thine evermore, most dear lady, whilst this
130   machine is to him,
                                 Hamlet.

This, in obedience, hath my daughter shown me;
And more above, hath his solicitings,
As they fell out by time, by means, and place,
135   All given to mine ear.

KING: But how hath she
    Receiv'd his love?

POLONIUS: What do you think of me?

KING: As of a man faithful and honourable.

140   POLONIUS: I would fain prove so. But what might you think,
       When I had seen this hot love on the wing—
       As I perceiv'd it, I must tell you that,
       Before my daughter told me—what might you,
       Or my dear Majesty your queen here, think,
145   If I had play'd the desk or table-book,
       Or given my heart a winking, mute and dumb,
       Or look'd upon this love with idle sight?
       What might you think? No, I went round to work

QUEEN: *Did this come from Hamlet to her?*

POLONIUS: *Good madam, wait. I will read everything.* [He reads]
  "*Doubt the stars are fire;*
     doubt that the sun does move;
  suspect truth to be a liar;
     but never doubt I love you.
  Oh, dear Ophelia, I am a poor poet. I have no skill for recounting my longing.
  But believe that I love you more than anyone, more than anyone, believe this!
  Adieu! Yours forever, dearest lady, as long as I live,

                                        Hamlet."

My daughter has obediently given this to me, and, what's more, has informed me of the details of his courtship—the time, manner, and place of his requests. All this she told to me.

KING: *But how has she reacted to his love declarations?*

POLONIUS: *What do you think of me?*

KING: *I think you're a faithful and honorable man.*

POLONIUS: *I would willingly prove it. But what might you have thought, when I saw this hot passion growing—I realized it, I must tell you, before my daughter told me—what would you, or my dear Majesty, your queen, have thought, if I had been silent like a desk or book or had closed my eyes deliberately, if I had pretended I didn't hear, or if I had not paid attention to this love, what would you think? No, I went straight to work, and this is what I told my young daughter: "Young Hamlet is a prince, out of your league. This cannot happen!" And then, this is what I ordered: she must*

And my young mistress thus I did bespeak:
150 'Lord Hamlet is a prince, out of thy star.
This must not be.' And then I prescripts gave her,
That she should lock herself from his resort,
Admit no messengers, receive no tokens.
Which done, she took the fruits of my advice,
155 And he, repellèd—a short tale to make—
Fell into a sadness, then into a fast,
Thence to a watch, thence into a weakness,
Thence to a lightness, and, by this declension,
Into the madness wherein now he raves,
160 And all we mourn for.

KING: Do you think 'tis this?

QUEEN: It may be, very like.

POLONIUS: Hath there been such a time—I would fain know that—
That I have positively said ''Tis so,'
165 When it proved otherwise?

KING: Not that I know.

POLONIUS: *[Pointing to his head and shoulder.]* Take this from this, if
this be otherwise.
If circumstances lead me, I will find
170 Where truth is hid, though it were hid indeed
Within the centre.

KING: How may we try it further?

POLONIUS: You know, sometimes he walks four hours together
Here in the lobby.

175 QUEEN: So he does indeed.

POLONIUS: At such a time I'll loose my daughter to him.
Be you and I behind an arras then;

lock herself away from his advances, admit no messengers, and accept no gifts from him. She took my advice, and he, rejected—to cut a long story short—was overcome with sadness, then with fasting, then with an inability to sleep, then with weakness, then with lightheadedness, and by this decline, he fell into the madness that has hold of him now, which we all mourn.

KING: *Do you think that's what it is?*

QUEEN: *It may be; very likely.*

POLONIUS: *Has there ever been an occasion—I'd like to know—when I claimed something was definitely a certain way and it proved otherwise?*

KING: *Not that I know of.*

POLONIUS: [Pointing to his head his shoulders] *Take this away from this, if I'm not right. No matter where the facts lead me, I will find out the truth, even if it is at the center of the earth.*

KING: *How can we find out more?*

POLONIUS: *You know sometimes he walks for four hours here in the lobby?*

QUEEN: *So he does, indeed.*

POLONIUS: *At that time, I'll send my daughter to him. You and I will hide behind a wall covering and view the encounter. If he doesn't love*

Mark the encounter. If he love her not,
And he not from his reason fall'n thereon
180 Let me be no assistant for a state,
But keep a farm and carters.

KING: We will try it.

QUEEN: But look where sadly the poor wretch comes reading.

POLONIUS: Away, I do beseech you both, away.
185   I'll board him presently. O, give me leave.
                    [Exeunt King and Queen, and Attendants.]
[Enter Hamlet reading.]
        How does my good Lord Hamlet?

HAMLET: Well, God-a-mercy.

POLONIUS: Do you know me, my lord?

HAMLET: Excellent well. You are a fishmonger.

190 POLONIUS: Not I, my lord.

HAMLET: Then I would you were so honest a man.

POLONIUS: Honest, my lord?

HAMLET: Ay, sir. To be honest, as this world goes, is to be one man
        picked out of ten thousand.

195 POLONIUS: That's very true, my lord.

HAMLET: *[Reads]* For if the sun breed maggots in a dead dog, being a god-
        kissing carrion—Have you a daughter?

POLONIUS: I have, my lord.

her and has not lost his mind because of it, don't allow me to work for your government any longer, but order me to work on a farm, hauling carts.

KING: We will try it.

QUEEN: But look how sad-looking this poor wretch comes, reading.

POLONIUS: Go away, I beg you both, go! I'll talk to him immediately.

[The King, Queen, and Attendant exit]
[Hamlet enters, reading]
   How are you, my good lord Hamlet?

HAMLET: Well, thank God.

POLONIUS: Do you know me, my lord?

HAMLET: Very well. You are a fishseller.

POLONIUS: Not I, my lord.

HAMLET: Then I wish you were that honest a man.

POLONIUS: Honest, my lord?

HAMLET: Yes, sir. To be honest in this world is to be one man in ten thousand.

POLONIUS: That's very true, my lord.

HAMLET: [Reads] If the sun can produce maggots in a dead dog, the meat deserving kisses—Do you have a daughter?

POLONIUS: I do, my lord.

HAMLET: Let her not walk i' th' sun. Conception is a blessing, but not
200   as your daughter may conceive. Friend, look to't.

POLONIUS: [Aside.] How say you by that? Still harping on my daughter. Yet he knew me not at first. He said I was a fishmonger. He
is far gone. And truly in my youth I suffered much extremity
for love, very near this. I'll speak to him again.—What do you
205   read, my lord?

HAMLET: Words, words, words.

POLONIUS: What is the matter, my lord?

HAMLET: Between who?

POLONIUS: I mean, the matter that you read, my lord.

210 HAMLET: Slanders, sir; for the satirical rogue says here that old men
have grey beards; that their faces are wrinkled; their eyes purging thick amber and plum-tree gum; and that they have a plen-
tiful lack of wit, together with most weak hams. All which, sir,
though I most powerfully and potently believe, yet I hold it
215   not honesty to have it thus set down; for you yourself, sir, shall
grow old as I am if, if like a crab, you could go backward.

POLONIUS: [Aside.] Though this be madness, yet there is a method
in't.—Will you walk out of the air, my lord?

HAMLET: Into my grave?

220 POLONIUS: Indeed, that is out of the air. [Aside.] How pregnant sometimes his replies are! a happiness that often madness hits on,
which reason and sanity could not so prosperously be delivered
of. I will leave him and suddenly contrive the means of meeting
between him and my daughter.— My honourable lord, I will
225   most humbly take my leave of you.

96

HAMLET: *Don't let her walk in the sun! Conception is a blessing, but not as your daughter might conceive—friend, be careful!*

POLONIUS: [Aside] *What do you say to that? He is still dwelling on my daughter. Yet, he didn't even know me at first, saying I was a fish-monger. He has gone very mad. Certainly, I suffered greatly for love as a young man, much like this. I'll speak to him again [To Hamlet] What are you reading, my lord?*

HAMLET: *Words, words, words.*

POLONIUS: *What is the matter, my lord?*

HAMLET: *Between whom?*

POLONIUS: *I mean the subject that you're reading about, my lord.*

HAMLET: *Slanders, sir; the satirical writer says here that old men have gray beards, that their faces are wrinkled, that their eyes discharge a thick slime, and that they have a significant lack of common sense, as well as weak knees. I believe all of this with a powerful conviction, sir, but I don't think it's decent to write it down like this. As for yourself, sir, you would grow as old as I am now, if only you could walk backwards, like a crab does.*

POLONIUS: [Aside] *Though this is madness, there is some pattern to it.* [To Hamlet] *Will you walk out of the air, my lord?*

HAMLET: *Into my grave?*

POLONIUS: *Indeed, that's "out of the air." [Aside] How true his answers are at times! A luck that often comes with madness, which reason and sanity could not as easily develop. I will leave him and imme-diately arrange a meeting between him and my daughter—My honorable lord, allow me to leave!*

HAMLET: You cannot, sir, take from me anything that I will more willingly part withal—except my life, except my life, except my
life.

POLONIUS: Fare you well, my lord.

230 HAMLET: These tedious old fools!

[Enter Rosencrantz and Guildenstern.]

POLONIUS: You go to seek the Lord Hamlet. There he is.

ROSENCRANTZ: *[to Polonius.]* God save you, sir!
                                          [Exit Polonius.]

GUILDENSTERN: My honoured lord!

ROSENCRANTZ: My most dear lord!

235 HAMLET: My excellent good friends! How dost thou, Guildenstern?
          Ah, Rosencrantz! Good lads, how do ye both?

ROSENCRANTZ: As the indifferent children of the earth.

GUILDENSTERN: Happy, in that we are not over-happy.
          On Fortune's cap we are not the very button.

240 HAMLET: Nor the soles of her shoe?

ROSENCRANTZ: Neither, my lord.

HAMLET: Then you live about her waist, or in the middle of her
          favours?

GUILDENSTERN: Faith, her privates we.

245 HAMLET: In the secret parts of Fortune? O! most true! she is a strum-
          pet. What news?

HAMLET: *You cannot, sir, take anything from me that I will more willingly part with—except for my life, except for my life, except for my life.*

POLONIUS: *Goodbye, my lord!*

HAMLET: *These tedious old fools.*

[Rosencrantz and Guildenstern enter]

POLONIUS: *If you are looking for Lord Hamlet, there he is.*

ROSENCRANTZ: [To Polonius] *God save you, sir!*

[Polonius exits]

GUILDENSTERN: *My honored lord!*

ROSENCRANTZ: *My dearest lord!*

HAMLET: *My excellent friends! How are you, Guildenstern? Ah, Rosencrantz! Good fellows, how are you both?*

ROSENCRANTZ: *Not good, not bad.*

GUILDENSTERN: *We are happy about not being too happy. We are not on the top of Fate's cap today.*

HAMLET: *Nor under the soles of her shoe?*

ROSENCRANTZ: *Neither, my lord.*

HAMLET: *Then you're living right about her waist, or in the middle of her favors?*

GUILDENSTERN: *Well, we are her private parts!*

HAMLET: *The private parts of Lady Fortune? Oh, indeed, she is quite a prostitute! What news do you bring?*

ROSENCRANTZ: None, my lord, but that the world's grown honest.

HAMLET: Then is doomsday near. But your news is not true. Let me
question more in particular. What have you, my good friends,
250   deserved at the hands of Fortune that she sends you to prison
hither?

GUILDENSTERN: Prison, my lord?

HAMLET: Denmark's a prison.

ROSENCRANTZ: Then is the world one.

255 HAMLET: A goodly one; in which there are many confines, wards, and
dungeons, Denmark being one o' the worst.

ROSENCRANTZ: We think not so, my lord.

HAMLET: Why, then 'tis none to you; for there is nothing either good
or bad but thinking makes it so. To me it is a prison.

260 ROSENCRANTZ: Why, then your ambition makes it one. 'Tis too narrow
for your mind.

HAMLET: O God, I could be bounded in a nutshell and count myself a
king of infinite space, were it not that I have bad dreams.

GUILDENSTERN: Which dreams indeed are ambition; for the very sub-
265 stance of the ambitious is merely the shadow of a dream.

HAMLET: A dream itself is but a shadow.

ROSENCRANTZ: Truly, and I hold ambition of so airy and light a quality
that it is but a shadow's shadow.

HAMLET: Then are our beggars bodies, and our monarchs and out-

ROSENCRANTZ: *None, my lord, only that the world has become honest.*

HAMLET: *Then doomsday is near! But your news is not true. Let me ask you more directly. What have you done, my good friends, that Fortune has imprisoned you here?*

GUILDENSTERN: *Imprisoned, my lord?*

HAMLET: *Denmark's a prison.*

ROSENCRANTZ: *Then the whole world is one.*

HAMLET: *A very good one, in which there are many confines, cells, and dungeons. Denmark is one of the worst.*

ROSENCRANTZ: *We do not think so, my lord.*

HAMLET: *Well, then it is not a prison to you. Nothing is either good or bad unless your mind decides it is. To me, it is a prison.*

ROSENCRANTZ: *Well, then your ambition makes it one. It is too confining for your mind.*

HAMLET: *Oh, God, I could be confined inside a nutshell and still consider myself a king of infinite space, if it were not for the fact that I have bad dreams.*

GUILDENSTERN: *Indeed, dreams show ambition, because the essence of an ambitious man is merely the shadow of a dream.*

HAMLET: *A dream itself is only a shadow.*

ROSENCRANTZ: *Truly, and I believe ambition to be so airy and light that it is only a shadow's shadow.*

HAMLET: *Then only beggars have real bodies and our monarchs and over-*

270 stretched heroes the beggars' shadows. Shall we to the court?
For, by my fay, I cannot reason.

ROSENCRANTZ AND GUILDENSTERN: We'll wait upon you.

HAMLET: No such matter! I will not sort you with the rest of my
servants; for, to speak to you like an honest man, I am most
275 dreadfully attended. But in the beaten way of friendship, what
make you at Elsinore?

ROSENCRANTZ: To visit you, my lord; no other occasion.

HAMLET: Beggar that I am, I am even poor in thanks; but I thank you;
And sure, dear friends, my thanks are too dear a halfpenny.
280 Were you not sent for? Is it your own inclining? Is it a free visitation? Come, deal justly with me. Come, come! Nay, speak.

GUILDENSTERN: What should we say, my lord?

HAMLET: Why, anything, but to the purpose. You were sent for; and
there is a kind of confession in your looks, which your modes-
285 ties have not craft enough to colour. I know the good King and
Queen have sent for you.

ROSENCRANTZ: To what end, my lord?

HAMLET: That you must teach me. But let me conjure you by the
rights of our fellowship, by the consonancy of our youth, by
290 the obligation of our ever-preserved love, and by what more
dear a better proposer could charge you withal, be even and
direct with me, whether you were sent for or no.

ROSENCRANTZ: [Aside to Guildenstern.] What say you?

HAMLET: [Aside.] Nay then, I have an eye of you.—If you love me,
295 hold not off.

ambitious heroes are the shadows of the beggars. Shall we go to court? Because—by my faith, I cannot figure it out!

ROSENCRANTZ AND GUILDENSTERN: We'll escort you there.

HAMLET: No such thing! I will not associate you with the rest of my servants. To tell you honestly, I am taken care of horribly! But, talking between friends, what are you doing at Elsinore?

ROSENCRANTZ: To visit you, my lord. No other reason.

HAMLET: Beggar that I am, I can only thank you poorly. But I do thank you, and, surely, dear friends, my thanks aren't worth a penny. Were you sent for? Was it your idea to come here? Is it a visit without a purpose? Come, come, be honest with me. Come, come— now speak!

GUILDENSTERN: What should we say, my lord?

HAMLET: Well, anything, but explain the purpose of your visit. You were sent for. I perceive a confession in your eyes, which your decency cannot hide. I know the good King and Queen have sent for you.

ROSENCRANTZ: Why, my lord?

HAMLET: You need to tell me that. Let me reqiest, that by our long friendship, by our similar ages, by the bond of our well-established love, and by anything important that comes to mind that you will be honest and straightforward with me and let me know whether you were sent for or not.

ROSENCRANTZ: [Aside to Guildenstern] What do you say to that?

HAMLET: [Aside] Well, then, understand you. If you love me, don't hesitate to answer.

GUILDENSTERN: My lord, we were sent for.

HAMLET: I will tell you why. So shall my anticipation prevent your
discovery, and your secrecy to the King and Queen moult no
feather. I have of late—but wherefore I know not—lost all my
300   mirth, forgone all custom of exercises; and indeed, it goes so
heavily with my disposition that this goodly frame, the earth,
seems to me a sterile promontory; this most excellent canopy,
the air, look you, this brave o'erhanging firmament, this majes-
tical roof fretted with golden fire, why, it appears no other
305   thing to me than a foul and pestilent congregation of vapours.
What a piece of work is a man! how noble in reason! how
infinite in faculty! in form and moving how express and admirable! in action how like an angel! in apprehension how like
a god! the beauty of the world, the paragon of animals! And
310   yet to me what is this quintessence of dust? Man delights not
me—no, nor woman neither, though by your smiling you seem
to say so.

ROSENCRANTZ: My lord, there was no such stuff in my thoughts.

HAMLET: Why did you laugh then, when I said man delights not me?

315   ROSENCRANTZ: To think, my lord, if you delight not in man, what
lenten entertainment the players shall receive from you. We
coted them on the way, and hither are they coming to offer you
service.

HAMLET: He that plays the king shall be welcome; his Majesty shall
320   have tribute of me. The adventurous knight shall use his foil
and target; the lover shall not sigh gratis; the humorous man
shall end his part in peace; the clown shall make those laugh
whose lungs are tickle o' the sere; and the lady shall say her
mind freely, or the blank verse shall halt for't. What players are
325   they?

GUILDENSTERN: *My lord, we were sent for.*

HAMLET: *I will tell you why, so that my explanation will prevent your confession, and your secret with the King and Queen will not be harmed in the least. Lately—I don't know why—I have lost my happy disposition and neglected all my activities. Indeed, my spirits are so low that this beautiful structure, the earth, seems to me like a sterile cliff. This beautiful canopy, the air, this splendid overhanging starry sky, this majestic roof adorned with golden fire— well, it seems to me to be no more than a foul and toxic collection of vapors. What a masterpiece man is! How noble in his reasoning, how infinite in his abilities, how accurate and admirable in shape and movement, how angel-like in his actions, how god-like in his understanding—the beauty of the world, the most perfect creature of all animals! And yet, to me, what is this finest and purest particle of dust? Man does not give me happiness, neither does woman, though your smiles tell me you seem to think so.*

ROSENCRANTZ: *My lord, nothing like this was on my mind.*

HAMLET: *Why did you laugh, then, when I said that man does not give me happiness?*

ROSENCRANTZ: *I was only thinking that, if you do not find happiness in man, what a poor reception the actors will receive from you. We passed them on the way here, and they are coming to offer you their services.*

HAMLET: *Whoever plays the King will be welcome; I will give tribute to his Majesty. The adventurous knight must use his sword and shield, the lover must not sigh without a reward, the humorous man will play his role peacefully until the end, the clown will even tickle the lungs of people who shouldn't laugh, and the lady will speak her mind freely, or the poetry will be inadequate. What kind of actors are they?*

ROSENCRANTZ: Even those you were wont to take such delight in, the tragedians of the city.

HAMLET: How chances it they travel? Their residence, both in reputation and profit, was better both ways.

330   ROSENCRANTZ: I think their inhibition comes by the means of the late innovation.

HAMLET: Do they hold the same estimation they did when I was in the city? Are they so followed?

ROSENCRANTZ: No, indeed, are they not.

HAMLET: How comes it? Do they grow rusty?

335   ROSENCRANTZ: Nay, their endeavour keeps in the wonted pace; but there is, sir, an eyrie of children, little eyases, that cry out on the top of question and are most tyrannically clapped for't. These are now the fashion, and so berattle the common stag-es—so they call them—that many wearing rapiers are afraid of
340   goose-quills and dare scarce come thither.

HAMLET: What, are they children? Who maintains 'em? How are they escoted? Will they pursue the quality no longer than they can sing? Will they not say afterwards, if they should grow themselves to common players—as it is most like, if their means are
345   no better—their writers do them wrong to make them exclaim against their own succession.

ROSENCRANTZ: Faith, there has been much to do on both sides; and the nation holds it no sin to tarre them to controversy. There was, for a while, no money bid for argument unless the poet and the
350   player went to cuffs in the question.

HAMLET: Is't possible?

GUILDENSTERN: O, there has been much throwing about of brains.

ROSENCRANTZ: The ones whose performances you used to enjoy—the tragedians of the city.

HAMLET: Why are they traveling? Playing on their home stage guaranteed them better profits and a better reputation.

ROSENCRANTZ: I think they were prohibited due to a number of recent restrictive actions.

HAMLET: Do they enjoy the same reputation they did when I was in the city? Are they still popular?

ROSENCRANTZ: No, indeed, they are not.

HAMLET: Why? Have they turned boring?

ROSENCRANTZ: No, their work is still fresh, but there is, sir, a company of child actors, young fledglings, who raise their voices above all others and are outrageously popular. They are now very fashionable, and they badmouth the ordinary playhouses—as they call them—so that many men carrying swords are afraid to be satirized and don't dare to go there anymore.

HAMLET: What, they are children? Who organizes them? Who pays them? Will they pursue a career in acting only until their voices begin to change? Won't they say later, after joining the ranks of the common players—which is quite likely, since they cannot pursue any other career—that the playwrights were wrong to make them speak out against their own future profession?

ROSENCRANTZ: Yes, there has been much controversy on both sides, and the public doesn't seem to think it wrong to encourage further quarreling. For a while, no plays were commissioned that did not include this controversy in their plots.

HAMLET: Is it possible?

GUILDENSTERN: Oh, there have been many arguments about this issue.

HAMLET: Do the boys carry it away?

ROSENCRANTZ: Ay, that they do, my lord, Hercules and his load too.

355 HAMLET: It is not very strange; for my uncle is King of Denmark, and
those that would make mows at him while my father lived give
twenty, forty, fifty, a hundred ducats apiece for his picture in
little. 'Sblood, there is something in this more than natural, if
philosophy could find it out.

[Flourish for the Players.]

360 GUILDENSTERN: There are the players.

HAMLET: Gentlemen, you are welcome to Elsinore. Your hands, come!
Then appurtenance of welcome is fashion and ceremony. Let
me comply with you in this garb, lest my extent to the players—which, I tell you, must show fairly outwards— should
365 more appear like entertainment than yours. You are welcome.
But my uncle-father and aunt-mother are deceived.

GUILDENSTERN: In what, my dear lord?

HAMLET: I am but mad north-north-west. When the wind is southerly
I know a hawk from a handsaw.

[Enter Polonius.]

370 POLONIUS: Well be with you, gentlemen!

HAMLET: Hark you, Guildenstern, and you too—at each ear a hearer!
That great baby you see there is not yet out of his swaddling
clouts.

ROSENCRANTZ: Happily he's the second time come to them; for they
375 say an old man is twice a child.

HAMLET: Are the children winning?

ROSENCRANTZ: Yes, they are, my lord—like Hercules watching over the world.

HAMLET: It is not very strange. My uncle is King of Denmark, and the people who made ugly faces at him while my father was still alive, now give twenty, forty, fifty, a hundred coins apiece for a small painting of his picture. By God, there is something unnatural in this—if philosophy could only reveal it.

[A trumpet sounds inside]

GUILDENSTERN: There are the players.

HAMLET: Gentlemen, welcome to Elsinore. Shake hands with me, come! Ceremony is part of any welcoming ritual. Let me greet you in this manner, in case the courtesy I show to the actors—which, I can tell you, will be obvious—seems more like an entertainment than yours. You are welcome! But my uncle-father and my aunt-mother are mistaken.

GUILDENSTERN: How, my dear lord?

HAMLET: I am mad only when the wind blows from the north or north-west. When the wind blows from the south, I can tell a hawk from a handsaw.

[Polonuis enters]

POLONIUS: Greetings, gentlemen!

HAMLET: Listen, Guildenstern, and you, too—give me your ear. That big baby you see there has not yet outgrown his diapers.

ROSENCRANTZ: Perhaps he's wearing them for the second time. As they say, an old man is a child again.

HAMLET: I will prophesy he comes to tell me of the players. Mark it.
You say right, sir; o' Monday morning; 'twas so indeed.

POLONIUS: My lord, I have news to tell you.

HAMLET: My lord, I have news to tell you. When Roscius was an actor
380   in Rome—

POLONIUS: The actors are come hither, my lord.

HAMLET: Buzz, buzz!

POLONIUS: Upon my honour—

HAMLET: Then came each actor on his ass—

385 POLONIUS: The best actors in the world, either for tragedy, comedy,
history, pastoral, pastoral-comical, historical-pastoral, tragical-
historical, tragical-comical-historical-pastoral; scene individ-
able, or poem unlimited. Seneca cannot be too heavy, nor
Plautus too light. For the law of writ and the liberty, these are
390   the only men.

HAMLET: O Jephthah, judge of Israel, what a treasure hadst thou!

POLONIUS: What treasure had he, my lord?

HAMLET: Why,
               'One fair daughter, and no more,
395   The which he loved passing well.'

POLONIUS: *[Aside]* Still on my daughter.

HAMLET: Am I not i' the right, old Jephthah?

HAMLET: *I predict that he comes to tell me about the actors. [Aloud] You are right, sir. On Monday morning. It was then, indeed.*

POLONIUS: *My lord, I have news to tell you.*

HAMLET: *My lord, I have news to tell you. When Roscius was an actor in Rome—*

POLONIUS: *The actors have arrived, my lord.*

HAMLET: *Quiet! Quiet!*

POLONIUS: *Upon my honor—*

HAMLET: *"Then came each actor on his ass"—*

POLONIUS: *They are the best actors in the world, either for tragedy, comedy, history, pastoral, pastoral-comical, historical-pastoral, tragical-historical, tragical-comical-historical-pastoral, for plays observing the unity of place, or for plays ignoring all rules. The plays by Seneca are not too serious for them, and the plays by Plautus are not too light; for formal or informal plays, these are the best players.*

HAMLET: *[Reciting] Oh, Jephthah, judge of Israel, what a treasure you had!*

POLONIUS: *What treasure did he have, my lord?*

HAMLET: *Well,*
> *"one fair daughter, and no more,*
> *which he loved very much."*

POLONIUS: *[Aside] Still dwelling on my daughter.*

HAMLET: *Am I not correct, old Jephthah?*

POLONIUS: If you call me Jephthah, my lord, I have a daughter that I
love passing well.

400 HAMLET: Nay, that follows not.

POLONIUS: What follows then, my lord?

HAMLET: Why,
                     As by lot, God wot,
and then, you know,
405   It came to pass, as most like it was.—
The first row of the pious chanson will show you more; for
look where my abridgment comes.
[Enter four or five Players.]
You are welcome, masters; welcome, all. I am glad to see thee
well. Welcome, good friends. O, my old friend? Why, thy face
410 is valanced since I saw thee last. Com'st' thou to' beard me in
Denmark? What, my young lady and mistress? By'r lady, your
ladyship is nearer to heaven than when I saw you last by the
altitude of a chopine. Pray God, your voice, like a piece of
uncurrent gold, be not cracked within the ring. Masters, you
415 are all welcome. We'll e'en to't like French falconers, fly at any
thing we see. We'll have a speech straight. Come, give us a taste
of your quality. Come, a passionate speech.

FIRST PLAY: What speech, my good lord?

HAMLET: I heard thee speak me a speech once, but it was never acted;
420 or if it was, not above once; for the play, I remember, pleased
not the million, 'twas caviary to the general; but it was—as I
received it, and others, whose judgments in such matters cried
in the top of mine— an excellent play, well digested in the
scenes, set down with as much modesty as cunning. I remem-
425 ber one said there were no sallets in the lines to make the matter savoury, nor no matter in the phrase that might indict the
author of affectation; but called it an honest method, as wholesome as sweet, and by very much more handsome than fine.
One speech in't I chiefly loved; 'twas Æneas' tale to Dido, and

POLONIUS: *If you call me Jephthah, my lord, yes, I have a daughter that I love very much.*

HAMLET: *No, I don't think that follows.*

POLONIUS: *What follows then, my lord?*

HAMLET: *Well, "As if by fate, God knows," and then, you know, "It happened, as it was very likely...." The first stanza of the pious song will tell you more; look, here comes my own entertainment!*
[The Players enter]
You are welcome, gentlemen, all welcome! I am glad to see you are doing well. Welcome, good friends! Oh, my old friend! Why, you have grown a beard since the last time I saw you! Did you come to confront me here in Denmark? Well, my young lady and mistress. [Greeting a young actor who plays women] By the Virgin Mary, you are closer to heaven than when I saw you last—at least by the height of your high heel shoes! I pray to God that your voice has not cracked and turned into a worthless piece of gold! Gentlemen, you are all welcome. We'll celebrate every moment—like the French falconers, who allow their falcons to capture anything at all! We'll listen to a speech immediately. Come, give us a taste of your professional skills; come, let's hear a passionate speech!

FIRST PLAYER: *What kind of speech, my good lord?*

HAMLET: *I heard you deliver a speech to me once, but it has never been performed, or if it has been, only one time. The play, I remember, did not please the masses. It was too refined for the common people, but, as far as I or other people with more authority on the subject than I have could tell, it was an excellent play. The scenes were well arranged, and the play equally displayed modesty and skill. I remember that somebody said that there were no spicy lines to flavor the piece, nor were there any lines that could accuse the author of affectation. It was an honest piece, as wholesome as it was sweet, and altogether much more well-rounded than pretentious. I especially loved one speech Aneas made to Dido, most of all the*

430   thereabout of it especially where he speaks of Priam's slaughter.
       If it live in your memory, begin at this line—let me see, let me
       see—
       The rugged Pyrrhus, like th' Hyrcanian beast—
       'Tis not so; it begins with Pyrrhus—

435   The rugged Pyrrhus, he whose sable arms,
       Black as his purpose, did the night resemble
       When he lay couched in the ominous horse,
       Hath now this dread and black complexion smear'd
       With heraldry more dismal. Head to foot

440   Now is he total gules, horridly trick'd
       With blood of fathers, mothers, daughters, sons.
       Baked and impasted with the parching streets,
       That lend a tyrannous and a damned light
       To their lord's murder. Roasted in wrath and fire,

445   And thus o'er-sized with coagulate gore,
       With eyes like carbuncles, the hellish Pyrrhus
       Old grandsire Priam seeks.
       So, proceed you.

POLONIUS: 'Fore God, my lord, well spoken, with good accent and
450   good discretion.

FIRST PLAY: 'Anon he finds him,
       Striking too short at Greeks. His antique sword,
       Rebellious to his arm, lies where it falls,
       Repugnant to command. Unequal match'd,

455   Pyrrhus at Priam drives, in rage strikes wide;
       But with the whiff and wind of his fell sword
       The unnerved father falls. Then senseless Ilium,
       Seeming to feel this blow, with flaming top
       Stoops to his base, and with a hideous crash

460   Takes prisoner Pyrrhus' ear. For lo! his sword,
       Which was declining on the milky head
       Of reverend Priam, seem'd i' the air to stick.
       So, as a painted tyrant, Pyrrhus stood,
       And like a neutral to his will and matter,

465   Did nothing.

part when he explains the slaying of Priam. If you can remember it, start with this line—let me see: 'The rugged Pyrrhus, like the Hyrcanian tiger....'" No, that's not it; it begins with Pyrrhus. "The rugged Pyrrhus, whose black armor, as dark as his purpose, resembled the night, as he lay inside the Trojan horse, has now smeared his dreadful and black face in a manner even more frightening. From head to toe, he now wears red; adorned horribly with the blood of fathers, mothers, daughters, sons, caked and crusted by the heat from the burning streets, which casts a tyrannous and cursed light on their lord's murder. Glowing with fiery wrath, and covered with clotted blood, with eyes shining like carbuncles, the hellish Pyrrhus seeks old grandfather Priam." Go on from here!

POLONIUS: *By God, my lord, this was well-spoken, with a good intonation and with and much sense.*

FIRST PLAYER: *"Soon he finds him, fighting the Greeks ineffectively. His old sword, disobeying his hand, lies where it falls, resisting his command. In an unequal fight, Pyrrhus attacks Priam, misses him in his rage, yet, blown over by the gust and wind of his cruel sword, the weakened father falls. The unfeeling Ilium, having felt that blow, falls down with its towers on fire, and, with a hideous crash, captivates Pyrrhus' ear. For, behold! His sword, which was coming down onto the white head of the revered Priam, seemed to halt in midair. Pyrrhus stood, the picture of a tyrant, and, torn between his intentions and his actions, he did nothing. But, as we often observe just before a storm breaks out, there is a silence in the heavens, the clouds stand still, the harsh winds cease, and the earth below stands still as death, before the thunder fills the air. And so, after Pyrrhus' hesitation, vengeance reawakens him and drives him to action. The Cyclops' hammer never fell on*

But as we often see, against some storm,
A silence in the heavens, the rack stand still,
The bold winds speechless, and the orb below
As hush as death—anon the dreadful thunder
470   Doth rend the region; so, after Pyrrhus' pause,
Aroused vengeance sets him new a-work;
And never did the Cyclops' hammers fall
On Mars's armour, forged for proof eterne,
With less remorse than Pyrrhus' bleeding sword
475   Now falls on Priam.
      Out, out, thou strumpet, Fortune! All you gods,
In general synod take away her power;
Break all the spokes and fellies from her wheel,
And bowl the round nave down the hill of heaven,
480   As low as to the fiends!

POLONIUS: This is too long.

HAMLET: It shall to the barber's, with your beard. Prithee say on.
      He's for a jig or a tale of bawdry, or he sleeps. Say on; come to
      Hecuba.

485   FIRST PLAY: But who, O who, had seen the mobled queen—

HAMLET: 'The mobled queen'?

POLONIUS: That's good! 'mobled queen' is good.

FIRST PLAY: Run barefoot up and down, threatening the flames
      With bisson rheum; a clout upon that head
490   Where late the diadem stood, and for a robe,
      About her lank and all o'erteemed loins,
      A blanket, in the alarm of fear caught up—
      Who this had seen, with tongue in venom steep'd
      'Gainst Fortune's state would treason have pronounced.
495   But if the gods themselves did see her then,
      When she saw Pyrrhus make malicious sport
      In mincing with his sword her husband's limbs,

116

Mars' armor, which had been forged to last eternally, with less pity than Pyrrhus' bloddy sword fell on Priam. Be gone, leave, Lady Fortune, you whore! All you Gods, consent to take away her power! Break all spokes and the rim from her wheel, and roll the round hub down the hill of heaven all the way down to hell!

POLONIUS: This is too long.

HAMLET: It will be trimmed at the barber's, along with your beard. Please continue. He's only interested in a dance number or an indecent story; otherwise he falls asleep. Speak on, come to Hecuba!

FIRST PLAYER: "But who, oh sorrow, had seen the muffled queen—"

HAMLET: "The muffled queen"?

POLONIUS: That's good! "Muffled queen" is good.

FIRST PLAYER: "Run barefoot up and down, threatening the flames with her many tears, a cloth on her head where her crown used to sit, and, for royal robes, around her loose, worn-out waist is a blanket, picked up hastily in fear. Whoever had have seen this, with a tongue filled with venom, would have declared that Lady Fortune is treasonous. But if the Gods themselves had seen her then, when she saw Pyrrhus play an evil game by chopping her husband's limbs with his sword, her instant cries would have moved the stars to tears and grieved the Gods, unless no mortal things can move them at all.

The instant burst of clamour that she made
Unless things mortal move them not at all
500 Would have made milch the burning eyes of heaven
And passion in the gods.

POLONIUS: Look, whether he has not turned his colour, and has tears
in's eyes. Prithee no more!

HAMLET: 'Tis well. I'll have thee speak out the rest of this soon. Good
505 my lord, will you see the players well bestow'd? Do you hear?
Let them be well used; for they are the abstract and brief chron-
icles of the time. After your death you were better have a bad
epitaph than their ill report while you live.

POLONIUS: My lord, I will use them according to their desert.

510 HAMLET: God's bodykins, man, much better! Use every man after his
desert, and who shall 'scape whipping? Use them after your
own honour and dignity. The less they deserve, the more merit
is in your bounty. Take them in.

POLONIUS: Come, sirs.

515 HAMLET: Follow him, friends. We'll hear a play to-morrow.
[Exit Polonius with all the Players but the First.]
Dost thou hear me, old friend? Can you play 'The Murder of
Gonzago'?

FIRST PLAY: Ay, my lord.

HAMLET: We'll ha't tomorrow night. You could, for a need, study a
520 speech of some dozen or sixteen lines which I would set down
and insert in't, could you not?

FIRST PLAY: Ay, my lord.

POLONIUS: *Note how his color has changed, and how he has tears in his eyes. Please, no more.*

HAMLET: *It's all right. I'll have you speak the rest of this soon. My good lord, will you see to it that the actors receive comfortable lodging? Do you hear me? Let them be treated well! They are responsible to note and record the history of our time. You would rather have a bad epitaph after your death, than receive a bad reputation through them while you're alive.*

POLONIUS: *My lord, I will treat them the way they deserve to be treated.*

HAMLET: *By the body of Christ, treat them much better! If we treat all men the way they deserve to be treated, who would not earn a beating? Treat them according to your own honor and dignity. The less they deserve it, the more commendable is your generosity. Take them inside.*

POLONIUS: *Come, gentlemen.*

HAMLET: *Follow him, friends. We'll hear a play tomorrow.*
[Polonius exits with all Players except for the First Player]
Listen to me, old friend. Can you perform "The Murder of Gonzago"?

FIRST PLAYER: *Yes, my lord.*

HAMLET: *We'll have it tomorrow night. Could you, if necessary, learn about twelve or sixteen lines, which I would write down and insert into the play?*

FIRST PLAYER: *Yes, my lord.*

HAMLET: Very well. Follow that lord, and look you mock him not.
    [Exit First Player.] My good friends, I'll leave you till night.
525   You are welcome to Elsinore.

ROSENCRANTZ: Good my lord!

HAMLET: Ay, so, God be wi' ye!
                  [Exeunt Rosencrantz and Guildenstern.]
    Now I am alone.
    O, what a rogue and peasant slave am I!
530   Is it not monstrous that this player here,
    But in a fiction, in a dream of passion,
    Could force his soul so to his own conceit
    That from her working all his visage wann'd,
    Tears in his eyes, distraction in's aspect,
535   A broken voice, and his whole function suiting
    With forms to his conceit? And all for nothing!
    For Hecuba!
    What's Hecuba to him, or he to Hecuba,
    That he should weep for her? What would he do,
540   Had he the motive and the cue for passion
    That I have? He would drown the stage with tears
    And cleave the general ear with horrid speech;
    Make mad the guilty and appall the free,
    Confound the ignorant, and amaze indeed
545   The very faculties of eyes and ears.
    Yet I,
    A dull and muddy-mettled rascal, peak
    Like John-a-dreams, unpregnant of my cause,
    And can say nothing! No, not for a king,
550   Upon whose property and most dear life
    A damn'd defeat was made. Am I a coward?
    Who calls me villain? breaks my pate across?
    Plucks off my beard and blows it in my face?
    Tweaks me by the nose? gives me the lie i' the throat,
555   As deep as to the lungs? Who does me this? Ha!
    'Swounds, I should take it! for it cannot be
    But I am pigeon-liver'd and lack gall

HAMLET: *Very well. Follow that lord, and do not make fun of him.*
  [First Player exits] *My good friends, I'll leave you until night. You
  are welcome in Elsinore.*

ROSENCRANTZ: *Good, my lord!*

HAMLET: *Indeed, good-bye to you.*
                            [Rosencrantz and Guildenstern exit]
  *Now I am alone. Oh, what villain and petty slave I am! Is it not
  amazing that this actor here, in a fictional story, in a mere show
  of passion, can put his soul into expressing this imagined idea. His
  face went pale, tears stood in his eyes, his appearance displayed
  sorrow, his voice broke, and the actions of his entire body supported his acting. And all for nothing! For Hecuba! What's Hecuba
  to him, or he to Hecuba, that he should cry for her? What would he
  do, if he had the motive and the reason for passion that I have? He
  would drown the stage with tears and split the audience's ears with
  horrifying speech, drive guilty men insane, confuse the ignorant,
  and amaze everyone's eyes and ears. Yet I, dull and hesitant, sneak
  around, like someone in a dream, indifferent to my purpose and
  unable to say anything! No, not even on behalf of a king, whose
  possessions and dear life was destroyed. Am I a coward? Who calls
  me a villain, strikes my head, plucks at my beard, and blows it in
  my face; who grabs me by my nose and calls me a liar as if the word
  came from my own lungs? Who does this? Ha! By Jesus, I should
  accept it. It must be that I am weak and incapable of resentment.
  Otherwise, I would have fattened all the vultures in the region with
  this slave's organs. Bloody, dirty villain! Remorseless, treacherous,
  lecherous, unnatural villain! Why, what an ass I am! It is very
  brave that I, the son of a dear father who was murdered, called to
  revenge by heaven and hell alike, must relieve my heart with words
  and fall like a whore, cursing like a prostitute, a kitchen servant!
  Damn it! I must use my brain! Well, I have heard that guilty men
  watching a play, have been so passionately affected by a skillful
  performance that they have immediately proclaimed their own
  crimes. Murder, although it has no tongue, will speak in mysteri-
  ous ways. I'll have these players perform something similar to the
  murder of my father in front of my uncle. I'll observe his looks; I'll*

To make oppression bitter, or ere this
I should have fatted all the region kites
560   With this slave's offal. Bloody, bawdy villain!
Remorseless, treacherous, lecherous, kindless villain!
O, vengeance!
Why, what an ass am I! This is most brave,
That I, the son of a dear father murder'd,
565   Prompted to my revenge by heaven and hell,
Must, like a whore, unpack my heart with words
And fall a-cursing like a very drab,
A scullion! Fie upon't! Foh!
About, my brain! Hum, I have heard
570   That guilty creatures, sitting at a play,
Have by the very cunning of the scene
Been struck so to the soul that presently
They have proclaim'd their malefactions;
For murder, though it have no tongue, will speak
575   With most miraculous organ. I'll have these players
Play something like the murder of my father
Before mine uncle. I'll observe his looks;
I'll tent him to the quick. If he but blench,
I know my course. The spirit that I have seen
580   May be a devil; and the devil hath power
T' assume a pleasing shape; yea, and perhaps
Out of my weakness and my melancholy,
As he is very potent with such spirits,
Abuses me to damn me. I'll have grounds
585   More relative than this. The play's the thing
Wherein I'll catch the conscience of the King.

                                    [Exit.]

examine every detail. If he merely flinches, I'll know what I must do. The ghost that I have seen may be the Devil, and the Devil has the power to assume any pleasing shape. And, perhaps, taking advantage of my weakness and sadness, since he is most powerful in these situations, the Devil leads me into damnation. I'll have more conclusive evidence than this! I will use the play to uncover the conscience of the King!

[Hamlet exits]

ACT III

Scene 1

Elsinore. A room in the Castle.

[Enter King, Queen, Polonius, Ophelia, Rosencrantz, Guildenstern, and Lords.]

KING: And can you by no drift of conference
    Get from him why he puts on this confusion,
    Grating so harshly all his days of quiet
    With turbulent and dangerous lunacy?

5 ROSENCRANTZ: He does confess he feels himself distracted,
    But from what cause he will by no means speak.

GUILDENSTERN: Nor do we find him forward to be sounded,
    But with a crafty madness keeps aloof
    When we would bring him on to some confession
10   Of his true state.

QUEEN: Did he receive you well?

ROSENCRANTZ: Most like a gentleman.

GUILDENSTERN: But with much forcing of his disposition.

ROSENCRANTZ: Niggard of question, but of our demands
15   Most free in his reply.

ACT III

Scene 1

A room in the castle.

[The King, Queen, Polonius, Ophelia, Rosencrantz, and Guildenstern enter]

KING: *Can't you steer your conversation in a direction that would help you find out why he is in such a state of confusion, destroying his peace of mind with disorderly and dangerous madness?*

ROSENCRANTZ: *He does confess that he feels agitated, but he will not say why.*

GUILDENSTERN: *Nor do we find him willing to be questioned. In his skillful madness, he keeps his distance every time we want him to discuss the issue of his sanity.*

QUEEN: *Did he welcome you properly?*

ROSENCRANTZ: *Very much like a gentleman.*

GUILDENSTERN: *But with a forced kindness.*

ROSENCRANTZ: *He was reserved, but answered our questions freely.*

QUEEN:　　　　　　　Did you assay him
　　　To any pastime?

ROSENCRANTZ: Madam, it so fell out that certain players
　　　We o'erraught on the way. Of these we told him,
20　　And there did seem in him a kind of joy
　　　To hear of it. They are here about the court,
　　　And, as I think, they have already order
　　　This night to play before him.

POLONIUS: 'Tis most true;
25　　And he beseech'd me to entreat your Majesties
　　　To hear and see the matter.

KING: With all my heart, and it doth much content me
　　　To hear him so inclin'd.
　　　Good gentlemen, give him a further edge
30　　And drive his purpose on to these delights.

ROSENCRANTZ: We shall, my lord.
　　　　　　　　　[Exeunt Rosencrantz and Guildenstern.]

KING:　　　　Sweet Gertrude, leave us too;
　　　For we have closely sent for Hamlet hither,
　　　That he, as 'twere by accident, may here
35　　Affront Ophelia.
　　　Her father and myself, lawful espials,
　　　Will so bestow ourselves that, seeing unseen,
　　　We may of their encounter frankly judge
　　　And gather by him, as he is behaved,
40　　If't be the affliction of his love or no,
　　　That thus he suffers for.

QUEEN:　　　　　　　I shall obey you;
　　　And for your part, Ophelia, I do wish
　　　That your good beauties be the happy cause
45　　Of Hamlet's wildness. So shall I hope your virtues
　　　Will bring him to his wonted way again,
　　　To both your honours.

QUEEN: *Did you tempt him with any kind of entertainment?*

ROSENCRANTZ: *Madam, it so happens that we passed a number of actors on our way here. We told him about that, and he seemed somewhat happy to hear it. They are here at the court, and I believe they already have orders to perform for him tonight.*

POLONIUS: *That is certainly true, and he entreated me to ask your Majesties to attend the play.*

KING: *With all my heart. It makes me very glad to find him interested. Good gentlemen, give him further encouragement and stimulate his interest in happiness.*

ROSENCRANTZ: *We will, my lord.*

[Rosencrantz and Guildenstern exit]

KING: *Sweet Gertrude, leave the two of us. We have secretly sent for Hamlet, so that he, as if by accident, will meet Ophelia here. Her father and I, legitimate spies, will hide ourselves, so that we may observe and judge their encounter without being seen and conclude from his behavior whether or not love causes him to suffer in this manner.*

QUEEN: *I will obey you. For your part, Ophelia, I wish that your also beauty is the cause of Hamlet's mad behavior. I also hope that your virtuous qualities will return him to his normal self again, which will honor both of you.*

OPHELIA: Madam, I wish it may.

[Exit Queen.]

POLONIUS: Ophelia, walk you here. Gracious, so please you,
50   We will bestow ourselves. *[To Ophelia.]* Read on this book,
        That show of such an exercise may colour
        Your loneliness. We are oft to blame in this—
        'Tis too much proved—that with devotion's visage
        And pious action we do sugar o'er
55   The Devil himself.

KING: *[Aside.]* O, 'tis too true!
        How smart a lash that speech doth give my conscience!
        The harlot's cheek, beautied with plastering art,
        Is not more ugly to the thing that helps it
60   Than is my deed to my most painted word.
        O heavy burden!

POLONIUS: I hear him coming. Let's withdraw, my lord.

[Exeunt King and Polonius.]

[Enter Hamlet.]

HAMLET: To be, or not to be, that is the question:
65   Whether 'tis nobler in the mind to suffer
        The slings and arrows of outrageous fortune
        Or to take arms against a sea of troubles,
        And by opposing end them. To die, to sleep—
        No more—and by a sleep to say we end
70   The heartache, and the thousand natural shocks
        That flesh is heir to. 'Tis a consummation
        Devoutly to be wish'd. To die, to sleep—
        To sleep—perchance to dream. Ay, there's the rub!
        For in that sleep of death what dreams may come,
75   When we have shuffled off this mortal coil,
        Must give us pause—there's the respect
        That makes calamity of so long life.
        For who would bear the whips and scorns of time,

OPHELIA: *Madam, I hope so.*

[The Queen exits]

POLONIUS: *Ophelia, you walk here. Your Majesty, we will hide ourselves, if you please.* [To Ophelia] *Read from this book so that your solitude will appear natural. We are often to blame—it has been shown—that with a devout face and pious actions we try to hide the Devil himself.*

KING: [Aside] *Oh, it is too true! That speech tortures my conscience! A prostitute's painted face is not uglier underneath her make-up than my deeds are underneath my false words. Oh, heavy burden!*

POLONIUS: *I hear him coming. Let's hide, my lord.*

[The King and Polonius exit]

[Hamlet enters]

HAMLET: *To live, or not to live, that is the question. Whether it's nobler to endure the attacks of outrageous fate, or to oppose one's troubles, and by fighting, confront and end them. Dying is like sleeping, nothing more. If we could, by sleeping, end the thousands of heartaches and suffering that people endure—that would be a highly desire conclusion. Dying is like sleeping—to sleep—perhaps, to dream. Yes, that's the problem, because the kind of dreams we would have in that sleep of death, after we have cast off this life, must make us stop and think. That's the consideration that makes a long life miserable. Who would bear the hardships and troubles of our world—the enemy's offenses, the proud man's contempt, the pain of unrequited love, the lack of justice, the insolence of officials, and the pains humbly accepted by a commoner—if he could end his existence with a bare blade? Who would bear these burdens, who would suffer and sweat under the weight of a weary life, if there*

129

The oppressor's wrong, the proud man's contumely,
80　　The pangs of disprized love, the law's delay,
The insolence of office, and the spurns
That patient merit of the unworthy takes,
When he himself might his quietus make
With a bare bodkin? Who would fardels bear,
85　　To grunt and sweat under a weary life,
But that the dread of something after death
The undiscover'd country, from whose bourn
No traveller returns, puzzles the will,
And makes us rather bear those ills we have
90　　Than fly to others that we know not of?
Thus conscience does make cowards of us all,
And thus the native hue of resolution ·
Is sicklied o'er with the pale cast of thought,
And enterprises of great pitch and moment
95　　With this regard their currents turn awry
And lose the name of action. Soft you now!
The fair Ophelia! Nymph, in thy orisons
Be all my sins remembered.

OPHELIA:　　　　　　Good my lord,
100　　How does your honour for this many a day?

HAMLET: I humbly thank you; well, well, well.

OPHELIA: My lord, I have remembrances of yours
That I have longed long to redeliver.
I pray you, now receive them.

105　　HAMLET:　　　　　　No, not I!
I never gave you aught.

OPHELIA: My honour'd lord, you know right well you did,
And with them words of so sweet breath compos'd
As made the things more rich. Their perfume lost,
110　　Take these again; for to the noble mind
Rich gifts wax poor when givers prove unkind.
There, my lord.

130

were no dread of something after death, that unknown country from whose boundary no traveler ever returns? This paralyzes the will and forces us to endure the difficulties we have, instead of flying to others we do not understand. Therefore, our conscience turns us all into cowards, and our natural sense of bold action is compromised by too much thinking. Great possibilities and prospects are lost due to a lack of action. I must be quiet now. It's the beautiful Ophelia: May all my sins be remembered in your prayers!

OPHELIA: Hello, my lord. How are you these days?

HAMLET: I humbly thank you; well, well.

OPHELIA: My lord, I have some small gifts from you that I have meant to return for quite some time. Please take them now.

HAMLET: No, not I; I never gave you anything.

OPHELIA: My honored lord, you know very well that you did, and you added words, spoken sweetly, which made them even more valuable. The sweet fragrance of these words has gone, so take the gifts back. To a respectable person, rich gifts lose their value when the givers become cold. Here, my lord.

HAMLET: Ha, ha! Are you honest?

OPHELIA: My lord?

115 HAMLET: Are you fair?

OPHELIA: What means your lordship?

HAMLET: That if you be honest and fair, your honesty should admit no
      discourse to your beauty.

OPHELIA: Could beauty, my lord, have better commerce than with
120   honesty?

HAMLET: Ay, truly; for the power of beauty will sooner transform
      honesty from what it is to a bawd than the force of honesty can
      translate beauty into his likeness. This was sometime a para-
      dox, but now the time gives it proof. I did love you once.

125 OPHELIA: Indeed, my lord, you made me believe so.

HAMLET: You should not have believed me; for virtue cannot so inoc-
      ulate our old stock but we shall relish of it. I loved you not.

OPHELIA: I was the more deceived.

HAMLET: Get thee to a nunnery! Why wouldst thou be a breeder of
130   sinners? I am myself indifferent honest, but yet I could accuse
      me of such things that it were better my mother had not borne
      me.
      I am very proud, revengeful, ambitious; with more offences
      at my beck than I have thoughts to put them in, imagination
135   to give them shape, or time to act them in. What should such
      fellows as I do, crawling between earth and heaven? We are
      arrant knaves all; believe none of us. Go thy ways to a nunnery.
      Where's your father?

OPHELIA: At home, my lord.

HAMLET: *Ha, ha! Are you chaste?*

OPHELIA: *My lord?*

HAMLET: *Are you beautiful?*

OPHELIA: *What does your lordship mean?*

HAMLET: *That if you are pure and beautiful, your chastity should allow no access to your beauty.*

OPHELIA: *Could beauty, my lord, have a better companion than purity?*

HAMLET: *Yes, truly. The power of beauty can turn purity into a harlot more easily than the power of chastity can transform beauty into purity. This used to be a riddle, but our times prove that it's true. I loved you once.*

OPHELIA: *Indeed, my lord, you made me believe so.*

HAMLET: *You should not have believed me. Virtue cannot be grafted on an old plant to make it seem delicious. I did not love you.*

OPHELIA: *I was very much deceived.*

HAMLET: *Go to a convent! Do you want to breed sinners? I myself am somewhat virtuous, yet, I could accuse myself of such atrocities that it would be better if my mother had not given birth to me. I am very proud, revengeful, ambitious, with more wrongs yet to be committed than I can conceive of, than I can imagine in my mind, than I have time to carry out. Why should men like me linger between heaven and earth? We are all shameless scoundrels. Don't believe any of us! Go and become a nun! Where's your father?*

OPHELIA: *At home, my lord.*

140 HAMLET: Let the doors be shut upon him, that he may play the fool
nowhere but in's own house. Farewell.

OPHELIA: O, help him, you sweet heavens!

HAMLET: If thou dost marry, I'll give thee this plague for thy dowry:
be thou as chaste as ice, as pure as snow, thou shalt not escape
145 calumny. Get thee to a nunnery. Go, farewell. Or if thou wilt
needs marry, marry a fool; for wise men know well enough
what monsters you make of them. To a nunnery, go; and
quickly too. Farewell.

OPHELIA: O heavenly powers, restore him!

150 HAMLET: I have heard of your paintings too, well enough. God hath
given you one face, and you make yourselves another. You jig,
you amble, and you lisp; and nickname God's creatures and
make your wantonness your ignorance. Go to, I'll no more on't!
it hath made me mad. I say, we will have no more marriages.
155 Those that are married already—all but one—shall live; the rest
shall keep as they are. To a nunnery, go. *[Exit.]*

OPHELIA: O, what a noble mind is here o'erthrown!
The courtier's, scholar's, soldier's, eye, tongue, sword,
The expectancy and rose of the fair state,
160 The glass of fashion and the mould of form,
The observed of all observers, quite, quite down!
And I, of ladies most deject and wretched,
That suck'd the honey of his music vows,
Now see that noble and most sovereign reason,
165 Like sweet bells jangled, out of tune and harsh;
That unmatch'd form and feature of blown youth
Blasted with ecstasy. O, woe is me,
To have seen what I have seen, see what I see!

[Enter King and Polonius.]

HAMLET: Shut the doors on him, so that he can play the fool nowhere but in his own house. Goodbye.

OPHELIA: Oh, help him, dear God!

HAMLET: If you marry, I'll give you this curse as your wedding gift—whether you are as chaste as ice, as pure as snow, you will not escape slander. Go to a convent. Goodbye. Or if you have to marry, marry a fool. Wise men know too well that you will turn them into deformed creatures. Go to a convent, and go quickly, too. Goodbye.

OPHELIA: Oh, God, make him better!

HAMLET: I have heard of your made up faces, too. God has given you one face and you paint yourself another one. You dance, you stroll, you talk in an affected manner; you call God's creatures perverse names and excuse your affection as ignorance. Go away, I have nothing more to say. It has made me mad. I propose that we have no more marriages. Those who are married already—all, except for one—will be permitted to live. They rest will remain the way they are. To a convent! Go!

[Hamlet exits]

OPHELIA: Oh, what a noble mind has lost its balance! A courtier's fine eye, a soldier's skills, and a scholar's words, the hope and promise of his kingdom, an example of good taste, and a model of courtly behavior, the most honored of all honorable people—entirely lost! And I, of the most dejected and wretched women, who tasted the honey of his sweet vows, now see his noble and powerful mind out of reason, like sweet bells ringing harshly out of tune. The unsurpassed shape and appearance of blossoming youth has been destroyed by madness. Oh, poor me, that I have seen what I have seen, and what I realize.

[King and Polonius enter]

135

KING: Love? His affections do not that way tend;
170   Nor what he spake, though it lack'd form a little,
Was not like madness. There's something in his soul
O'er which his melancholy sits on brood;
And I do doubt the hatch and the disclose
Will be some danger; which for to prevent,
175   I have in quick determination
Thus set it down: he shall with speed to England
For the demand of our neglected tribute.
Haply the seas, and countries different,
With variable objects shall expel
180   This something-settled matter in his heart,
Whereon his brains still beating puts him thus
From fashion of himself. What think you on't?

POLONIUS: It shall do well. But yet do I believe
The origin and commencement of his grief
185   Sprung from neglected love. How now, Ophelia?
You need not tell us what Lord Hamlet said.
We heard it all. My lord, do as you please;
But, if you hold it fit, after the play,
Let his queen mother all alone entreat him
190   To show his grief. Let her be round with him;
And I'll be placed, so please you, in the ear
Of all their conference. If she find him not,
To England send him; or confine him where
Your wisdom best shall think.

195 KING: It shall be so.
Madness in great ones must not unwatch'd go.

                            [Exeunt.]

KING: Love? His feelings are not like love; nor were the words he said, although they lacked coherence, pure madness. There's something breeding melancholy within his mind, and I fear that if it hatches, the result will be dangerous. To prevent this, I have quickly determined the following: He must immediately leave for England in order to collect our unpaid tribute money. Perhaps, the sea, different countries with varying scenery, and other kinds of entertainment, will expel the somewhat unsettled matter in his heart, which has disordered his mind and made him different from the way we knew him. What do you think?

POLONIUS: It should work. Yet, I still believe the source and origin of his grief is unrequited love. How are you, Ophelia? You do not need to tell us what Lord Hamlet said. We heard it all. My lord, do as you please, but if you agree, after the play, let the Queen confront him all alone, and plainly ask him to explain his misery. Let her be direct with him. I will, with your permission, eavesdrop on their conversation. If she cannot find out the truth about him, send him to England, or confine him in a place your wisdom deems suitable.

KING: That's what we will be done. Madness in the great must not go unobserved.

[They exit]

137

Scene 2

Elsinore. A hall in the Castle.

[Enter Hamlet and three of the Players.]

HAMLET: Speak the speech, I pray you, as I pronounced it to you, trip-
pingly on the tongue. But if you mouth it, as many of our players do, I had as lief the town-crier spoke my lines. Nor do not
saw the air too much with your hand, thus, but use all gently;
5   for in the very torrent, tempest, and, as I may say, whirlwind
of your passion, you must acquire and beget a temperance that
may give it smoothness. O, it offends me to the
soul to hear a robustious periwig-pated fellow tear a passion
to tatters, to very rags, to split the ears of the groundlings,
10   who, for the most part, are capable of nothing but inexplicable
dumb-shows and noise. I would have such a fellow whipped
for o'erdoing Termagant. It out-Herods Herod. Pray you avoid
it.

FIRST PLAYER: I warrant your honour.

15   HAMLET: Be not too tame neither; but let your own discretion be your
tutor. Suit the action to the word, the word to the action; with
this special observance, that you o'erstep not the modesty of
nature: for anything so overdone is from the purpose of playing, whose end, both at the first and now, was and is, to hold,
20   as 'twere, the mirror up to nature; to show virtue her own feature, scorn her own image, and the very age and body of the
time his form and pressure. Now this overdone, or come tardy
off, though it make the unskilful laugh, cannot but make the
judicious grieve; the censure of the which one must in your
25   allowance o'erweigh a whole theatre of others. O, there be
players that I have seen play, and heard others praise, and that
highly, not to speak it profanely, that, neither having the accent
of Christians, nor the gait of Christian, pagan, nor man, have
so strutted and bellowed that I have thought some of Nature's

Scene 2

A hall in the castle.

[Hamlet and the Players enter]

HAMLET: *I ask you to please perform the speech as I recited it to you, spoken lightly. But if you exaggerate the words, I might as well have the town crier speak my lines. Also, don't wave your hands too much, like this, but use gestures sparingly. When your passion overpowers you like a storming whirlwind, you must use restraint, in order to speak naturally. Oh, it offends me deeply to hear a rude, overdressed fellow tear a passion apart, into pieces, splitting the ears of the commoners on the ground, who, for the most part, are unable to appreciate anything but nonsensical pantomimes and loud entertainment. I would have any actor whipped who overplayed the role of Termagant. It outdoes a ranting Herod! Please, avoid it.*

FIRST PLAYER: *I certainly will, your honor.*

HAMLET: *But don't be too calm, either. Act according to your own discretion. Let your actions agree with your words, and your words with your actions, especially taking care that you keep a natural balance. Anything that's overdone goes against the purpose of acting, which is and always has been, to hold a mirror up to reality, in order to reveal virtue, to recognize evil, and to represent the shape and image of our times. If this is overplayed or performed inadequately, although it might make the commoners laugh, it will cause the enlightened to scream; their critical judgment must, in your estimation, outweigh an entire theater full of all the others. Oh, I have seen actors, praised very highly, who did not talk like decent Christians, nor did they walk like a Christian, a pagan, or any man. They strutted around and bellowed in a way that made me think nature had not made them herself, but some*

30 journeymen had made men, and not made them well, they imi-
tated humanity so abominably.

FIRST PLAYER: I hope we have reformed that indifferently with us, sir.

HAMLET: O, reform it altogether! And let those that play your clowns
speak no more than is set down for them. For there be of them
35 that will themselves laugh, to set on some quantity of barren
spectators to laugh too, though in the meantime some necessary question of the play be then to be considered. That's vil-
lainous and shows a most pitiful ambition in the fool that uses
it. Go make you ready.

[Exeunt Players.]

[Enter Polonius, Rosencrantz, and Guildenstern.]
40 How now, my lord? Will the King hear this piece of work?

POLONIUS: And the Queen too, and that presently.

HAMLET: Bid the players make haste,   *[Exit Polonius.]*
Will you two help to hasten them?

ROSENCRANTZ AND GUILDENSTERN: We will, my lord.

[Exeunt they two.]

45 HAMLET: What, ho, Horatio!

[Enter Horatio.]

HORATIO: Here, sweet lord, at your service.

HAMLET: Horatio, thou art e'en as just a man
As e'er my conversation cop'd withal.

HORATIO: O, my dear lord!

50 HAMLET: Nay, do not think I flatter;
For what advancement may I hope from thee,

assistant made them, and he did not make them well. That's how horribly they resembled humanity.

FIRST PLAYER: *I hope we have remedied that tolerably well, sir.*

HAMLET: *Oh, remedy it altogether! And let your clowns speak no more then what has been written for them to say. There are some comedians who laugh in order to make a number of dull spectators laugh as well. In the meantime, some necessary part of the play may be overshadowed. That's awful and shows an unnecessary ambition in the fool who does it. Go, get ready!*

[Players exit]

[Polonius, Rosencrantz, and Guildenstern enter]
How are you, my lord? Will the King attend the play?

POLONIUS: *And the Queen, too, immediately.*

HAMLET: *Ask the players to hurry up,*   [Polonius exits]
Will you two help to hurry them on?

ROSENCRANTZ and GUILDENSTERN: *We will, my lord.*

[Rosencrantz and Guildenstern exit]

HAMLET: *Hello Horatio!*

[Horatio enters]

HORATIO: *Here, my dear lord, at your service.*

HAMLET: *Horatio, you come as close to being exactly what a man should be, as far as I can tell.*

HORATIO: *Oh, my dear lord!*

HAMLET: *No, do not think I flatter you. What advantage could I gain from someone who has only his good will to feed and clothe him?*

That no revenue hast but thy good spirits
To feed and clothe thee? Why should the poor be flatter'd?
No, let the candied tongue lick absurd pomp,
55 And crook the pregnant hinges of the knee
Where thrift may follow fawning. Dost thou hear?
Since my dear soul was mistress of her choice,
And could of men distinguish her election,
Sh'hath seal'd thee for herself. For thou hast been
60 As one, in suff'ring all, that suffers nothing;
A man that Fortune's buffets and rewards
Hast ta'en with equal thanks; and blest are those
Whose blood and judgment are so well commeddled
That they are not a pipe for Fortune's finger
65 To sound what stop she please. Give me that man
That is not passion's slave, and I will wear him
In my heart's core, ay, in my heart of heart,
As I do thee. Something too much of this.
There is a play tonight before the King.
70 One scene of it comes near the circumstance,
Which I have told thee, of my father's death.
I prithee, when thou seest that act afoot,
Even with the very comment of thy soul
Observe my uncle. If his occulted guilt
75 Do not itself unkennel in one speech,
It is a damned ghost that we have seen,
And my imaginations are as foul
As Vulcan's stithy. Give him heedful note;
For I mine eyes will rivet to his face,
80 And after we will both our judgments join
In censure of his seeming.

HORATIO: Well, my lord.
If he steal aught the whilst this play is playing,
And 'scape detecting, I will pay the theft.

*[Sound a flourish. Enter Trumpets and Kettledrums. Danish march.
Enter King, Queen, Polonius, Ophelia, Rosencrantz, Guildenstern, and
other Lords attendant, with the Guard carrying torches.]*

Why should anyone flatter the poor? No, let those with a flattering tongue stick to the rich and kneel willingly, if a quick profit can be gained. Do you understand me? Ever since my soul has been able to distinguish between men of quality and other men, I have chosen you as my close friend. You have been a man who, having suffered so much, bears every hardship and accepts his fate, whether good or bad. Those men are blessed, whose emotions and good judgment are so well balanced that they are not an instrument for the finger of Fate to play whatever way she wishes. Show me a man who is no slave to his emotions, and I will embrace him deeply, with all my heart, like I do you. But enough of this. There is a play that will be performed in front of the King tonight. One scene closely resembles the circumstances of my father's death, as I have told them to you. When you see that scene acted, please, even in the judgment of your sould, observe my uncle very closely. If his hidden guilt will not come out into the open during this speech, we have seen an evil spirit, and my imagination is as foul as the forge of hell. Pay very close attention to him, while I will study his face, and, afterwards, we will compare our observations and draw a conclusion regarding his behavior.

HORATIO: *Well, my lord. If he steals anything while this play is performed, and escapes undetected, I will pay for the stolen goods.*

[A trumpet sounds. A Danish march is played. The King, Queen, Polonius, Ophelia, Rosencrantz, Guildenstern and other Attendants enter, with the Guard carrying torches]

143

85 HAMLET: They are coming to the play. I must be idle.
  Get you a place.

KING: How fares our cousin Hamlet?

HAMLET: Excellent, i' faith; of the chameleon's dish. I eat the air,
  promise-cramm'd. You cannot feed capons so.

90 KING: I have nothing with this answer, Hamlet. These words are not
  mine.

HAMLET: No, nor mine now. *[To Polonius.]* My lord, you play'd once i'
  th' university, you say?

POLONIUS: That did I, my lord, and was accounted a good actor.

95 HAMLET: What did you enact?

POLONIUS: I did enact Julius Caesar; I was killed i' the Capitol; Brutus
  killed me.

HAMLET: It was a brute part of him to kill so capital a calf there. Be
  the players ready.

100 ROSENCRANTZ: Ay, my lord. They stay upon your patience.

QUEEN: Come hither, my dear Hamlet, sit by me.

HAMLET: No, good mother. Here's metal more attractive.

POLONIUS: *[To the King.]* O, ho! do you mark that?

HAMLET: Lady, shall I lie in your lap? *[Lying down at Ophelia's feet.]*

105 OPHELIA: No, my lord.

HAMLET: I mean, my head upon your lap?

HAMLET: *They are coming to see the play. I must appear mad. Find a seat!*

KING: *How is our nephew Hamlet?*

HAMLET: *Excellent, honestly. Eating like the chameleon: I feed on air stuffed with promises. Chickens don't eat better.*

KING: *I don't understand your answer, Hamlet; The words are not for me.*

HAMLET: *Nor are they for me, now.* [To Polonius] *My lord, you say that you acted once at the university?*

POLONIUS: *That I did, my lord, and I had the reputation of being a good actor.*

HAMLET: *What role did you play?*

POLONIUS: *I played Julius Caesar. I was killed in the Capitol; Brutus killed me.*

HAMLET: *It was brutish of him to kill such an important calf there. Are the players ready?*

ROSENCRANTZ: *Yes, my lord. They are ready at your command.*

QUEEN: *Come here, my dear Hamlet, sit with me.*

HAMLET: *No, good mother. Here's someone more attractive.*

POLONIUS: [To the King] *Oh, listen, do you hear that?*

HAMLET: *Lady, shall I lie in your lap?* [Lying down at Ophelia's feet]

OPHELIA: *No, my lord.*

HAMLET: *I mean, with my head upon your lap?*

OPHELIA: Ay, my lord.

HAMLET: Do you think I meant country matters?

OPHELIA: I think nothing, my lord.

110   HAMLET: That's a fair thought to lie between maids' legs.

OPHELIA: What is, my lord?

HAMLET: Nothing.

OPHELIA: You are merry, my lord.

HAMLET: Who, I?

115   OPHELIA: Ay, my lord.

HAMLET: O God, your only jig-maker! What should a man do but be
     merry? For, look you, how cheerfully my mother looks, and
     my father died within's two hours.

OPHELIA: Nay 'tis twice two months, my lord.

120   HAMLET: So long? Nay then, let the devil wear black, for I'll have a
     suit of sables. O heavens! die two months ago, and not forgot-
     ten yet? Then there's hope a great man's memory may outlive
     his life half a year. But, by'r lady, he must build churches then;
     or else shall he suffer not thinking on, with the hobby-horse,
125   whose epitaph is, 'For, O, for O, the hobby-horse is forgot!'

[Hautboys play. The dumb-show enters.

*Enter a King and a Queen very lovingly; the Queen embracing him and he
her. She kneels, and makes show of protestation unto him. He takes her
up, and declines his head upon her neck. He lays him down upon a bank
of flowers. She, seeing him asleep, leaves him. Anon comes in a fellow,*

OPHELIA: *Yes, my lord.*

HAMLET: *Do you think I meant something indecent?*

OPHELIA: *I think nothing, my lord.*

HAMLET: *It's a nice thought, lying between a maiden's legs.*

OPHELIA: *What is, my lord?*

HAMLET: *Nothing.*

OPHELIA: *You are in good spirits, my lord.*

HAMLET: *Who, I?*

OPHELIA: *Yes, my lord.*

HAMLET: *Oh God, you are very funny! What can a man do but be in good spirits? Look how happy my mother looks, and my father died only two hours ago.*

OPHELIA: *No, it was four months ago, my lord.*

HAMLET: *So long? Well, then let the devil wear black clothes, because I have a fine fur coat. Oh heavens, died two months ago, and not yet forgotten? Then there's hope that the memory of a great man may live on for six months after his death! But, by the virgin Mary, he must build churches, then, or he will be forgotten, like the hobbyhorse in the old song, whose epitaph reads "For nothing, for aught, the hobbyhorse has been forgot."*

[Trumpets sound. The pantomime actors enter. A King and a lovely Queen enter. They embrace each other. She kneels and makes promises to him. He lifts her up and leans his head on her neck. Then he lies down on a bed of flowers. Seeing him asleep, she leaves him. Before long, a man enters, takes off the King's crown, kisses it, pours poison into the King's ear, and leaves. The Queen returns, finds the

takes off his crown, kisses it, pours poison in the King's ears, and leaves him. The Queen returns, finds the King dead, and makes passionate action. The Poisoner with some three or four Mutes, comes in again, seeming to lament with her. The dead body is carried away. The Poisoner woos the Queen with gifts; she seems loath and unwilling awhile, but in the end accepts his love. Exeunt.]

OPHELIA: What means this, my lord?

HAMLET: Marry, this is miching mallecho; it means mischief.

OPHELIA: Belike this show imports the argument of the play.

[Enter Prologue.]

HAMLET: We shall know by this fellow. The players cannot keep
130   counsel; they'll tell all.

OPHELIA: Will he tell us what this show meant?

HAMLET: Ay, or any show that you'll show him. Be not you ashamed
      to show, he'll not shame to tell you what it means.

OPHELIA: You are naught, you are naught! I'll mark the play.

135 PROLOGUE: For us, and for our tragedy,
      Here stooping to your clemency,
      We beg your hearing patiently.
                           [Exit.]

HAMLET: Is this a prologue, or the posy of a ring?

OPHELIA: 'Tis brief, my lord.

140 HAMLET: As woman's love.

[Enter two Players as King and Queen]

King dead and cries passionately. The Poisoner returns with two or three others and appears to grieve with her. The dead body is carried away. The Poisoner woos the Queen with gifts. For a while, she seems reluctant and unwilling, but, in the end, accepts his love. They exit]

OPHELIA: *What does this mean, my lord?*

HAMLET: *Well, this is insidious calamity. It means more mischief.*

OPHELIA: *Most likely this pantomime show introduces the plot of the play.*

[The Prologue enters]

HAMLET: *We will find out from this fellow. The actors cannot keep secrets. They'll explain everything.*

OPHELIA: *Will he tell us what this pantomime show meant?*

HAMLET: *Yes, or any show that you'll show him. Anything you are not too ashamed to show him, he'll explain to you.*

OPHELIA: *You are wicked, you are wicked. I'll watch the play.*

PROLOGUE: *On behalf of ourselves and our tragedy, we are begging for your kindness, and we ask that you listen patiently.*
[Prologue Exits]

HAMLET: *Is this a prologue, or the short inscription in a ring?*

OPHELIA: *It is very brief, my lord.*

HAMLET: *Like the love of a woman.*

[Two actors, "King" and "Queen," enter]

P. KING: Full thirty times hath Phoebus' cart gone round
   Neptune's salt wash and Tellus' orbed ground,
   And thirty dozen moons with borrowed sheen
   About the world have times twelve thirties been,
145   Since love our hearts, and Hymen did our hands,
   Unite commutual in most sacred bands.

P. QUEEN: So many journeys may the sun and moon
   Make us again count o'er ere love be done!
   But woe is me! you are so sick of late,
150   So far from cheer and from your former state.
   That I distrust you. Yet, though I distrust,
   Discomfort you, my lord, it nothing must;
   For women's fear and love holds quantity,
   In neither aught, or in extremity.
155   Now, what my love is, proof hath made you know;
   And as my love is sized, my fear is so.
   Where love is great, the littlest doubts are fear;
   Where little fears grow great, great love grows there.

P. KING: Faith, I must leave thee, love, and shortly too;
160   My operant powers their functions leave to do.
   And thou shalt live in this fair world behind,
   Honour'd, belov'd, and haply one as kind
   For husband shalt thou—

P. QUEEN: O, confound the rest!
165   Such love must needs be treason in my breast.
   In second husband let me be accurst!
   None wed the second but who killed the first.

HAMLET: [Aside.] Wormwood, wormwood!

P. QUEEN: The instances that second marriage move
170   Are base respects of thrift, but none of love.
   A second time I kill my husband dead
   When second husband kisses me in bed.

PLAYER KING: *For thirty years has the sun god Phoebus circled Neptune's seas and Tellus' earth. And thirty dozen moons have reflected their radiance onto the world twelve times thirty times, since love has brought our hearts together and the God of marriage has joined our hands in the holy bond of matrimony.*

PLAYER QUEEN: *May the same amount of time go by until our love fades away! But I worry, because, lately, you have been sick, unhappy, and changed, and I fear for your health. Yet, though I am concerned for you, it must not trouble you, my lord. In women, worry and love go together: either they don't feel anything, or they feel too much. Now, experience has shown you the extent of my love, and my concern for you is as extensive as my love. Where love is great, the smallest doubts become a source of concern. Where small concerns grow great, great love grows likewise.*

PLAYER KING: *Well, I must leave you very soon, my dear. My vital powers are fading, and you will be left behind in this beautiful world, honored, beloved, and, perhaps, you will find an equally kind husband—*

ACTOR QUEEN: *Oh, don't say any more! I would consider such love treason! If I take a second husband, I will be cursed! Nobody would take a second husband, unless that man killed the first!*

HAMLET: [Aside] *Bitterness! Bitterness!*

PLAYER: *The reasons that give rise to second marriages are material considerations, not love. I would kill my first husband a second time, when my second husband first kisse me in my bed.*

P. KING: I do believe you think what now you speak;
    But what we do determine oft we break.
175   Purpose is but the slave to memory,
    Of violent birth, but poor validity;
    Which now, like fruit unripe, sticks on the tree,
    But fall unshaken when they mellow be.
    Most necessary 'tis that we forget
180   To pay ourselves what to ourselves is debt.
    What to ourselves in passion we propose,
    The passion ending, doth the purpose lose.
    The violence of either grief or joy
    Their own enactures with themselves destroy.
185   Where joy most revels, grief doth most lament;
    Grief joys, joy grieves, on slender accident.
    This world is not for aye, nor 'tis not strange
    That even our loves should with our fortunes change;
    For 'tis a question left us yet to prove,
190   Whether love lead fortune, or else fortune love.
    The great man down, you mark his favorite flies,
    The poor advanced makes friends of enemies;
    And hitherto doth love on fortune tend,
    For who not needs shall never lack a friend,
195   And who in want a hollow friend doth try,
    Directly seasons him his enemy.
    But, orderly to end where I begun,
    Our wills and fates do so contrary run
    That our devices still are overthrown;
200   Our thoughts are ours, their ends none of our own.
    So think thou wilt no second husband wed;
    But die thy thoughts when thy first lord is dead.

P. QUEEN: Nor earth to me give food, nor heaven light,
    Sport and repose lock from me day and night,
205   To desperation turn my trust and hope,
    An anchor's cheer in prison be my scope,
    Each opposite, that blanks the face of joy,
    Meet what I would have well, and it destroy,
    Both here and hence pursue me lasting strife,
210   If, once a widow, ever I be wife!

152

PLAYER KING: *I do believe you mean what you are saying right now. But we often change our minds. One's purpose is easily forgotten; strong at first, it has no lasting power. Like an unripe fruit firmly sticking to a tree, it falls as soon as it becomes ripe. These resolutions are a debt we owe to ourselves, and we easily forget to honor these debts. Our passionate resolutions fade as soon as the passion cools. Violent grief and violent joy destroy themselves. If joy is great, grief is deep. Yet, just as easily, grief can rejoice and joy can grieve. This world will not last, and it is only natural that our ability to love changes with our fortunes. This is a question left for us to prove: whether love determines fate, or fate determines love. When a great man is out of luck, watch his friends disappear. When a poor man gains power, he makes friends out of all his enemies. Until now, love depended on fate. A rich man will never lack friends; a poor man must seek an unworthy friend, but turns him into an enemy. But, to end as I have begun, our will and our fate contradict each other too often, so that our plans always change. Our thoughts belong to us, but their outcome is beyond our control. Now you think that you will never marry a second time, but this resolution will die once your first husband has died.*

PLAYER QUEEN: *May the earth refuse to provide me with food and heaven deny me light, may day and night refuse to offer amusements or rest to me, may my trust and hope turn into desperation, may the fare of a hermit be the only comfort to me, may everything be marked by grief or destroyed, may I be punished by an eternal struggle now and forever, if, once I become a widow, I should ever marry again.*

HAMLET: If she should break it now!

P. KING: 'Tis deeply sworn. Sweet, leave me here awhile.
My spirits grow dull, and fain I would beguile
The tedious day with sleep.   *[He sleeps.]*

215   P. QUEEN: Sleep rock thy brain,
And never come mischance between us twain!
                                              [Exit.]

HAMLET: Madam, how like you this play?

QUEEN: The lady doth protest too much, methinks.

HAMLET: O, but she'll keep her word.

220   KING: Have you heard the argument? Is there no offence in't?

HAMLET: No, no! They do but jest, poison in jest; no offence i' the
world.

KING: What do you call the play?

HAMLET: *The Mousetrap.* Marry, how? Tropically. This play is the
225   image of a murder done in Vienna. Gonzago is the Duke's
name; his wife, Baptista. You shall see anon. 'Tis a knavish
piece of work; but what o' that? Your Majesty, and we that
have free souls, it touches us not. Let the galled jade winch; our
withers are unwrung.
[Enter Lucianus.]
230   This is one Lucianus, nephew to the King.

OPHELIA: You are as good as a chorus, my lord.

HAMLET: I could interpret between you and your love, if I could see
the puppets dallying.

OPHELIA: You are keen, my lord, you are keen.

HAMLET: *If she should break that promise now!*

ACTOR KING: *You have made a profound vow. Dear, leave me here for a while; I am feeling tired, and I wish to fool the day by sleepimg leep.*   [He sleeps]

ACTOR QUEEN: *May you sleep comfort you; may no bad luck ever come between us!*

[They exit]

HAMLET: *Madam, how do you like this play?*

QUEEN: *The lady states her feelings too strongly, I think.*

HAMLET: *Oh, but she'll keep her word.*

KING: *Are you familiar with the plot? Is it offensive?*

HAMLET: *No, no! They are only pretending! The poison is fake. No offense committed at all!*

KING: *What is the play called?*

HAMLET: *"The Mousetrap." Indeed, how. It's metaphorical! This play is based on a murder committed in Vienna. Gonzago is the Duke's name; his wife's name is Baptista. You will soon see. It's an unscrupulous piece of work. But that doesn't matter. It doesn't affect your Majesty or any innocent person. Let guilty people flinch; our consciences are clear.*
[Lucianus enters]
This is Lucianus, the King's nephew.

OPHELIA: *You explain the play well, like a chorus my lord.*

HAMLET: *I could explain the relationship between you and your lover, if I could watch you.*

OPHELIA: *You are sharp, my lord; you are sharp.*

235   HAMLET: It would cost you a groaning to take off my edge.

OPHELIA: Still better, and worse.

HAMLET: So you must take your husbands. Begin, murderer. Pox,
    leave thy damnable faces, and begin! Come, the croaking raven
    doth bellow for revenge.

240   LUCIANUS: Thoughts black, hands apt, drugs fit, and time agreeing;
    Confederate season, else no creature seeing;
    Thou mixture rank, of midnight weeds collected,
    With Hecate's ban thrice blasted, thrice infected,
    Thy natural magic and dire property
245   On wholesome life usurp immediately.
    [Pours the poison into the sleeper's ears.]

HAMLET: He poisons him i' the garden for his estate. His name's
    Gonzago.
    The story is extant, and written in very choice Italian. You shall
    see anon how the murderer gets the love of Gonzago's wife.

250   OPHELIA: The King rises.

HAMLET: What, frighted with false fire?

QUEEN: How fares my lord?

POLONIUS: Give o'er the play.

KING: Give me some light! Away!

255   ALL: Lights, lights, lights!
                          [Exeunt all but Hamlet and Horatio.]

HAMLET: Why, let the strucken deer go weep,
        The hart ungalled play;
      For some must watch, while some must sleep:
        Thus runs the world away.

HAMLET: *It would cost you your virginity to take off my edge.*

OPHELIA: *Sharper still, and indecent.*

HAMLET: *That's how you fool your husbands. Begin, murderer! Stop making ugly faces, and begin! Come, the croaking raven bellows for revenge.*

LUCIANUS: *Black thoughts, skilled hands, potent drugs, and perfect timing—everything works in my favor. No creature is anywhere near. You rotten poison, brewed from midnight weeds, cursed and infected three times by Hecate may your magical nature and dreadful effects destroy this healthy life immediately!*
[Pours the poison in the sleeping King's ears]

HAMLET: *He poisons him in the garden to gain his fortune. His name's Gonzago. The story is very popular and written in excellent Italian. You will soon see how the murderer wins the love of Gonzago's wife.*

OPHELIA: *The King rises.*

HAMLET: *What, frightened by a false alarm?*

QUEEN: *How is my lord?*

POLONIUS: *Stop the play!*

KING: *Give me some light! Let's leave!*

ALL: *Lights, lights, lights!*
[All except for Hamlet and Horatio exit]

HAMLET: *"Well, let the wounded doe cry, the buck, uninjured, play. Some must stand guard, while others sleep. This is how the world works."*

260   Would not this, sir, and a forest of feathers—if the rest of my fortunes turn Turk with me—with two Provincial roses on my razed shoes, get me a fellowship in a cry of players, sir?

HORATIO: Half a share.

HAMLET: A whole one, I!

265   For thou dost know, O Damon dear,
        This realm dismantled was
     Of Jove himself; and now reigns here
        A very, very—pajock.

HORATIO: You might have rhymed.

270 HAMLET: O good Horatio, I'll take the ghost's word for a thousand pound!
     Didst perceive?

HORATIO: Very well, my lord.

HAMLET: Upon the talk of the poisoning?

275 HORATIO: I did very well note him.

HAMLET: Ah, ha! Come, some music! Come, the recorders!

     For if the King like not the comedy,
     Why then, belike, he likes it not, perdy.

Come, some music!

[Enter Rosencrantz and Guildenstern.]

280 GUILDENSTERN: Good my lord, vouchsafe me a word with you.

HAMLET: Sir, a whole history.

If my fortunes turn bad, sir, wouldn't this speech, with some stage props, two roses on my decorated shoes, get me a share in a company of actors if my luck leaves me?

HORATIO: *Half a share.*

HAMLET: *I deserve a whole share!*

"For you know, dear Damon, Jove destroyed this country and now a peacock reigns here."

HORATIO: *You should have rhymed it.*

HAMLET: *Oh, good Horatio, I'll believe the ghost's word for a thousand dollars! Did you notice?*

HORATIO: *Very much so, my lord.*

HAMLET: *When poison came up in the play?*

HORATIO: *I observed him well.*

HAMLET: *Ah, yes! Come, some music! Come—bring the flutes!*

"For if the King does not like this comedy, he certainly seems like he doesn't like it at all."

Come, some music!

[Rosencrantz and Guildenstern enter]

GUILDENSTERN: *My good lord, allow me to have a word with you.*

HAMLET: *Sir, a whole history if you like.*

GUILDENSTERN: The King, sir—

HAMLET: Ay, sir, what of him?

GUILDENSTERN: Is in his retirement, marvellous distempered.

285　HAMLET: With drink, sir?

GUILDENSTERN: No, my lord; rather with choler.

HAMLET: Your wisdom should show itself more richer to signify this
　　　　to the doctor; for, me to put him to his purgation would per-
　　　　haps plunge him into far more choler.

290　GUILDENSTERN: Good my lord, put your discourse into some frame,
　　　　and start not so wildly from my affair.

HAMLET: I am tame, sir. Pronounce.

GUILDENSTERN: The Queen, your mother, in most great affliction of
　　　　spirit hath sent me to you.

295　HAMLET: You are welcome.

GUILDENSTERN: Nay, good my lord, this courtesy is not of the right
　　　　breed. If it shall please you to make me a wholesome answer, I
　　　　will do your mother's commandment; if not, your pardon and
　　　　my return shall be the end of my business.

300　HAMLET: Sir, I cannot.

GUILDENSTERN: What, my lord?

HAMLET: Make you a wholesome answer. My wit's diseased. But, sir,
　　　　such answer as I can make, you shall command; or rather, as
　　　　you say, my mother. Therefore no more, but to the matter! My
305　　mother, you say—

160

GUILDENSTERN: The King, sir—

HAMLET: Yes, sir, what about him?

GUILDENSTERN: He retired to his bedroom—extremely upset.

HAMLET: Because of drink, sir?

GUILDENSTERN: No, my lord, with anger.

HAMLET: It would be wiser for you to tell this to the doctor. If I were to cleanse him, he might get even more angry.

GUILDENSTERN: My good lord, give some sense to your words and don't wander off wildly on a different subject.

HAMLET: I am calm, sir. Speak!

GUILDENSTERN: The Queen, your mother, in greatest spiritual grief, has sent me to you.

HAMLET: You are welcome here.

GUILDENSTERN: No, my good lord; this false courtesy is not the right kind. If you can please give me a sensible answer, I will obey your mother's instructions. If not, I ask for permission to leave, and my business will be done.

HAMLET: Sir, I cannot.

GUILDENSTERN: What, my lord?

HAMLET: Give you a sensible answer. My mind is confused. But, sir, any answer I can give you, is yours to order, or rather, as you say, my mother's. Therefore, no more of that. But to continue, my mother, you say—

ROSENCRANTZ: Then thus she says: your behaviour hath struck her into amazement and admiration.

HAMLET: O wonderful son, that can so astonish a mother! But is there no sequel at the heels of this mother's admiration? Impart.

310 ROSENCRANTZ: She desires to speak with you in her closet, ere you go to bed.

HAMLET: We shall obey, were she ten times our mother. Have you any further trade with us?

ROSENCRANTZ: My lord, you once did love me.

315 HAMLET: So I do still, by these pickers and stealers!

ROSENCRANTZ: Good my lord, what is your cause of distemper? You do surely bar the door upon your own liberty, if you deny your griefs to your friend.

HAMLET: Sir, I lack advancement.

320 ROSENCRANTZ: How can that be, when you have the voice of the King himself for your succession in Denmark?

HAMLET: Ay, sir, but 'while the grass grows'—the proverb is something musty.

[Enter the Players with recorders.]
325 O, the recorders! Let me see one. To withdraw with you—why do you go about to recover the wind of me, as if you would drive me into a toil?

GUILDENSTERN: O, my lord, if my duty be too bold, my love is too unmannerly.

330 HAMLET: I do not well understand that. Will you play upon this pipe?

ROSENCRANTZ: *In that case, she says that your conduct has amazed and bewildered her.*

HAMLET: *Oh, it is a wonderful son who can so astound a mother! But is there nothing to follow this motherly admiration? Speak!*

ROSENCRANTZ: *She desires to speak to you in her bedroom before you go to bed.*

HAMLET: *I will obey, even if she were ten times my mother. Do you have any further business to discuss with us?*

ROSENCRANTZ: *My lord, you used to like me.*

HAMLET: *And do still, by these thieving hands!*

ROSENCRANTZ: *Good lord, what is the cause of your ill-humor? You prevent your own happiness if you don't share your worries with your friend.*

HAMLET: *Sir, I lack promotion.*

ROSENCRANTZ: *How can that be, when the King himself has named you his successor and the future King of Denmark?*

HAMLET: *Yes, sir, but, "While the grass grows,"—the old proverb is stale.*

[The Players enter with instruments]
Oh, the flutes! Let me see one. Let the two of us walk. Why are you trying to find me out and force me into a trap?

GUILDENSTERN: *Oh, my lord, if I seem impertinent, it is my love that causes me to act this way.*

HAMLET: *I do not quite understand that. Will you play this instrument?*

GUILDENSTERN: My lord, I cannot.

HAMLET: I pray you.

GUILDENSTERN: Believe me, I cannot.

335 HAMLET: I do beseech you.

GUILDENSTERN: I know no touch of it, my lord.

HAMLET: It is as easy as lying. Govern these ventages with your fingers and thumbs, give it breath with your mouth, and it will discourse most eloquent music. Look you, these are the stops.

340 GUILDENSTERN: But these cannot I command to any utterance of harmony. I have not the skill.

HAMLET: Why, look you now, how unworthy a thing you make of me! You would play upon me; you would seem to know my stops; you would pluck out the heart of my mystery; you
345 would sound me from my lowest note to the top of my compass; and there is much music, excellent voice, in this little organ, yet cannot you make it speak. 'Sblood, do you think I am easier to be played on than a pipe? Call me what instrument you will, though you can fret me, you cannot play upon
350 me.

[Enter Polonius.]
God bless you, sir!

POLONIUS: My lord, the Queen would speak with you, and presently.

HAMLET: Do you see yonder cloud that's almost in shape of a camel?

POLONIUS: By the mass, and 'tis like a camel, indeed.

355 HAMLET: Methinks it is like a weasel.

GUILDENSTERN: *My lord, I cannot.*

HAMLET: *Please do!*

GUILDENSTERN: *Believe me, I cannot.*

HAMLET: *I'm begging you.*

GUILDENSTERN: *I don't know how to play, my lord.*

HAMLET: *It is as easy as lying. Cover these holes with your fingers and thumbs, breathe into it, and it will play wonderful music. Look, here are the openings.*

GUILDENSTERN: *I cannot make it sound harmonious. I do not have the skill.*

HAMLET: *Well, look, how worthless you make me seem. You want to play me; you pretend to know where my openings are; you want to rob me of all my heart's secrets; you want to play me, like this flute, from the lowest note to the highest that I carry inside of me. There's plenty of music and excellent melodies hidden inside this little instrument, yet, you cannot make it play. By God, why do you think I am easier to play than a flute? Call me whatever instrument you want to call me, but, though you can anger me, you cannot play on me.*

[Polonius enters]
   God bless you, sir!

POLONIUS: *My lord, the Queen wants to speak with you immediately.*

HAMLET: *Do you see that cloud shaped like a camel?*

POLONIUS: *Indeed, it looks like a camel.*

HAMLET: *I think it looks like a weasel.*

POLONIUS: It is backed like a weasel.

HAMLET: Or like a whale.

POLONIUS: Very like a whale.

HAMLET: Then will I come to my mother by and by. They fool me to
360   the top of my bent.—I will come by and by.

POLONIUS: I will say so. *[Exit Polonius.]*

HAMLET: 'By and by' is easily said. Leave me, friends.
                         [Exeunt all but Hamlet.]
    'Tis now the very witching time of night,
    When churchyards yawn, and hell itself breathes out
365   Contagion to this world. Now could I drink hot blood,
    And do such bitter business as the day
    Would quake to look on. Soft! now to my mother!
    O heart, lose not thy nature; let not ever
    The soul of Nero enter this firm bosom.
370   Let me be cruel, not unnatural;
    I will speak daggers to her, but use none.
    My tongue and soul in this be hypocrites
    How in my words soever she be shent,
    To give them seals never, my soul, consent!   *[Exit.]*

POLONIUS: It has a back like a weasel.

HAMLET: Or like a whale.

POLONIUS: Very much a whale.

HAMLET: Then will I come to my mother by-and-by. [Aside] They mock me to my upper limits. I will come by-and-by.

POLONIUS: I will inform her.   [He exits]

HAMLET: "By-and-by" is easily said. Leave me, my friends.
                              [All except for Hamlet exit]
It is now almost midnight, close to the witching hour, when graves open and hell itself breathes disease into this world. Now, I could drink hot blood, and commit evil deeds that daylight would shudder to reveal. Quiet, now I'll go to my mother. Oh heart, do not forget your filial affection! Don't ever allow the soul of Nero take over my thinking! Let me be cruel, but not unnaturally cruel. I will speak Sharply to her, but I will not use violence. My words and my feelings must not agree with each other. No matter how much I will blame her with words, my soul will not allow me to put these words into action.

                              [Hamlet exits]

Scene 3

A room in the Castle.

[Enter King, Rosencrantz, and Guildenstern.]

KING: I like him not, nor stands it safe with us
    To let his madness range. Therefore prepare you.
    I your commission will forthwith dispatch,
    And he to England shall along with you.
5   The terms of our estate may not endure
    Hazard so near us as doth hourly grow
    Out of his brows.

GUILDENSTERN: We will ourselves provide.
    Most holy and religious fear it is
10   To keep those many many bodies safe
    That live and feed upon your Majesty.

ROSENCRANTZ: The single and peculiar life is bound
    With all the strength and armour of the mind
    To keep itself from noyance; but much more
15   That spirit upon whose weal depends and rests
    The lives of many. The cess of majesty
    Dies not alone, but like a gulf doth draw
    What's near it with it. It is a massy wheel,
    Fix'd on the summit of the highest mount,
20   To whose huge spokes ten thousand lesser things
    Are mortised and adjoin'd; which, when it falls,
    Each small annexment, petty consequence,
    Attends the boisterous ruin. Never alone
    Did the King sigh, but with a general groan.

25 KING: Arm you, I pray you, to this speedy voyage;
    For we will fetters put upon this fear,
    Which now goes too free-footed.

Scene 3

A room in the castle.

[The King, Rosencrantz, and Guildenstern enter]

KING: *I don't like him, and it will not be safe for me to let his madness get out of control. Therefore, prepare yourselves. I will write down your instructions at once, and he must accompany you to England. My royal position cannot bear the dangers that grow out of his mind by the hour.*

GUILDENSTERN: *We will prepare ourselves. It is your holy and righteous concern to protect the many people who depend on your Majesty's generosity.*

ROSENCRANTZ: *Private individuals must protect themselves, with all their strength and power, from all harm. It is even more important that the King, on whom so many lives depend and rely, must protect himself. A king doesn't die alone; like a whirlpool, his death affects everybody around him. It is a massive wheel, fastened to the summit of the highest mountain. Ten thousand lesser beings are solidly attached to the enormous spokes of this wheel. When it falls, each small part, each minor component, accompanies the turbulent ruination. The King never sighs alone: If he does, his subjects do the same.*

KING: *Please prepare yourselves for this voyage, because we must restrain this object of our fear, which now is too free.*

ROSENCRANTZ AND GUILDENSTERN: We will haste us.
[Exeunt Rosencrantz and Guildenstern.]

[Enter Polonius.]

POLONIUS: My lord, he's going to his mother's closet.
30   Behind the arras I'll convey myself,
To hear the process. I'll warrant she'll tax him home;
And, as you said, and wisely was it said,
'Tis meet that some more audience than a mother,
Since nature makes them partial, should o'erhear
35   The speech, of vantage. Fare you well, my liege.
I'll call upon you ere you go to bed
And tell you what I know.

KING: Thanks, dear my lord.
[Exit Polonius.]

O, my offence is rank, it smells to heaven;
40   It hath the primal eldest curse upon't,
A brother's murder! Pray can I not,
Though inclination be as sharp as will;
My stronger guilt defeats my strong intent,
And, like a man to double business bound,
45   I stand in pause where I shall first begin,
And both neglect. What if this cursed hand
Were thicker than itself with brother's blood,
Is there not rain enough in the sweet heavens
To wash it white as snow? Whereto serves mercy
50   But to confront the visage of offence?
And what's in prayer but this twofold force,
To be forestalled ere we come to fall,
Or pardon'd being down? Then I'll look up;
My fault is past. But, O, what form of prayer
55   Can serve my turn? 'Forgive me my foul murder?'
That cannot be; since I am still possess'd
Of those effects for which I did the murder—
My crown, mine own ambition, and my queen.
May one be pardon'd and retain the offence?

ROSENCRANTZ *and* GUILDENSTERN: *We will hurry.*
[Rosencrantz and Guildenstern exit]

[Polonius enters]

POLONIUS: *My lord, he's going to his mother's room. I'll hide behind the drapes in order to hear their conversation. I'm certain she'll question him seriously. And, as you said so wisely, it is a good idea if someone other than a mother—as mother's are naturally biased—will overhear the conversation. Goodbye, my lord, I'll call on you before you go to bed and tell you what I have found out.*

KING: *Thanks, my dear lord*
[Polonius exits]
Oh, my crime is awful; it smells to heaven. It has the oldest, the first, the curse of Cain, a brother murder. I cannot pray, though my desire is as strong as my resolve to do so. My guilt is stronger and defeats my good intentions. And, like a man committed to two ideas, I stand and wonder what I should do first, and neglect both. What if this cursed hand is covered with my brother's blood? Is there not enough rain in the sweet heavens to wash it white as snow? Why does mercy exist, if not to confront the face of sin? What good is prayer if not for its double purpose—to prevent us from sinning and to pardon us after we have sinned. Then I can look up! My crime is in the past. But, oh, what kind of prayer would help me? "Forgive my foul murder?" This is not possible, since I still have what I gained through the murder: my crown, my ambitions, and my queen. Can one be pardoned and keep the fruits of the offense? In our corrupt world, a disguised crime can deceive justice, and we often see the rewards of corruption dominate the law system. But it is not this way in heaven! There is no trickery, there, every charge is considered in its true light, and we must provide evidence and come face to face with our faults. What then? What remains? Find out what repentance can do and what can it not do? Yet, what can it do when one cannot repent? Oh, what a

60 In the corrupted currents of this world
 Offence's gilded hand may shove by justice,
 And oft 'tis seen the wicked prize itself
 Buys out the law; but 'tis not so above:
 There is no shuffling; there the action lies
65 In his true nature, and we ourselves compell'd,
 Even to the teeth and forehead of our faults,
 To give in evidence. What then? What rests?
 Try what repentance can. What can it not?
 Yet what can it when one cannot repent?
70 O wretched state! O bosom black as death!
 O limed soul, that, struggling to be free,
 Art more engaged! Help, angels! Make assay.
 Bow, stubborn knees; and heart with strings of steel,
 Be soft as sinews of the new-born babe!
75 All may be well.   *[He kneels.]*

[Enter Hamlet.]

Hamlet: Now might I do it pat, now he is praying;
 And now I'll do't. And so he goes to heaven,
 And so am I revenged. That would be scann'd.
 A villain kills my father; and for that,
80 I, his sole son, do this same villain send
 To heaven.
 O, this is hire and salary, not revenge!
 He took my father grossly, full of bread,
 With all his crimes broad blown, as flush as May;
85 And how his audit stands, who knows save heaven?
 But in our circumstance and course of thought,
 'Tis heavy with him; and am I then revenged,
 To take him in the purging of his soul,
 When he is fit and seasoned for his passage?
90 No.
 Up, sword, and know thou a more horrid hent.
 When he is drunk asleep; or in his rage;
 Or in the incestuous pleasure of his bed;
 At game, a-swearing, or about some act

horrible situation! Oh, my conscience is as black as death! Oh, my imprisoned soul, entangling itself more and more while struggling to be free! Help, oh, angels! See what you can do! Bow, my stubborn knees! And heart, with strings of steel, be soft as the muscles of a newborn baby! All may yet turn out well. [He kneels]

[Hamlet enters]

HAMLET: *Now might I do it nicely, now as he prays. And now I'll do it. And he would go to heaven. That's how I would be revenged. This must be carefully considered. A villain kills my father, and for that, I, his only son, send this same villain to heaven. Oh, this will be relief, not revenge! He killed my father unprepared, after feasting, with all his sins in full bloom, full of lust! Who knows his history other than God? But, judging from a human standpoint, it does not look good for him. How his account adds up, only heaven knows. As far as I can see, his sins are great. Can I be revenged if he is prepared and ready for his passing, while he is cleansing his soul? No! Back into the sheath, sword, until we catch him during a more sinful time. When he is drunk and sleeping, or is angry, or while enjoying incestuous pleasures in bed, or while he is gambling, or swearing, or occupied with some kind of deed that has no trace of salvation! Then I will attack him, so that his heels will kick against the entrance to heaven, and his soul will be as damned and black as hell, where it is going. My mother waits. Prayers just prolong your dreadful life.*

[He exits]

95   That has no relish of salvation in't
Then trip him, that his heels may kick at heaven,
And that his soul may be as damn'd and black
As hell, whereto it goes. My mother stays.
This physic but prolongs thy sickly days.   *[Exit.]*

100   KING: *[Rising]* My words fly up, my thoughts remain below.
Words without thoughts never to heaven go.

                                       [Exit.]

Scene 4

The Queen's closet.

[Enter Queen and Polonius.]

POLONIUS: He will come straight. Look you lay home to him.
Tell him his pranks have been too broad to bear with,
And that your Grace hath screen'd and stood between
Much heat and him. I'll silence me even here.
5   Pray you, be round with him.

QUEEN: I'll warrant you;
Fear me not. Withdraw; I hear him coming.
      [Polonius hides behind the arras.]

[Enter Hamlet.]

HAMLET: Now, mother, what's the matter?

QUEEN: Hamlet, thou hast thy father much offended.

10 HAMLET: Mother, you have my father much offended.

QUEEN: Come, come, you answer with an idle tongue.

KING: [Rising] *My words fly to heaven, but my thoughts remain here. Words without remorse never go to heaven.*

[Exits]

Scene 4

The Queen's bedroom.

[The Queen and Polonius enter]

POLONIUS: *He will come soon. Speak firmly to him. Tell him his mischief has been too undisciplined to bear and that the King has protected him from a great deal of trouble. I won't say any more. Please, speak plainly with him.*

QUEEN: *I guarantee you that you don't have to worry. Hide yourself! I hear him coming.*
[Polonius hides behind the tapestry]

[Hamlet enters]

HAMLET: *Well, mother, what's the matter?*

QUEEN: *Hamlet, you have offended your father very much.*

HAMLET: *Mother, you have offended my father very much.*

QUEEN: *Come, come, you answer foolishly.*

HAMLET: Go, go, you question with a wicked tongue.

QUEEN: Why, how now, Hamlet?

HAMLET: What's the matter now?

15   QUEEN: Have you forgot me?

HAMLET: No, by the rood, not so!
     You are the Queen, your husband's brother's wife,
     And—would it were not so—you are my mother.

QUEEN: Nay, then, I'll set those to you that can speak.

20   HAMLET: Come, come, and sit you down. You shall not budge.
     You go not till I set you up a glass
     Where you may see the inmost part of you.

QUEEN: What wilt thou do? Thou wilt not murder me?
     Help, help, ho!

25   POLONIUS: [Behind.] What, ho! Help, help, help!

HAMLET: [Drawing.] How now, a rat? Dead for a ducat, dead!
     [Makes a pass through the arras]

POLONIUS: [Behind.] O, I am slain! [falls and dies]

QUEEN: O me, what hast thou done?

HAMLET: Nay, I know not. Is it the King?

30   QUEEN: O, what a rash and bloody deed is this!

HAMLET: A bloody deed. Almost as bad, good mother,
     As kill a king, and marry with his brother.

HAMLET: *Well, you question me with an evil tongue.*

QUEEN: *Why, how so, Hamlet?*

HAMLET: *What's the matter now?*

QUEEN: *Have you forgotten who I am?*

HAMLET: *No, by the cross, I haven't! You are the Queen, your husband's brother's wife, and, though I wish it weren't so, you are my mother.*

QUEEN: *Well then, I'll send for somebody else you can speak to.*

HAMLET: *Come, come, and sit down. You mustn't go. You mustn't leave until I show you your inner self in a mirror.*

QUEEN: *What are you going to do? You will not kill me? Help, help here!*

POLONIUS: [From behind the drapes] *What! Help!*

HAMLET: [Drawing his sword] *What? A rat? Dead, easily, dead!*
    [Stabs Polonius through the drapes]

POLONIUS: [From behind the drapes] *Oh, I am killed!*
                                        [He falls and dies]

QUEEN: *Oh, my God, what have you done?*

HAMLET: *I don't know; is it the King?*

QUEEN: *Oh, what a foolish and bloody deed!*

HAMLET: *A bloody deed! Almost as bad, good mother, as killing a king and marrying his brother.*

QUEEN: As kill a king?

HAMLET: Ay, lady, it was my word.
       [Lifts up the arras and sees Polonius.]
35   Thou wretched, rash, intruding fool, farewell!
       I took thee for thy better. Take thy fortune.
       Thou find'st to be too busy is some danger.
       Leave wringing of your hands. Peace! sit you down,
       And let me wring your heart; for so I shall,
40   If it be made of penetrable stuff;
       If damned custom have not braz'd it so
       That it be proof and bulwark against sense.

QUEEN: What have I done, that thou darest wag thy tongue
       In noise so rude against me?

45 HAMLET: Such an act
       That blurs the grace and blush of modesty;
       Calls virtue hypocrite; takes off the rose
       From the fair forehead of an innocent love,
       And sets a blister there; makes marriage vows
50   As false as dicers' oaths—O, such a deed
       As from the body of contraction plucks
       The very soul, and sweet religion makes
       A rhapsody of words! Heaven's face doth glow;
       Yea, this solidity and compound mass,
55   With tristful visage, as against the doom,
       Is thought-sick at the act.

QUEEN: Ay me, what act,
       That roars so loud and thunders in the index?

HAMLET: Look here upon this picture, and on this,
60   The counterfeit presentment of two brothers.
       See what a grace was seated on this brow;
       Hyperion's curls; the front of Jove himself;
       An eye like Mars, to threaten and command;
       A station like the herald Mercury

QUEEN: *Killing a king?*

HAMLET: *Yes, lady, those were my words.*
     [Lifts up the drapes and sees Polonius]
     You wretched, reckless, intruding fool, farewell! I mistook you for the king. Accept your fate. You have learned that it's dangerous to be too curious. Stop wringing your hands. Be quiet and sit down, and let me wring your heart. That's what I will do, if your heart can be penetrated at all, and your evil deeds have not hardened you against all good sense.

QUEEN: *What have I done that you dare to speak to me in this loud and rude manner?*

HAMLET: *An act that blemishes the graceful reputation of modesty, calls virtue a hypocrite, removes idealism from innocent love and turns it into prostitution, makes marriage vows as false as a gambler's promise—oh, a deed that takes honesty out of the marriage commitment, and turns sacred vows into meaningless words. The face of God glares sadly and angrily at the entire mass of sin, preparing for Judgment Day, sick at the thought of your deed.*

QUEEN: *Oh, me! What act can cause such a loud and thundering introduction?*

HAMLET: *Look at this picture, and at this, the painted pictures of two brothers. See what grace is evident in this face: Hyperion's curls, the forehead of Jove himself, an eye like Mars, to threaten and command, a stance like the herald Mercury landing on a beautiful hill, a character and shape, indeed, approved by all Gods as a model for mankind. This was your husband. Look what follows. Here is your*

65 New lighted on a heaven-kissing hill:
A combination and a form indeed
Where every god did seem to set his seal
To give the world assurance of a man.
This was your husband. Look you now what follows.
70 Here is your husband, like a mildew'd ear
Blasting his wholesome brother. Have you eyes?
Could you on this fair mountain leave to feed,
And batten on this moor? Ha! have you eyes?
You cannot call it love; for at your age
75 The heyday in the blood is tame, it's humble,
And waits upon the judgment; and what judgment
Would step from this to this? Sense sure you have,
Else could you not have motion; but sure that sense
Is apoplex'd; for madness would not err,
80 Nor sense to ecstacy was ne'er so thrall'd
But it reserv'd some quantity of choice
To serve in such a difference. What devil was't
That thus hath cozen'd you at hoodman-blind?
Eyes without feeling, feeling without sight,
85 Ears without hands or eyes, smelling sans all,
Or but a sickly part of one true sense
Could not so mope.
O shame! where is thy blush? Rebellious hell,
If thou canst mutine in a matron's bones,
90 To flaming youth let virtue be as wax
And melt in her own fire. Proclaim no shame
When the compulsive ardour gives the charge,
Since frost itself as actively doth burn,
And reason panders will.

95 QUEEN: O Hamlet, speak no more!
Thou turn'st mine eyes into my very soul,
And there I see such black and grained spots
As will not leave their tinct.

HAMLET: Nay, but to live
100 In the rank sweat of an enseamed bed,

180

husband, like mildewed corn contaminating his healthy brother. Do you have eyes? Could you cease to feed on this beautiful mountain and feast on this wasteland? Ha! Do you have eyes? You cannot call it love. At your age, the passion in your blood is calm; it is submissive and waits upon thought; but what thought would move from this to this? You certainly have all your senses, otherwise you wouldn't be able to move. But clearly your senses are paralyzed, because madness itself could not go wrong and rapture was never so enslaved as to be unable to perceive this difference. What devil was it that tricked you at blindman's bluff? Seeing without feeling, feeling without seeing, hearing without touching, or only smelling—just one tiny part of one sense must have been functioning. Oh, shame, why are you not blushing? Rebellious devil, if you can live inside a lady, virtue in the young will cease to exist. Don't censure the young when they pursue desire because passion burns within the old also, and lust makes a pimp out of thought.

QUEEN: Oh, Hamlet, don't say anything else! You turn my eyes inward to see my inner soul, where I see black and permanent spots that will not fade.

HAMLET: No—but to live in the rotten sweat of a filthy bed, covered with corruption, playing and making love in a nasty pigsty.

Stew'd in corruption, honeying and making love
Over the nasty sty!

QUEEN: O, speak to me no more!
These words like daggers enter in mine ears.
105   No more, sweet Hamlet!

HAMLET: A murderer and a villain!
A slave that is not twentieth part the tithe
Of your precedent lord; a vice of kings;
A cutpurse of the empire and the rule,
110   That from a shelf the precious diadem stole
And put it in his pocket!

QUEEN: No more!

[Enter the Ghost in his nightgown.]

HAMLET: A king of shreds and patches!
Save me and hover o'er me with your wings,
115   You heavenly guards! What would your gracious figure?

QUEEN: Alas, he's mad!

HAMLET: Do you not come your tardy son to chide,
That, lapsed in time and passion, lets go by
The important acting of your dread command?
120   O, say!

GHOST: Do not forget. This visitation
Is but to whet thy almost blunted purpose.
But look, amazement on thy mother sits.
O, step between her and her fighting soul!
125   Conceit in weakest bodies strongest works.
Speak to her, Hamlet.

HAMLET: How is it with you, lady?

QUEEN: *Oh, don't say anything else! These words penetrate my ears like daggers. No more, sweet Hamlet!*

HAMLET: *A murderer and a villain! A slave that is not worth a twentieth of a tenth of your former husband, a buffoon among kings, a thief who took the empire and the leadership, and stole the precious crown from a shelf to put it in his own pocket.*

QUEEN: *No more!*

[The Ghost enters in his nightgown]

HAMLET: *A king dressed in rags! Save me and keep me under your wings, oh heavenly guards! What does your Majesty wish?*

QUEEN: *Alas, he's mad!*

HAMLET: *Do you not come to scold your slow-acting son, who has allowed time and emotions to go by without fulfilling your royal command? Tell me!*

GHOST: *Do not forget! This visit is to remind you of your purpose, which is almost dulled. But look, your mother is bewildered and amazed. Oh, stop her soul from the torture it causes in her. Imagination takes the strongest hold of the weak! Speak to her, Hamlet!*

HAMLET: *How are you, lady?*

QUEEN: Alas, how is't with you,
    That you do bend your eye on vacancy,
130   And with the incorporal air do hold discourse?
    Forth at your eyes your spirits wildly peep;
    And, as the sleeping soldiers in the alarm,
    Your bedded hairs, like life in excrements,
    Start up and stand an end. O gentle son,
135   Upon the heat and flame of thy distemper
    Sprinkle cool patience! Whereon do you look?

HAMLET: On him, on him! Look you how pale he glares!
    His form and cause conjoin'd, preaching to stones,
    Would make them capable.—Do not look upon me,
140   Lest with this piteous action you convert
    My stern effects. Then what I have to do
    Will want true colour—tears perchance for blood.

QUEEN: To whom do you speak this?

HAMLET: Do you see nothing there?

145   QUEEN: Nothing at all; yet all that is I see.

HAMLET: Nor did you nothing hear?

QUEEN: No, nothing but ourselves.

HAMLET: Why, look you there! Look how it steals away!
    My father, in his habit as he liv'd!
150   Look where he goes even now out at the portal!

                                     [Exit Ghost.]

QUEEN: This is the very coinage of your brain.
    This bodiless creation ecstasy
    Is very cunning in.

HAMLET: Ecstasy?
155   My pulse as yours doth temperately keep time

QUEEN: *Alas, how are you; why do you stare at empty space and talk to the air? Spirits seem to look from your eyes, and your smooth hair, like soldiers in a call to battle, like a living beard, rise up and stand at attention. Oh, gentle son, pour the cool water of understanding on the heat and flames of your disturbance. What are you looking at?*

HAMLET: *At him, at him! Look how his pale eyes glare! His appearance and his purpose together could control stones if he addressed them. Don't look at me, or your pitiful state of mind may change my intentions. In that case, what I have to do will lack commitment—tears instead of revenge!*

QUEEN: *Who are you speaking to?*

HAMLET: *Don't you see anything?*

QUEEN: *Nothing at all; yet I see everything that's there.*

HAMLET: *Did you hear nothing?*

QUEEN: *No, nothing but ourselves.*

HAMLET: *Why, look there! Look how it sneaks away! My father, in the same clothes he used to wear! Look, how he goes right out of the door!*

[The Ghost exits]

QUEEN: *This is made up in your imagination; madness is very cunning in creating hallucinations.*

HAMLET: *Madness? My pulse keeps proper time, just like yours, and it beats rhythmically. I have not spoken any madness. Test me, and*

And makes as healthful music. It is not madness
That I have utt'red. Bring me to the test,
And I the matter will reword; which madness
Would gambol from. Mother, for love of grace,
160   Lay not that flattering unction to your soul
That not your trespass but my madness speaks.
It will but skin and film the ulcerous place,
Whilst rank corruption, mining all within,
Infects unseen. Confess yourself to heaven;
165   Repent what's past; avoid what is to come;   -
And do not spread the compost on the weeds
To make them ranker. Forgive me this my virtue;
For in the fatness of these pursy times
Virtue itself of vice must pardon beg
170   Yea, curb and woo for leave to do him good.

QUEEN: O Hamlet, thou hast cleft my heart in twain.

HAMLET: O, throw away the worser part of it,
And live the purer with the other half,
Good night- but go not to my uncle's bed.
175   Assume a virtue, if you have it not.
That monster, custom, who all sense doth eat
Of habits evil, is angel yet in this,
That to the use of actions fair and good
He likewise gives a frock or livery,
180   That aptly is put on. Refrain to-night,
And that shall lend a kind of easiness
To the next abstinence; the next more easy;
For use almost can change the stamp of nature,
And either [master] the devil, or throw him out
185   With wondrous potency. Once more, good night;
And when you are desirous to be blest,
I'll blessing beg of you. For this same lord, *[Points to Polonius.]*
I do repent; but heaven hath pleas'd it so,
To punish me with this, and this with me,
190   That I must be their scourge and minister.
I will bestow him, and will answer well

186

I'll repeat everything. Madness could run from that! Mother, for the love of God, don't soothe your conscience by telling yourself that it is not your sin, but my madness that has spoken. That will only cover up the sore offense, while foul corruption, spreading quickly, will infect everything unseen. Confess your sins to heaven, repent the past, avoid what will come, and don't spread fertilizer on the weeds of your sin to make them even more foul. Forgive my moral speech. In the depravity of these odd times, even virtue must ask vice for forgiveness; yes, bow and ask for permission to do vice a favor.

QUEEN: Oh, Hamlet, you have split my heart in two!

HAMLET: Oh, throw away the worse part, and live a purer life with the other half. Good night. But don't go to my uncle's bed. Pretend to be virtuous, though you are not. Custom, that monster, which everyone supposes lives off evil habits, can be an angel through this: Through good and just actions, custom can allow us to put on clothing that is proper to wear. Abstain tonight, and the next abstinence will be easier, as will the one after that. A habit can change a person's natural inclination. It will either serve the devil himself, or throw him out of one's life with amazing power. Once again, good night. And when you are repentant, I'll beg a blessing from you. As far as this lord is concerned [Pointing to Polonius], I am sorry, but heaven chose to punish me with this, and him through me, by making me a force to administer heavenly justice. I will dispose of him and explain why I killed him. So, again, good night. I must be cruel, only to be kind. Bad times have started this way, and worse things remain to be seen. One more word, good lady.

The death I gave him. So again, good night.
I must be cruel, only to be kind;
Thus bad begins, and worse remains behind.
195   One word more, good lady.

QUEEN: What shall I do?

HAMLET: Not this, by no means, that I bid you do:
Let the bloat King tempt you again to bed;
Pinch wanton on your cheek; call you his mouse;
200   And let him, for a pair of reechy kisses,
Or paddling in your neck with his damn'd fingers,
Make you to ravel all this matter out,
That I essentially am not in madness,
But mad in craft. 'Twere good you let him know;
205   For who that's but a queen, fair, sober, wise,
Would from a paddock, from a bat, a gib
Such dear concernings hide? Who would do so?
No, in despite of sense and secrecy,
Unpeg the basket on the house's top,
210   Let the birds fly, and like the famous ape,
To try conclusions, in the basket creep
And break your own neck down.

QUEEN: Be thou assur'd, if words be made of breath,
And breath of life, I have no life to breathe
215   What thou hast said to me.

HAMLET: I must to England; you know that?

QUEEN: Alack,
I had forgot! 'Tis so concluded on.

HAMLET: There's letters seal'd; and my two schoolfellows,
220   Whom I will trust as I will adders fang'd,
They bear the mandate; they must sweep my way
And marshal me to knavery. Let it work;
For 'tis the sport to have the enginer

QUEEN: *What do you want me to do?*

HAMLET: *Not by any means should you do what I'm telling to you. Let the bloated king tempt you to join him in bed again, pinch lustfully at your cheek, call you his mouse; don't let him, for a few filthy kisses, or a few caresses on your neck with his damned fingers, make you explain everything: That I am not really mad, but only pretending to be. It would be good if you told him. After all, would a queen, beautiful, level-headed, and wise, hide these matters of utmost concern from a toad, a bat, a tomcat? Who would do that? Do not ignore common sense and secrecy and let everything out. If you let birds fly loose in your home, and, like an ape, play in their house, you will fall and break your neck.*

QUEEN: *Be assured, if words are made of breath, and breath made of life, that I have no life to breathe what you have said to me.*

HAMLET: *I must go to England; do you know that?*

QUEEN: *Alas, I had forgotten! It was decided.*

HAMLET: *Letters have been sealed, and my two colleagues from school, whom I trust as if they were poisonous snakes, are in command. They must lead me into a trap. Let it be. It will be fun to see the engineer blown up with his own explosives. And it would be horrible, if I did not hide myself one yard beneath their traps and blow them to the moon. Oh, it is best when two different plots*

Hoist with his own petar; and shall go hard
225 But I will delve one yard below their mines
And blow them at the moon. O, 'tis most sweet
When in one line two crafts directly meet.
This man shall set me packing:
I'll lug the guts into the neighbour room.
230 Mother, good night. Indeed, this counsellor
Is now most still, most secret, and most grave,
Who was in life a foolish prating knave.
Come, sir, to draw toward an end with you.
Good night, mother.

[Exit the Queen. Then Exit Hamlet, tugging on Polonius.]

collide head on! This man will send me off in a hurry. I'll carry the remains of Polonius into the next room. Mother, good night, indeed. This counselor is now very quiet, very secretive, and very grave. In life, he was a foolish, talkative scoundrel. Come, sir, to end my business with you. Good night, mother.

[The Queen exits. Hamlet exits, dragging Polonius]

ACT IV

Scene 1

Elsinore. A room in the Castle.

[Enter King and Queen, with Rosencrantz and Guildenstern.]

KING: There's matter in these sighs. These profound heaves
You must translate; 'tis fit we understand them.
Where is your son?

QUEEN: Bestow this place on us a little while.
[Exeunt Rosencrantz and Guildenstern.]
Ah, mine own lord, what have I seen to-night!

5

KING: What, Gertrude? How does Hamlet?

QUEEN: Mad as the sea and wind when both contend
Which is the mightier. In his lawless fit
Behind the arras hearing something stir,
Whips out his rapier, cries 'A rat, a rat!'
10   And in this brainish apprehension kills
The unseen good old man.

KING: O heavy deed!
It had been so with us, had we been there.
His liberty is full of threats to all,
15   To you yourself, to us, to every one.
Alas, how shall this bloody deed be answer'd?
It will be laid to us, whose providence

ACT IV

Scene 1

A room in the castle.

[The King, Queen, Rosencrantz, and Guildenstern enter]

KING: *There's meaning to these sighs: You must explain these profound heaves. It is important that I should be informed. Where is your son?*

QUEEN: *Leave us alone here for a little while.*
                              [Rosencrantz and Guildenstern exit]
Ah, my own lord. What I have seen tonight!

KING: *What, Gertrude? How is Hamlet?*

QUEEN: *Mad as the sea and wind, when they fight to decide who is more powerful. In his fit of confusion, he heard something move behind the drapes, ripped out his sword, and cried, "A rat! A rat!" In his madness, he killed the hidden good, old man.*

KING: *Oh, what a terrible deed! It would have happened to me, had I been there! His freedom is a threat to all—to you, yourself, to us, to everyone. Alas, how can this bloody deed be accounted for? We will be held responsible, because we should have had the foresight to keep this mad young man on a shorter leash, to restrain him, and keep him away from other people. But we loved him so much,*

Should have kept short, restrain'd, and out of haunt
This mad young man. But so much was our love
20   We would not understand what was most fit,
But, like the owner of a foul disease,
To keep it from divulging, let it feed
Even on the pith of life. Where is he gone?

QUEEN: To draw apart the body he hath kill'd;
25   O'er whom his very madness, like some ore
Among a mineral of metals base,
Shows itself pure. He weeps for what is done.

KING: O Gertrude, come away!
The sun no sooner shall the mountains touch
30   But we will ship him hence; and this vile deed
We must with all our majesty and skill
Both countenance and excuse. Ho, Guildenstern!

[Enter Rosencrantz and Guildenstern.]
Friends both, go join you with some further aid.
Hamlet in madness hath Polonius slain,
35   And from his mother's closet hath he dragg'd him.
Go seek him out; speak fair, and bring the body
Into the chapel. I pray you haste in this.
                    [Exeunt Rosencrantz and Guildenstern.]
Come, Gertrude, we'll call up our wisest friends
And let them know both what we mean to do
40   And what's untimely done. So haply slander
Whose whisper o'er the world's diameter,
As level as the cannon to his blank,
Transports his poisoned shot, may miss our name
And hit the woundless air.—O, come away!
45   My soul is full of discord and dismay.
                                        [Exeunt.]

we did not understand what had to be done, but, like a sick person who tries to keep his disease hidden, we allowed him to consume the essence of life itself. Where has he gone?

QUEEN: *To remove the body he has killed. In his madness, like a gold mine among more primitive metals, he seems pure: he weeps for what he has done.*

KING: *Oh, Gertrude, come away! As soon as the morning rises, we will send him away, and we must explain and repent this evil deed using our authority and all our abilities. Hello, Guildenstern!*

[Rosencrantz and Guildenstern enter]
> *My friends, find others to help you. Hamlet, in his madness, has killed Polonius and dragged him from his mother's room. Go find him, speak kindly, and bring the body into the chapel. I beg you, please hurry!*

[Rosencrantz and Guildenstern exit]
> *Come, Gertrude, we'll call our wisest friends together and tell them what we are planning to do and what has, unfortunately, already happened. Maybe we can completely avoid slander's poisonous effects from traveling across the entire world like a cannon shot and hitting us directly. Oh, come away, my soul is full of confusion and anger.*

[They exit]

Scene 2

Elsinore. A passage in the Castle.

[Enter Hamlet.]

HAMLET: Safely stow'd.

ROSENCRANTZ AND GUILDENSTERN: *[Without.]* Hamlet! Lord Hamlet!

HAMLET: But soft! What noise? Who calls on Hamlet? O, here they
come.

[Enter Rosencrantz and Guildenstern.]

5   ROSENCRANTZ: What have you done, my lord, with the dead body?

HAMLET: Compounded it with dust, whereto 'tis kin.

ROSENCRANTZ: Tell us where 'tis, that we may take it thence
And bear it to the chapel.

HAMLET: Do not believe it.

10   ROSENCRANTZ: Believe what?

HAMLET: That I can keep your counsel, and not mine own. Besides, to
be demanded of a sponge, what replication should be made by
the son of a king?

ROSENCRANTZ: Take you me for a sponge, my lord?

15   HAMLET: Ay, sir; that soaks up the King's countenance, his rewards,
his authorities. But such officers do the King best service in the
end. He keeps them, like an ape, in the corner of his jaw; first
mouth'd, to be last swallowed. When he needs what you have
glean'd, it is but squeezing you and, sponge, you shall be dry
20   again.

196

Scene 2

Another room in the castle.

[Hamlet enters]

HAMLET: *Safely stowed away.*

ROSENCRANTZ *and* GUILDENSTERN: [Offstage] *Hamlet! Lord Hamlet!*

HAMLET: *Wait! What's that sound? Who's calling Hamlet? Oh, here they come.*

[Rosencrantz and Guildenstern enter]

ROSENCRANTZ: *What have you done with the dead body, my lord?*

HAMLET: *Joined it with dust, that it now is a part of.*

ROSENCRANTZ: *Tell us where it is, so that we can take it away and carry it to the chapel.*

HAMLET: *Do not believe it.*

ROSENCRANTZ: *Believe what?*

HAMLET: *That I can keep your secrets and not my own. Besides, what reply would you expect from the son of a king to a question asked by people who suck up every answer like a sponge?*

ROSENCRANTZ: *Do you think I am a sponge, my lord?*

HAMLET: *Yes, sir. One that soaks up the King's favors, his rewards, his power. Officers like that serve the King best in the end. Like an ape, he puts them into his mouth first to be tasted and swallows them last. When he needs to find out the information you have gathered, he will only have to squeeze you, and, like a sponge, you will be dry again.*

ROSENCRANTZ: I understand you not, my lord.

HAMLET: I am glad of it. A knavish speech sleeps in a foolish ear.

ROSENCRANTZ: My lord, you must tell us where the body is and go
    with us to the King.

25   HAMLET: The body is with the King, but the King is not with the
        body.
    The King is a thing—

GUILDENSTERN: A thing, my lord?

HAMLET: Of nothing. Bring me to him. Hide fox, and all after.

[Exeunt.]

Scene 3

Elsinore. A room in the Castle.

[Enter King, attended.]

KING: I have sent to seek him, and to find the body.
    How dangerous is it that this man goes loose!
    Yet must not we put the strong law on him.
    He's loved of the distracted multitude,
5   Who like not in their judgment, but their eyes;
    And where 'tis so, the offender's scourge is weigh'd,
    But never the offence. To bear all smooth and even,
    This sudden sending him away must seem
    Deliberate pause. Diseases desperate grown
10   By desperate appliance are relieved,
    Or not at all.

ROSENCRANTZ: *I don't understand you, my lord.*

HAMLET: *I'm glad. A clever speech is meaningless to a foolish ear.*

ROSENCRANTZ: *My lord, you must tell us where the body is and go with us to the King.*

HAMLET: *The body is with the King, but the King is not with the body. The King is a thing—*

GUILDENSTERN: *A thing, my lord?*

HAMLET: *He is unimportant. Bring me to him. Hide the fox, and all search after it.*

[They exit]

Scene 3

Another room in the castle.

[King enters with Attendants]

KING: *I have given orders to look for him and to find the body. It is dangerous that this man walks free! Yet, we must not enforce the strict law on him. He's loved by the unstable masses, who judge him only by his appearance. the punishment is questioned, but the crime is ignored. In order to guarantee that everything is smooth, our sudden decision to send him away must appear like the result of careful consideration. Hopeless diseases are cured by desperate remedies or are not cured at all.*

[Enter Rosencrantz.]
> How now, what hath befall'n?

ROSENCRANTZ: Where the dead body is bestow'd, my lord,
> We cannot get from him.

15 KING: But where is he?

ROSENCRANTZ: Without, my lord; guarded, to know your pleasure.

KING: Bring him before us.

ROSENCRANTZ: Ho, Guildenstern! Bring in my lord.

[Enter Hamlet and Guildenstern with Attendants.]

KING: Now, Hamlet, where's Polonius?

20 HAMLET: At supper.

KING: At supper? Where?

HAMLET: Not where he eats, but where he is eaten. A certain convoca-
> tion of politic worms are e'en at him. Your worm is your only
> emperor for diet. We fat all creatures else to fat us, and we fat
25 ourselves for maggots. Your fat king and your lean beggar is but
> variable service, two dishes, but to one table. That's the end.

KING: Alas, alas!

HAMLET: A man may fish with the worm that hath eat of a king, and
> eat of the fish that hath fed of that worm.

30 KING: What dost thou mean by this?

HAMLET: Nothing but to show you how a king may go a progress
> through the guts of a beggar.

[Rosencrantz enters]
   Well, what has happened?

ROSENCRANTZ: *We cannot get him to tell us where he has disposed of the dead body, my lord.*

KING: *But where is he?*

ROSENCRANTZ: *Outside, my lord, with guards, waiting to hear your wishes.*

KING: *Bring him to me.*

ROSENCRANTZ: *Guildenstern, bring in Lord Hamlet!*

[Hamlet and Guildenstern enter]

KING: *Now, Hamlet, where's Polonius?*

HAMLET: *At supper.*

KING: *At supper? Where?*

HAMLET: *Not where he eats, but where he is eaten. A certain gathering of governmental worms are enjoying him as we speak. Worms are the supreme eaters. We fatten all creatures to make us fat, and we, in turn, become fat for maggots. Your fat king and your lean beggar are two different courses of the same meal. That's it.*

KING: *Alas, alas!*

HAMLET: *A man may fish with the worm that has eaten a king, and eat the fish that has fed on that worm.*

KING: *What do you mean by this?*

HAMLET: *Nothing, except but to show you how a king may take a journey through the guts of a beggar.*

KING: Where is Polonius?

HAMLET: In heaven. Send thither to see. If your messenger find him
35   not there, seek him i' the other place yourself. But indeed, if
       you find him not within this month, you shall nose him as you
       go up the stair, into the lobby.

KING: *[To some Attendants.]* Go seek him there.

HAMLET: He will stay till you come.

                                   [Exeunt Attendants.]

40 KING: Hamlet, this deed, for thine especial safety—
       Which we do tender as we dearly grieve
       For that which thou hast done—must send thee hence
       With fiery quickness. Therefore prepare thyself.
       The bark is ready and the wind at help,
45   The associates tend, and everything is bent
       For England.

HAMLET: For England?

KING: Ay, Hamlet.

HAMLET: Good.

50 KING: So is it, if thou knew'st our purposes.

HAMLET: I see a cherub that sees them. But come, for England!
       Farewell, dear mother.

KING: Thy loving father, Hamlet.

HAMLET: My mother! Father and mother is man and wife; man and
55   wife is one flesh; and so, my mother. Come, for England!
                                   [Exit.]

KING: Follow him at foot. Tempt him with speed aboard.

KING: Where   nius?

HAMLET: In h   . Send for him there. If your messenger can't find him there, see him in hell yourself. But indeed, if you don't find him within th month, you will smell him going up the stairs, into the lobby.

KING: [To Attendants] *Go look for him there!*

HAMLET: He will wait until you get there.

[Attendants exit]

KING: Hamlet, because of this deed, and for your own safety, which is as important to us as our grief over your crime, we must send you away extre nely quickly. Therefore, prepare yourself. The boat is ready, and e wind favorable, your comrades are waiting, and everythin repared for your trip to E land.

HAMLET: To   and?

KING: Yes, Han

HAMLET: Good.

KING: So it is, if you know our intentions.

HAMLET: Heaven knows them! But come, off to England! Goodbye, dear mother!

KING: I remain your loving father, Hamlet.

HAMLET: My m er: Father and mother are man and wife; man and wife are on sh—and so, you are my mother, come along to England!

[He exits]

KING: Foll m closely! Hurry him aboard! I want him gone tonight.

Delay it not; I'll have him hence tonight.
Away! for every thing is seal'd and done
That else leans on the affair. Pray you, make haste.

[Exeunt Rosencrantz and Guildenstern.]

60 And, England, if my love thou hold'st at aught—
As my great power thereof may give thee sense,
Since yet thy cicatrice looks raw and red
After the Danish sword, and thy free awe
Pays homage to us—thou mayst not coldly set
65 Our sovereign process, which imports at full,
By letters congruing to that effect,
The present death of Hamlet. Do it, England;
For like the hectic in my blood he rages,
And thou must cure me. Till I know 'tis done,
70 Howe'er my haps, my joys were ne'er begun.

[Exit.]

Scene 4

A plain in Denmark.

[Enter Fortinbras with his Army over the stage.]

Fortinbras: Go, Captain, from me greet the Danish king.
Tell him that by his license Fortinbras
Craves the conveyance of a promised march
Over his kingdom. You know the rendezvous.
5 If that his Majesty would aught with us,
We shall express our duty in his eye;
And let him know so.

Captain: I will do't, my lord.

Fortinbras: Go softly on.

[Exeunt Fortinbras and Soldiers.]

Away! Everything relating to this trip has been decided. Please, hurry!

[Rosencrantz and Guildenstern exit]

And, dear King of England, if you value my friendship—and you know my power, since the scar you acquired in a fight against the Danes is still raw and red, and your fear forces you to pay for your defeat—you will not delay our royal command. I request, as described in these letters, the immediate death of Hamlet. Do it, King of England! He rages like a fever in my blood, and you must cure me! Until I know it has been done, I will never be happy again, no matter what my fortunes bring.

[He exits]

Scene 4

A plain in Denmark.

[Fortinbras, a Captain, and Soldiers enter, marching]

FORTINBRAS: *Captain, go convey my greetings to the Danish king. Tell him that Fortinbras asks to march with his escorts across Denmark, as it has been agreed upon. You are familiar with our understanding. If his Majesty wants to see us, we will pay our respects in person. Let him know this.*

CAPTAIN: *I will, my lord.*

FORTINBRAS: *Move quickly!*

[Fortinbras and Soldiers exit]

[Enter Hamlet, Rosencrantz, Guildenstern, and others.]

10   HAMLET: Good sir, whose powers are these?

CAPTAIN: They are of Norway, sir.

HAMLET: How purposed, sir, I pray you?

CAPTAIN: Against some part of Poland.

HAMLET: Who commands them, sir?

15   CAPTAIN: The nephew to old Norway, Fortinbras.

HAMLET: Goes it against the main of Poland, sir,
    Or for some frontier?

CAPTAIN: Truly to speak, and with no addition,
    We go to gain a little patch of ground
20   That hath in it no profit but the name.
    To pay five ducats, five, I would not farm it;
    Nor will it yield to Norway or the Pole
    A ranker rate, should it be sold in fee.

HAMLET: Why, then the Polack never will defend it.

25   CAPTAIN: Yes, it is already garrison'd.

HAMLET: Two thousand souls and twenty thousand ducats
    Will not debate the question of this straw.
    This is the imposthume of much wealth and peace,
    That inward breaks, and shows no cause without
30   Why the man dies. I humbly thank you, sir.

CAPTAIN: God be wi' you, sir.   *[Exit.]*

ROSENCRANTZ: Will't please you go, my lord?

[Hamlet, Rosencrantz, Guildenstern, and others enter]

HAMLET: *Good sir, whose army is this?*

CAPTAIN: *They belong to the King of Norway, sir.*

HAMLET: *What is the purpose?*

CAPTAIN: *To fight against some part of Poland.*

HAMLET: *Who commands them, sir?*

CAPTAIN: *The nephew to old Fortinbras, King of Norway.*

HAMLET: *Are you going to fight against the main territory of Poland, sir, or at some frontier?*

CAPTAIN: *To speak honestly and directly, we are trying to gain a little patch of land that has no benefit other than its name. I wouldn't pay five ducats a year to lease it. It wouldn't yield much more for the King of Norway or for Poland if it were sold outright.*

HAMLET: *Why, then the Polish will never defend it.*

CAPTAIN: *Yes, it is already garrisoned.*

HAMLET: *Two thousand men and twenty thousand ducats will scarcely be enough to settle this fight! It is an abscess—fueled by wealth and peace—that bursts inside of men, which does not explain why a man must die. I give you humble thanks, sir.*

CAPTAIN: *May God be with you, sir.*   [He exits]

ROSENCRANTZ: *Will you come along, my lord?*

HAMLET: I'll be with you straight. Go a little before.

[Exeunt all but Hamlet.]

How all occasions do inform against me
35 And spur my dull revenge! What is a man,
If his chief good and market of his time
Be but to sleep and feed? A beast, no more.
Sure, he that made us with such large discourse,
Looking before and after, gave us not
40 That capability and godlike reason
To fust in us unused. Now, whether it be
Bestial oblivion, or some craven scruple
Of thinking too precisely on the event—
A thought which, quarter'd, hath but one part wisdom
45 And ever three parts coward—I do not know
Why yet I live to say this 'Thing's to do,'
Sith I have cause, and will, and strength, and means
To do't. Examples gross as earth exhort me.
Witness this army, of such mass and charge,
50 Led by a delicate and tender prince,
Whose spirit with divine ambition puff'd,
Makes mouths at the invisible event,
Exposing what is mortal and unsure
To all that fortune, death, and danger dare,
55 Even for an eggshell. Rightly to be great
Is not to stir without great argument,
But greatly to find quarrel in a straw
When honour's at the stake. How stand I then,
That have a father kill'd, a mother stain'd,
60 Excitements of my reason and my blood,
And let all sleep, while to my shame I see
The imminent death of twenty thousand men
That for a fantasy and trick of fame
Go to their graves like beds, fight for a plot
65 Whereon the numbers cannot try the cause,
Which is not tomb enough and continent
To hide the slain? O, from this time forth,
My thoughts be bloody, or be nothing worth!

[Exit.]

HAMLET: *I'll be w... 1 you soon. Go ahead a little.*

[All except for Hamlet exit]

All events seem to speak to me and encourage my revenge. What is a man, if sleeping and eating occupy all his time? No more than a beast. Certainly God, who has given us the power to reason, to look at the past and envision the future, does not want us to allow our abilities and our divine reason to be neglected and grow moldy. I don't know whether it is my awful forgetfulness or a cowardly uneasiness of thinking too much about my plan—a thought that always consists of one part wisdom and three parts cowardice— that has made me live and still say, "This thing's yet to be done." I certainly have the reason, the willpower, the strength, and means to do it. Many simple examples encourage me. Observe this large and powerful army, led by a delicate and tender prince, whose spirit—spurned by divine ambition—disregards all unforeseeable events. Risking his life, he confronts fate, death, and danger—all for something as trivial as an eggshell. To be great does not mean to attack without a worthy cause, but to find a reason for fighting in anything, even straw, if honor is at stake? What about me, I'm the son of a murdered father and an unfaithful mother, urged on by my reason, as well as my passion. Yet, I allow it to continue, while, to my shame, I see twenty thousand men who willingly go to their graves, spurred on by some fantasty and trivial gains as if they were going to sleep. They fight over a territory that is not large enough to accommodate a battle, or bury the dead. Oh, from now on, I must think abo... blood, or be nothing at all.

[He exits]

Scene 5

Elsinore. A room in the Castle.

[Enter Horatio, Queen, and a Gentleman.]

QUEEN: I will not speak with her.

GENTLEMAN: She is importunate, indeed distract. Her
    mood will needs be pitied.

QUEEN: What would she have?

5   GENTLEMAN: She speaks much of her father; says she hears
    There's tricks i' the world, and hems, and beats her heart;
    Spurns enviously at straws; speaks things in doubt,
    That carry but half sense. Her speech is nothing,
    Yet the unshaped use of it doth move
10   The hearers to collection; they aim at it,
    And botch the words up fit to their own thoughts;
    Which, as her winks and nods and gestures yield them,
    Indeed would make one think there might be thought,
    Though nothing sure, yet much unhappily.

15   HORATIO: 'Twere good she were spoken with; for she may strew
    Dangerous conjectures in ill-breeding minds.

QUEEN: Let her come in.   *[Exit Gentleman.]*
    [Aside.] To my sick soul, as sin's true nature is,
    Each toy seems prologue to some great amiss.
20   So full of artless jealousy is guilt
    It spills itself in fearing to be spilt.

[Enter Gentleman, with Ophelia distracted.]

OPHELIA: Where is the beauteous Majesty of Denmark?

Scene 5

Elsinore. A room in the castle.

[The Queen, Horatio, and a Gentleman enter]

QUEEN: *I will not speak with her.*

GENTLEMAN: *She is persistent and confused. Her situation should certainly be pitied.*

QUEEN: *What does she want?*

GENTLEMAN: *She speaks a lot about her father. Says she has heard there is corruption in this world, and she mumbles and strikes her chest; she shows contempt at pieces of straw, speaks obscurely, and makes little sense although her confused mumbling tempts her listeners to find some meaning. Her listeners do their best to make sense of her words; her winks and nods and gestures seem to give them meaning, but nothing is certain, and much is sad.*

HORATIO: *It would be good if somebody would talk to her, since she may put dangerous ideas into evil minds.*

QUEEN: *Let her come in.* [Gentleman exits]
[Aside] To my blemished conscience, as it usually happens when sin is involved, it seems like every trivial event foreshadows some great tragedy. Guilt is accompanied by uncontrolled anxiety. It shows itself by trying not to be shown.

[Ophelia enters]

OPHELIA: *Where is the beautiful Majesty of Denmark?*

QUEEN: How now, Ophelia?

OPHELIA: *[Sings.]*
25   How should I your true love know
            From another one?
        By his cockle bat and staff
            And his sandal shoon.

QUEEN: Alas, sweet lady, what imports this song?

30 OPHELIA: Say you? Nay, pray you, mark.
            [Sings.]   He is dead and gone, lady,
                He is dead and gone;
            At his head a grass-green turf,
                At his heels a stone.
35   O, ho!

QUEEN: Nay, but Ophelia—

OPHELIA: Pray you, mark.
        [Sings.] White his shroud as the mountain snow

[Enter King.]

QUEEN: Alas, look here, my lord!

40 OPHELIA: *[Sings.]*
            Larded all with sweet flowers;
        Which bewept to the grave did not go
            With true-love showers.

KING: How do you, pretty lady?

45 OPHELIA: Well, God 'ild you! They say the owl was a baker's
                daughter.
        Lord, we know what we are, but know not what we may be.
        God be at your table!

QUEEN: *What is it, Ophelia?*

OPHELIA: [Singing]
> *"How should I know true love from untrue love? By his pilgrim's hat and staff and his woven sandals."*

QUEEN: *Alas, sweet lady, why are you singing this song?*

OPHELIA: *Do you speak? No, pay attention, please!*
> [Singing] *"He is dead and gone, lady, he is dead and gone. At his head a mound of grass, at his heels a gravestone. Oh, oh!"*

QUEEN: *No, but Ophelia—*

OPHELIA: *Pay attention!* [Singing] *"His shroud is as white as the mountain snow."*

[The King enters]

QUEEN: *Alas, look here, my lord!*

OPHELIA: [Singing]
> *"Adorned with sweet flowers, which did not find their tearful grave with showers of true love."*

KING: *How are you, pretty lady?*

OPHELIA: *Well, may God reward you! They say the baker's daughter was turned into an owl. Lord, we know what we are, but we don't know what we may be. May God watch over your table!*

KING: Conceit upon her father.

50 OPHELIA: Pray let's have no words of this; but when they ask, you
   what it means, say you this:
   [Sings.]
       Tomorrow is Saint Valentine's day,
           All in the morning betime,
       And I a maid at your window,
55   To be your Valentine.

       Then up be rose and donn'd his clo'es
           And dupp'd the chamber door,
       Let in the maid, that out a maid
           Never departed more.

60 KING: Pretty Ophelia!

OPHELIA: Indeed, without an oath, I'll make an end on't!
   [Sings.]
       By Gis and by Saint Charity,
           Alack, and fie for shame!
       Young men will do't if they come to't
65   By Cock, they are to blame.

       Quoth she, 'Before you tumbled me,
           You promis'd me to wed.'

   He answers:

       'So would I 'a' done, by yonder sun,
70   An thou hadst not come to my bed.'

KING: How long hath she been thus?

OPHELIA: I hope all will be well. We must be patient. But I cannot choose but weep, to think they would lay him i' the cold
   ground. My brother shall know of it. And so I thank you for
75 your good counsel. Come, my coach! Good night, ladies. Good
   night, sweet ladies. Good night, good night.   *[Exit]*

KING: *Brooding about her father.*

OPHELIA: *Please let's not talk about this. But when they ask you what it means, say this:* [Singing]
"*Tomorrow is Saint Valentine's day. Early in the morning, I will be a maid at your window, waiting to be your valentine. Then he got up, put on his clothes, and opened his door, and let in a maid that never again was pure.*"

KING: *That's pretty Ophelia!*

OPHELIA: *Indeed, without swearing an oath, I'll finish it!*
[Singing] "*By Jesus and by Saint Charity, alas, and forget about shame; young men will do it if they can. By God, they are to blame! She quotes, 'Before you seduced me, you promised to wed.' He answers: 'That I would have done, by the sun, if you had not come to my bed.'*"

KING: *How long has she been like this?*

OPHELIA: *I hope all will be well. We must be patient. But I must cry when I think that they will lay him in the cold ground. My brother will hear of it! And so, I thank you for your good advice. Come, my coach! Good night, ladies! Good night, sweet ladies! Good night, good night!* [She exits]

KING: Follow her close; give her good watch, I pray you.

[Exit Horatio.]

O, this is the poison of deep grief; it springs
All from her father's death. O Gertrude, Gertrude,
80 When sorrows come, they come not single spies,
But in battalions! First, her father slain;
Next, your son gone, and he most violent author
Of his own just remove; the people muddied,
Thick and unwholesome in their thoughts and whispers,
85 For good Polonius' death, and we have done but greenly,
In hugger-mugger to inter him; poor Ophelia
Divided from herself and her fair judgment,
Without the which we are pictures, or mere beasts;
Last, and as much containing as all these,
90 Her brother is in secret come from France;
Feeds on his wonder, keeps himself in clouds,
And wants not buzzers to infect his ear
With pestilent speeches of his father's death,
Wherein necessity, of matter beggar'd,
95 Will nothing stick our person to arraign
In ear and ear. O my dear Gertrude, this,
Like to a murdering-piece, in many places
Gives me superfluous death.   *[A noise within.]*

QUEEN: Alack, what noise is this?

100 KING: Where are my Switzers? Let them guard the door.

[Enter another Gentleman.]
What is the matter?

GENTLEMAN: Save yourself, my lord.
The ocean, overpeering of his list,
Eats not the flats with more impetuous haste
105 Than young Laertes, in a riotous head,
O'erbears your offices. The rabble call him lord;
And, as the world were now but to begin,
Antiquity forgot, custom not known—

KING: *Please, follow her closely, observe her well.*

[Horatio exits]

Oh, these are the dire consequences of deep grief. It is all caused by her father's death. Oh, Gertrude, Gertrude, when sorrows come, they do not come alone, but in armies. First, her father is killed. Then, your son, who caused his own banishment through his violent actions, is gone. The people are confused, doubtful, and suspicious in their thoughts and hear rumors about the death of good Polonius. We buried him too quickly, and in secret. Poor Ophelia has lost her reason and her good judgment, without which, we are merely images of ourselves, or beasts. Last, but as important as everything else, her brother has secretly arrived from France. He is consumed with the lack of order, engages in his own wild speculations, and doesn't lack gossips to fill his ears with horrible stories about his father's death. They, because of the lack of facts, will not hesitate to accuse me as they spread their rumor from person to persons. Oh, my dear Gertrude, this is like a cannon firing multiple shots, killing me many times

[A noise is heard inside]

QUEEN: *Alas, what is this noise?*

KING: *Where are my Swiss guards? Let them watch the door.*

[Another Gentleman enters]

What is the matter?

GENTLEMAN: *Save yourself, my lord! The ocean rising above the shoreline does not devour the plains more quickly than young angry Laertes and his armed forces overpower your soldiers. The mob calls him "lord," as if the world had just begun, the accomplishments of antiquity forgotten, traditions meaningless, and all ratified, supported, and established customs lost! People shout, "we*

217

110 The ratifiers and props of every word—
They cry 'Choose we! Laertes shall be king!'
Caps, hands and tongues applaud it to the clouds,
'Laertes shall be king! Laertes king!'   *[A noise within.]*

QUEEN: How cheerfully on the false trail they cry.
O, this is counter, you false Danish dogs!

115 KING: The doors are broke.

[Enter Laertes, armed; Danes following.]

LAERTES: Where is this King? Sirs, stand you all without.

DANES: No, let's come in!

LAERTES: I pray you give me leave.

DANES: We will, we will!   *[Exeunt his Followers.]*

120 LAERTES: I thank you. Keep the door.
O thou vile king,
Give me my father!

QUEEN: Calmly, good Laertes.

LAERTES: That drop of blood that's calm proclaims me bastard;
125 Cries cuckold to my father; brands the harlot
Even here, between the chaste unsmirched brows
Of my true mother.

KING: What is the cause, Laertes,
That thy rebellion looks so giant-like?
130 Let him go, Gertrude. Do not fear our person.
There's such divinity doth hedge a king
That treason can but peep to what it would,
Acts little of his will. Tell me, Laertes,
Why thou art thus incensed. Let him go, Gertrude.
135 Speak, man.

218

choose! Laertes shall be king." caps, hands, and tongues cheer
toward heaven, *"Laertes shall be king! Laertes, king!"*

QUEEN: *Like a pack of dogs, they gleefully follow this false trail. This is wrong,*
    you traitorous Danish dogs!   [A noise is heard within]

KING: *The doors have been broken down.*

[Laertes enters, armed; other Danes follow]

LAERTES: *Where is this king? Gentlemen, wait outside!*

DANES: *No, let's go in!*

LAERTES: *Please, let me go alone!*

DANES: *We will, we will!*   [The Danish followers exit]

LAERTES: *Thank you. Guard the door!*
    Oh, you evil king, give me my father!

QUEEN: *Calm down, good Laertes.*

LAERTES: *The one drop of blood that remains calm would proclaim me a*
    bastard, accuse my father of adultery, and call my chaste mother
    a harlot!

KING: *What is the cause of this enormous rebellion, Laertes? Let him go,*
    Gertrude, Don't fear for our safety! A king receives such divine
    protection that treason barely understand its intended actions.
    Tell me, Laertes, why are you so enraged? Let him go, Gertrude.
    Speak, man!

LAERTES: Where is my father?

KING: Dead.

QUEEN: But not by him!

KING: Let him demand his fill.

140 LAERTES: How came he dead? I'll not be juggled with:
         To hell, allegiance! Vows, to the blackest devil!
         Conscience and grace, to the profoundest pit!
         I dare damnation. To this point I stand,
         That both the worlds, I give to negligence,
145   Let come what comes; only I'll be revenged
         Most throughly for my father.

KING: Who shall stay you?

LAERTES: My will, not all the world!
         And for my means, I'll husband them so well,
150   They shall go far with little.

KING: Good Laertes,
         If you desire to know the certainty
         Of your dear father's death, is't writ in your revenge
         That, swoopstake, you will draw both friend and foe,
155   Winner and loser?

LAERTES: None but his enemies.

KING: Will you know them then?

LAERTES: To his good friends thus wide I'll ope my arms
         And, like the kind life-rendering pelican,
160   Repast them with my blood.

KING: Why, now you speak
         Like a good child and a true gentleman.

LAERTES: *Where is my father?*

KING: *Dead.*

QUEEN: *But not killed by him!*

KING: *Let him ask for answers!*

LAERTES: *How did he die? I will not be trifled with. To hell with duty! My vows belong to the devil! Conscience and salvation are condmened to hell! I can withstand damnation. I am not afraid of the consequences in this world or in the next. No matter what happens—I will fully avenge my father's death!*

KING: *Who would stop you?*

LAERTES: *No one's will in the entire world, other than my own! As far as my means of revenge are concerned, I will use them carefully so that a little will go a long way.*

KING: *Good Laertes, if you desire to know the circumstances of your father's death, does your revenge require you to fight indiscriminately against everyone, whether friend or foe, winner or loser?*

LAERTES: *Only against my enemies.*

KING: *Do you want to know them?*

LAERTES: *I'll open my arms wide to his good friends, and, like the pelican sacrificing her life for her young, I will feed them with my own blood.*

That I am guiltless of your father's death,
And am most sensibly in grief for it,
165   It shall as level to your judgment pierce
As day does to your eye. *[A noise without]*

DANES: Let her come in.

LAERTES: How now? What noise is that?

[Enter Ophelia.]
O heat, dry up my brains! Tears seven times salt,
170   Burn out the sense and virtue of mine eye!
By heaven, thy madness shall be paid with weight,
Till our scale turn the beam. O rose of May!
Dear maid, kind sister, sweet Ophelia!
O heavens! is't possible a young maid's wits
175   Should be as mortal as an old man's life?
Nature is fine in love, and where 'tis fine,
It sends some precious instance of itself
After the thing it loves.

OPHELIA: *[Sings.]* They bore him barefac'd on the bier
180   Hey non nonny, nonny, hey nonny
And on his grave rain'd many a tear.

Fare you well, my dove!

LAERTES: Hadst thou thy wits, and didst persuade revenge,
It could not move thus.

185 OPHELIA: You must sing 'down a-down,' and you 'Call him a-down-a.'
O, how the wheel becomes it! It is the false steward, that stole
his master's daughter.

LAERTES: This nothing's more than matter.

OPHELIA: There's rosemary, that's for remembrance. Pray you, love,
190   remember. And there is pansies, that's for thoughts.

KING: *Well, now you speak like a good child and a true gentleman. I am guiltless of your father's death and grieve most profoundly for it. This will become as clear your mind as daylight to your eyes.*
[Heard outside]

DANES: *Let her come in.*

LAERTES: *What? What is this noise?*

[Ophelia enters]
Oh, heat, dry up my brains! Tears, seven times saltier, burn away the sense and clarity of my eyes! By heaven, your madness will be paid for dearly until our revenge alters the scale of justice. Oh, rose of May! Dear maid, kind sister, sweet Ophelia! Oh, heavens, is it possible that the sanity of a young maid's mind should be as flimsy as the life of an old man? Nature is tender in love, and when it's tender, it buries a piece of itself with a departed loved one.

OPHELIA: [Singing] *"They laid him barefaced onto the bier and shed many tears on his grave. Farewell, my dove!"*

LAERTES: *If you had your wits and persuaded me to revenge his death, it could not be as moving as this.*

OPHELIA: *You must sing "down-a-down," and you call him "a-down-a." Oh, how fitting is fortune! The false servant stole his master's daughter.*

LAERTES: *This is nothing more than rambling.*

OPHELIA: *There's rosemary; it's for remembrance. I am begging you, love, remember! And there are pansies; they are for thoughts.*

LAERTES: A document in madness! Thoughts and remembrance fitted.

OPHELIA: There's fennel for you, and columbines. There's rue for
you, and here's some for me. We may call it herb of grace o'
Sundays. O, you must wear your rue with a difference! There's
195   a daisy. I would give you some violets, but they wither'd all
when my father died. They say a made a good end—
[Sings.] For bonny sweet Robin is all my joy.

LAERTES: Thought and affliction, passion, hell itself,
She turns to favour and to prettiness.
200

OPHELIA: [Sings.]
And will he not come again?
And will he not come again?
No, no, he is dead;
Go to thy deathbed;
205   He never will come again.

His beard was as white as snow,
All flaxen was his poll.
He is gone, he is gone,
And we cast away moan.
210   God 'a'mercy on his soul!

And of all Christian souls, I pray God. God be wi' you.

[Exit.]

LAERTES: Do you see this, O God?

KING: Laertes, I must commune with your grief,
Or you deny me right. Go but apart,
215   Make choice of whom your wisest friends you will,
And they shall hear and judge 'twixt you and me.
If by direct or by collateral hand
They find us touch'd, we will our kingdom give,
Our crown, our life, and all that we call ours,
220   To you in satisfaction; but if not,
Be you content to lend your patience to us,

LAERTES: *There is a lesson contained in this madness: thoughts and memories complement each other.*

OPHELIA: *There's fennel for you, and columbine. There's rue for you, and here's some for me. We can call it the herb of grace on Sundays. Oh, you must wear your rue differently! There's a daisy. I would give you some violets, but they all withered when my father died. They say he died well.* [Singing] *"For bonny sweet Robin is all my joy."*

LAERTES: *She turns sorrow and disease, grief, hell itself, into affection and beauty.*

OPHELIA: [Singing]

"And will he not come again? And will he not come again? No, no, he is dead. Go to your deathbed! He never will come back. His beard was as white as snow; his head was gray. He is gone, he is gone, and we moan and moan. May God have mercy on his soul! And on all Christian souls, I am praying to God. May God be with you."

[She exits]

LAERTES: *Do you see this? Oh, God!*

KING: *Laertes, I must join in your grief, unless you deny me my right. Leave me and choose your wisest friends, and they will listen and judge between you and me. If they find me guilty directly or indirectly, I will happily give my kingdom, my crown, my life, and everything I own, to you. But if not, you must be patient, and we will work together to satisfy the need of your soul to find peace.*

And we shall jointly labour with your soul
To give it due content.

LAERTES: Let this be so.
225 His means of death, his obscure burial—
No trophy, sword, nor hatchment o'er his bones,
No noble rite nor formal ostentation,
Cry to be heard, as 'twere from heaven to earth,
That I must call't in question.
230

KING: So you shall;
And where the offence is let the great axe fall.
I pray you go with me.   *[Exeunt.]*

Scene 6

Elsinore. Another room in the Castle.

[Enter Horatio with an Attendant.]

HORATIO: What are they that would speak with me?

SERVANT: Seafaring men, sir. They say they have letters for you.

HORATIO: Let them come in.   *[Exit Attendant.]*
I do not know from what part of the world
I should be greeted, if not from Lord Hamlet.
5
[Enter Sailors.]

SAILOR: God bless you, sir.

HORATIO: Let him bless thee too.

LAERTES: *So it shall be. The circumstances of his death and the reasons for his secretive funeral—no monument, no sword, no coat of arms displayed, no rites of nobility, nor formal ceremony—cry to heaven to be looked into, and I must investigate it.*

KING: *So you shall, and whoever is guilty shall be disciplined accordingly. Please come with me.*

[They exit]

Scene 6

Another room in the castle.

[Horatio and a Servant enter]

HORATIO: *Who wants to speak to me?*

SERVANT: *Sailors, sir. They say they have letters for you.*

HORATIO: *Let them come in.*   [Servant exits]
I do not know who should send me greetings from another part of the world, if not Lord Hamlet.

[Sailors enter]

SAILOR: *May God bless you, sir.*

HORATIO: *May he bless you, too.*

SAILOR: He shall, sir, an't please him. There's a letter for you, sir. It
comes from the ambassador that was bound for England—if
10   your name be Horatio, as I am let to know it is.

HORATIO: *[Reads the letter]* 'Horatio, when thou shalt have overlook'd
this, give these fellows some means to the King. They have letters
for him. Ere we were two days old at sea, a pirate of very warlike
appointment gave us chase. Finding ourselves too slow of sail, we
15   put on a compelled valour, and in the grapple I boarded them. On
the instant they got clear of our ship; so I alone became their prisoner. They have dealt with me like thieves of mercy; but they knew
what they did: I am to do a good turn for them. Let the King have
the letters I have sent, and repair thou to me with as much speed as
20   thou wouldst fly death. I have words to speak in thine ear will make
thee dumb; yet are they much too light for the bore of the matter.
These good fellows will bring thee where I am. Rosencrantz and
Guildenstern hold their course for England. Of them I have much to
tell thee. Farewell.
25   'He that thou knowest thine, Hamlet.'

Come, I will give you way for these your letters,
And do't the speedier that you may direct me
To him from whom you brought them.   *[Exeunt.]*

Scene 7

Elsinore. Another room in the Castle.

[Enter King and Laertes.]

KING: Now must your conscience my acquittance seal,
And you must put me in your heart for friend,
Sith you have heard, and with a knowing ear,
That he which hath your noble father slain
5   Pursued my life.

SAILOR: *He shall, sir, if it pleases Him. There's a letter for you, sir. It came from the ambassador who was on his way to England—if your name is really Horatio, as I am led to believe.*

HORATIO: [Reading the letter] *"Horatio, when you have read this, give these fellows an escort to the King. They have letters for him. We had not been at sea for two days, when a hostile pirate ship chased us. Realizing that our ship was too slow, we put up a brave fight. During the battle, I boarded their ship. At that instant, they moved away from our ship, so I became their only prisoner. They have treated me as merciful thieves would. But they knew why they did it. I have to do them a favor. Make sure the King receives the letters I have sent, and come to me as though you were flying from death. I have something to tell you that will make you speechless, yet the words are far less important than the heart of the matter. These good fellows will bring you to me. Rosencrantz and Guildenstern continue on their course to England. I have much to tell you about them. Farewell. Always your dear friend, Hamlet."*

Come, I will give you passage for these letters, and do it quickly, so that you can take me to the man from whom you received them.

[They exit]

Scene 7

Another room in the castle.

[The King and Laertes enter]

KING: *Now you must acknowledge my innocence in your father's death. You must consider me your friend, since you have heard from reliable sources that the man who killed your noble father intended to kill me.*

LAERTES: It well appears. But tell me
     Why you proceeded not against these feats
     So crimeful and so capital in nature,
     As by your safety, wisdom, all things else,
10   You mainly were stirr'd up.

KING: O, for two special reasons,
     Which may to you, perhaps, seem much unsinew'd,
     But yet to me they are strong. The Queen his mother
     Lives almost by his looks; and for myself—
15   My virtue or my plague, be it either which—
     She's so conjunctive to my life and soul
     That, as the star moves not but in his sphere,
     I could not but by her. The other motive
     Why to a public count I might not go
20   Is the great love the general gender bear him,
     Who, dipping all his faults in their affection,
     Would, like the spring that turneth wood to stone,
     Convert his gyves to graces; so that my arrows,
     Too slightly timber'd for so loud a wind,
25   Would have reverted to my bow again,
     And not where I had aim'd them.

LAERTES: And so have I a noble father lost;
     A sister driven into desperate terms,
     Whose worth, if praises may go back again,
30   Stood challenger on mount of all the age
     For her perfections. But my revenge will come.

KING: Break not your sleeps for that. You must not think
     That we are made of stuff so flat and dull
     That we can let our beard be shook with danger,
35   And think it pastime. You shortly shall hear more.
     I loved your father, and we love ourself,
     And that, I hope, will teach you to imagine—

[Enter a Messenger with letters.]
     How now? What news?

LAERTES: It seems that way. But tell me why you did not prosecute these truly criminal and murderous deeds? riminal and should be punished? Your safety, greatness, wisdom, and everything else, should have forcefully driven you into action.

KING: Oh, there are two special reasons, which may seem insignificant to you, but they are important to me. The Queen, his mother, lives for him, and, as for myself—to my advantage or as a curse; one or the other—she is so closely joined to my life that, just as a star moves only in its own orbit, I could not act without her. The other reason why I could not publicly explain for the incident is the great love the common people feel for him. They weigh all his faults against their affection for him, and, like the spring that makes wood become petrified they would consider his deficiencies to be virtues. My accusations, too trivial for the understanding of the masses, would have turned against me instead of the target I aimed at.

LAERTES: So I have lost my noble father, and my sister has been driven into madness. Her virtues, if I make may praise the way she was, rivaled anyone else's because of her perfection. But I will have my revenge.

KING: Do not lose sleep over this. You mustn't think that I'm so weak and stupid that I will take this personal insolence as a joke. You will soon hear more of this. I loved your father, and I love myself. That, I hope, will make you understand—

[A Messenger enters with letters]
Yes? What news?

MESSENGER: Letters, my lord, from Hamlet.
40   This to your Majesty; this to the Queen.

KING: From Hamlet? Who brought them?

MESSENGER: Sailors, my lord, they say; I saw them not.
          They were given me by Claudio; he receiv'd them
          Of him that brought them.

45   KING: Laertes, you shall hear them.
          Leave us.   *[Exit Messenger.]*
          [Reads] High and mighty, you shall know I am set naked on your
          kingdom. Tomorrow shall I beg leave to see your kingly eyes, when I
          shall, first asking your pardon, thereunto recount the occasion of my
50   sudden and more strange return.
                                             HAMLET.

          What should this mean? Are all the rest come back?
          Or is it some abuse, and no such thing?

LAERTES: Know you the hand?

KING: 'Tis Hamlet's character. 'Naked'—
55   And in a postscript here, he says 'Alone.'
          Can you advise me?

LAERTES: I'm lost in it, my lord. But let him come.
          It warms the very sickness in my heart
          That I shall live and tell him to his teeth,
60   'Thus didst thou.'

KING: If it be so, Laertes
          As how should it be so? how otherwise?—
          Will you be ruled by me?

LAERTES: Ay my lord,
65   So you will not o'errule me to a peace.

MESSENGER: *Letters from Hamlet, my lord. This one is for your Majesty; this one is for the Queen.*

KING: *From Hamlet? Who brought them?*

MESSENGER: *They say they are sailors, my lord. I did not see them. Claudio gave them to me. He received them from the man who brought them.*

KING: *Laertes, you shall hear them. Leave us!*

[Messenger exits]

[Reading] *"High and mighty Majesty, you shall know that I have returned to your kingdom poor and unarmed. Tomorrow, I will ask for permission to appear before you. At this point I will ask your forgiveness first, and, afterwards, explain to you the circumstances of my sudden and extraordinary return. Hamlet."*

What does this mean? Have the other returned as well? Is this a trick and a lie?

LAERTES: *Do you recognize the handwriting?*

KING: *It is Hamlet's handwriting. Poor and unarmed, and in a postscript here, he says "alone." Can you explain it?*

LAERTES: *I am confused by it, my lord. But let him come. It relieves my ill heart to know that I will live to tell him face to face: "This is what you did."*

KING: *If this is true, Laertes—how can it be otherwise—will you obey to me?*

LAERTES: *Yes, my lord, if you will not force me to make peace with him.*

KING: To thine own peace. If he be now return'd
    As checking at his voyage, and that he means
    No more to undertake it, I will work him
    To an exploit, now ripe in my device,
70   Under the which he shall not choose but fall;
    And for his death no wind of blame shall breathe,
    But even his mother shall uncharge the practice,
    And call it accident.

LAERTES: My lord, I will be ruled;
75   The rather, if you could devise it so
    That I might be the organ.

KING: It falls right.
    You have been talk'd of since your travel much,
    And that in Hamlet's hearing, for a quality
80   Wherein they say you shine. Your sum of parts
    Did not together pluck such envy from him
    As did that one; and that, in my regard,
    Of the unworthiest siege.

85 LAERTES: What part is that, my lord?

KING: A very ribbon in the cap of youth,
    Yet needful too; for youth no less becomes
    The light and careless livery that it wears
    Than settled age his sables and his weeds,
90   Importing health and graveness. Two months since
    Here was a gentleman of Normandy—
    I have seen myself, and served against, the French,
    And they can well on horseback; but this gallant
    Had witchcraft in't. He grew unto his seat,
95   And to such wondrous doing brought his horse
    As had he been incorpsed and demi-natured
    With the brave beast. So far he topp'd my thought
    That I, in forgery of shapes and tricks,
    Come short of what he did.

KING: *Only your own peace of mind. If he has indeed returned, turning from his voyage with no intentions of going back, I have a plan ready that will guarantee his downfall. We will not be blamed for his death, and even his mother will fail to recognize our scheme and call his death an accident.*

LAERTES: *My lord, I will obey you. But I am asking you to plan everything so that I can be the agent of his death.*

KING: *It is exactly right. Many have spoken about you since you have traveled abroad, and Hamlet heard it, too. They say you possess a skill in which you excel. All your other accomplishments put together did not cause Hamlet to envy you so much, even though I think this skill is the least important of all.*

LAERTES: *What skill is that, my lord?*

KING: *It's one of the accomplishments of youth, yet, it is also necessary. Light and carefree clothing suits youthfulness, as dark, somber garments signifying prosperity and dignity are proper for old age. Two months ago, a gentleman from Normandy came here. I have seen the French, and I have served in battle against them, and they are skilled riders. But this fellow was magical. He grew into his saddle and performed such amazing feats with his horse that it seemed as if he was one with the brave horse. He exceeded all my expectations, and any tricks I came up with fell short of his performance.*

100 **LAERTES:**   A Norman was't?

KING: A Norman.

LAERTES: Upon my life, Lamord.

KING: The very same.

LAERTES: I know him well. He is the brooch indeed
105   And gem of all the nation.

KING: He made confession of you;
         And gave you such a masterly report,
         For art and exercise in your defence,
         And for your rapier most especial,
110   That he cried out 'twould be a sight indeed
         If one could match you. The scrimers of their nation
         He swore had neither motion, guard, nor eye,
         If you opposed them. Sir, this report of his
         Did Hamlet so envenom with his envy
115   That he could nothing do but wish and beg
         Your sudden coming o'er to play with you.
         Now, out of this–

LAERTES: What out of this, my lord?

KING: Laertes, was your father dear to you?
120   Or are you like the painting of a sorrow,
         A face without a heart?

LAERTES: Why ask you this?

KING: Not that I think you did not love your father;
         But that I know love is begun by time,
125   And that I see, in passages of proof,
         Time qualifies the spark and fire of it.
         There lives within the very flame of love
         A kind of wick or snuff that will abate it;

236

LAERTES: He was a Norman?

KING: A Norman.

LAERTES: I know him—Lamord!

KING: The very same man.

LAERTES: I know him well. He is the ornament and jewel of his entire nation.

KING: He acknowledged your excellence and gave a wonderful report on the skill and execution of your swordsmanship. He especially praised your handling of the rapier and declared that it would be a show worth seeing if somebody else engaged in a match with you. He swore that duelists from his country did not have the motion, eye, or ability that you possess. Sir, his report filled Hamlet with such envy that he wished and begged for your speedy return, so that he could fence with you. Now, from this...

LAERTES: What "from this," my lord?

KING: Laertes, did you love your father? Or are you merely pretending to feel sorrow—putting on a sad face without feeling the pain?

LAERTES: Why do you ask this?

KING: Not that I think you did not love your father, but I know that love begins at a certain point, and I know, from experience, that time diminishes the spark and powerful passion that comes with love. The flame of love contains a wick or snuff that extinguishes itself. Nothing can remain at the same level forever. Goodness that grows too much fades because of its own excess. What we want to do, we

And nothing is at a like goodness still;
130   For goodness, growing to a pleurisy,
Dies in his own too much. That we would do,
We should do when we would; for this 'would' changes,
And hath abatements and delays as many
As there are tongues, are hands, are accidents;
135   And then this 'should' is like a spendthrift sigh,
That hurts by easing. But to the quick o' the ulcer!
Hamlet comes back. What would you undertake
To show yourself your father's son in deed
More than in words?

140   LAERTES: To cut his throat i' the church.

KING: No place indeed should murder sanctuarize;
Revenge should have no bounds. But, good Laertes,
Will you do this? Keep close within your chamber.
Hamlet return'd shall know you are come home.
145   We'll put on those shall praise your excellence
And set a double varnish on the fame
The Frenchman gave you; bring you in fine together
And wager on your heads. He, being remiss,
Most generous and free from all contriving,
150   Will not peruse the foils; so that with ease,
Or with a little shuffling, you may choose
A sword unbated, and in a pass of practice,
Requite him for your father.

  LAERTES: I will do't!
155   And for that purpose I'll anoint my sword.
I bought an unction of a mountebank,
So mortal that but dip a knife in it,
Where it draws blood no cataplasm so rare,
Collected from all simples that have virtue
160   Under the moon, can save the thing from death
This is but scratch'd withal. I'll touch my point
With this contagion, that, if I gall him slightly,
It may be death.

must do soon because this "want" will change and has as many modifications and delays as there are words, actions, and circumstances. Then, this "should have" is like an extravagant sigh that hurts us by making us feel better. But now to the point of this painful sore: Hamlet is back. What would you do that would prove, in action rather than in words, that you are your father's son?

LAERTES: *I would cut his throat, even in the church!*

KING: *Yes, no place should offer a sanctuary for murder. Revenge should have no boundaries. But, good Laertes, please do this: Stay in your room. Hamlet, recently returned, will soon hear that you have come home. I will put those people who praise your excellence to work and, that way, strengthen the fame you have earned because of the Frenchman. We will bring you together in a match and place bets on you. He, being unsuspecting, noble-minded, and naïve, will not inspect the rapiers, and you can very easily, or with a little trickery, choose a sharpened sword and, with a skilled thrust, avenge your father's death.*

LAERTES: *I will do it, and, for that purpose, I will prepare my sword. I bought a poison from a false doctor. It is so deadly that, if you just dip a knife in it, and you draw blood, not even the rarest ointment, gathered from medicinal herbs with the great healing power of the moon can save a person from certain death, even if he has been merely scratched with it. I will cover the tip of my rapier with this poison, so that, if I scrape him slightly, it will be his death.*

KING: Let's further think of this,
165   Weigh what convenience both of time and means
        May fit us to our shape. If this should fail,
        And that our drift look through our bad performance.
        'Twere better not assay'd. Therefore this project
        Should have a back or second, that might hold
170   If this did blast in proof. Soft! let me see.
        We'll make a solemn wager on your cunnings—
        I ha't!
        When in your motion you are hot and dry—
        As make your bouts more violent to that end—
175   And that he calls for drink, I'll have prepared him
        A chalice for the nonce; whereon but sipping,
        If he by chance escape your venom'd stuck,
        Our purpose may hold there. But stay, what noise?

[Enter Queen.]
180   How now, sweet Queen?

QUEEN: One woe doth tread upon another's heel,
        So fast they follow. Your sister's drown'd, Laertes.

LAERTES: Drown'd! O, where?

QUEEN: There is a willow grows aslant a brook,
185   That shows his hoary leaves in the glassy stream.
        Therewith fantastic garlands did she make
        Of crow-flowers, nettles, daisies, and long purples,
        That liberal shepherds give a grosser name,
        But our cold maids do dead men's fingers call them.
190   There on the pendant boughs her crownet weeds
        Clambering to hang, an envious sliver broke,
        When down her weedy trophies and herself
        Fell in the weeping brook. Her clothes spread wide
        And, mermaid-like, awhile they bore her up;
195   Which time she chaunted snatches of old lauds,
        As one incapable of her own distress,
        Or like a creature native and indued

KING: *Let me consider this further and decide what time and means will best suit our purpose. If this plan should fail, and our scheme becomes apparent through bad execution, it would be better if we hadn't tried it at all. Therefore, we need a second plan that will work, in case this one fails. Wait... let me see. I'll make a serious wager on your specific skills—I have it! During the fight, when you become hot and thirsty—and you should fight fiercely in order to achieve that—he will ask for a drink. I'll already have prepared a glass for this occasion. If he only sips on it—in case he has escaped a hit from your poisoned sword—we will reach our goal. But wait, what is that noise?*

[The Queen enters]
What now, sweet Queen?

QUEEN: *One sorrow quickly follows the next. They pursue each other rapidly! Your sister has drowned, Laertes.*

LAERTES: *Drowned! Oh, where?*

QUEEN: *There is a willow that grows over the brook. Its gray leaves glimmer in the translucent water. With willow branches, she made strange garlands from crow flowers, nettles, daisies, and wild orchids, which rude shepherds call by a sexual name, but our chaste maidens call them "dead men's fingers." When she climbed to hang these wreaths on the overhanging branches, a malicious branch broke, and she fell into the weeping brook along with her weedy garlands. Her clothes spread wide, and, for a while, kept her afloat like a mermaid, while she sang pieces of old hymns, as if she was unaware of her own dangerous situation, or as if she was a creature that is used to living in water. But it did not take long till her garments, soaking wet and heavy, pulled the poor thing from her sweet song to a muddy death.*

Unto that element; but long it could not be
Till that her garments, heavy with their drink,
200   Pull'd the poor wretch from her melodious lay
To muddy death.

LAERTES: Alas, then she is drown'd?

QUEEN: Drown'd, drown'd.

LAERTES: Too much of water hast thou, poor Ophelia,
205   And therefore I forbid my tears; but yet
It is our trick; nature her custom holds,
Let shame say what it will. When these are gone,
The woman will be out. Adieu, my lord.
I have a speech of fire, that fain would blaze
210   But that this folly drowns it.   *[Exit.]*

KING: Let's follow, Gertrude.
How much I had to do to calm his rage.
Now fear I this will give it start again;
Therefore let's follow.   *[Exeunt.]*

LAERTES: *Alas, then she has drowned?*

QUEEN: *Drowned, drowned!*

LAERTES: *You have had too much water, Opheli, so I forbid myself to cry. Yet, weeping is in our nature, and nature forces us to obey, no matter how shameful it may be. Once these tears are gone, I will stop acting like a woman. Adieu, my lord. I have an angry speech that wants to be heard, but these tears drown my words.*

[He exits]

KING: *Let's follow, Gertrude! How much I had to do to calm his rage! Now I fear this "will cause it to start all over again. Therefore, let's follow him.*

[They exit]

ACT V

Scene 1

Elsinore. A churchyard.

[Enter two Clowns, with spades and pickaxes.]

FIRST CLOWN: Is she to be buried in Christian burial that wilfully seeks her own salvation?

SECOND CLOWN: I tell thee she is; therefore make her grave straight. The crowner hath sat on her, and finds it Christian burial.

5 FIRST CLOWN: How can that be, unless she drown'd herself in her own defence?

SECOND CLOWN: Why, 'tis found so.

FIRST CLOWN: It must be *se offendendo*; it cannot be else. For here lies the point: if I drown myself wittingly, it argues an act; and an act hath three branches: it is to act, to do, and to perform;
10 argal, she drown'd herself wittingly.

SECOND CLOWN: Nay, but hear you, goodman delver—

FIRST CLOWN: Give me leave. Here lies the water—good. Here stands the man—good. If the man go to this water and drown himself,
15 it is, will he, nill he, he goes. Mark you that. But if the water

ACT V

Scene 1

A churchyard.

[Two Gravediggers enter with spades and picks]

FIRST CLOWN: Is she to be receive a Christian burial, although she committed suicide?

SECOND CLOWN: I tell you she is. Therefore, make her grave immediately. The coroner has ruled in her case, and he finds she deserves a Christian burial.

FIRST CLOWN: How can that be, unless she drowned herself in her own defense?

SECOND CLOWN: Well, it's been decided that way.

FIRST CLOWN: It must be in "self-offense"; everything else is impossible. Here is the point: If I drown myself deliberately, it becomes an act, and an act has three parts: to act, to do, and to perform. Therefore, she drowned herself on purpose.

SECOND CLOWN: No, let me tell you, good digger—

FIRST CLOWN: Allow me to explain: Here lies the water—good. Here stands the man—good. If the man goes to the water and drowns himself, it is he who goes, of his own will or not. Pay attention to that. But if the water comes to him and drowns him, he doesn't

come to him and drown him, he drowns not himself. Argal, he
that is not guilty of his own death shortens not his own life.

SECOND CLOWN: But is this law?

FIRST CLOWN: Ay, marry, is't; crowner's quest law.

20 SECOND CLOWN: Will you ha' the truth on't? If this had not been a
gentlewoman, she should have been buried out o' Christian
burial.

FIRST CLOWN: Why, there thou say'st! And the more pity that great
folk should have countenance in this world to drown or hang
25 themselves more than their even Christian. Come, my spade!
There is no ancient gentlemen but gardeners, ditchers, and
grave-makers. They hold up Adam's profession.

SECOND CLOWN: Was he a gentleman?

FIRST CLOWN: A was the first that ever bore arms.

30 SECOND CLOWN: Why, he had none.

FIRST CLOWN: What, art a heathen? How dost thou understand the
Scripture?
The Scripture says Adam digged. Could he dig without arms?
I'll put another question to thee. If thou answerest me not to
35 the purpose, confess thyself—

SECOND CLOWN: Go to!

FIRST CLOWN: What is he that builds stronger than either the mason,
the shipwright, or the carpenter?

SECOND CLOWN: The gallows-maker; for that frame outlives a thou-
40 sand tenants.

FIRST CLOWN: I like thy wit well, in good faith. The gallows does

drown himself. Therefore, whoever is not guilty of his own death does not shorten his own life.

SECOND CLOWN: But is this law?

FIRST CLOWN: Yes, indeed. Coroner's inquest law.

SECOND CLOWN: Do you want to know the truth? If this had not been a gentlewoman, she would not have received a Christian burial.

FIRST CLOWN: Well, you say it. It is a pity that great folk should be allowed to drown or hang themselves in this world, unlike their poorer fellow Christians. Come, give me my spade. In ancient times, there were no gentlemen, except for gardeners, ditch diggers, and gravediggers. They continue Adam's profession.

SECOND CLOWN: Was he a gentleman?

FIRST CLOWN: He was the first that man who ever bore arms.

SECOND CLOWN: Why, he had no arms.

FIRST CLOWN: What, are you a heathen? How do you interpret the Scripture? The Scripture says "Adam dug." Could he dig without arms? I'll ask you another question. If you can't answer me correctly, confess your sins!

SECOND CLOWN: Go ahead.

FIRST CLOWN: Who is it that builds stronger than either the mason, the shipmaker, or the carpenter?

SECOND CLOWN: The gallows-maker, because his construction outlives a thousand tenants.

FIRST CLOWN: I like your wit truly. The gallows works well as an answer. But

well. But how does it well? It does well to those that do ill.
Now, thou dost ill to say the gallows is built stronger than
the church. Argal, the gallows may do well to thee. To't again,
45   come!

SECOND CLOWN: Who builds stronger than a mason, a shipwright, or a
carpenter?

FIRST CLOWN: Ay, tell me that, and unyoke.

SECOND CLOWN: Marry, now I can tell!

50   FIRST CLOWN: To't.

SECOND CLOWN: Mass, I cannot tell.

[Enter Hamlet and Horatio afar off.]

FIRST CLOWN: Cudgel thy brains no more about it, for your dull ass
will not mend his pace with beating; and when you are asked
this question next, say 'A grave-maker.' The houses that he
55   makes last till doomsday. Go, get thee to Yaughan; fetch me a
stoup of liquor.
                [Exit Second Clown.First Clown digs and sings.]
In youth when I did love, did love,
   Methought it was very sweet;
To contract—O—the time for—a—my behove,
60   O, methought there—a—was nothing—a meet.

HAMLET: Has this fellow no feeling of his business, that he sings at
grave-making?

HORATIO: Custom hath made it in him a property of easiness.

HAMLET: 'Tis e'en so. The hand of little employment hath the daintier
65   sense.

how does it work well? It does good to those who do bad. However, you are wrong to say the gallows is built stronger than the church. Therefore, the gallows may do you well. Go for the answer again!

SECOND CLOWN: *Who builds stronger than a mason, a shipmaker, or a carpenter?*

FIRST CLOWN: *Yes, tell me that, and then your work is done.*

SECOND CLOWN: *Indeed, now I can tell you!*

FIRST CLOWN: *Tell me!*

SECOND CLOWN: *By God, I don't know.*

[Hamlet and Horatio enter far in the distance]

FIRST CLOWN: *Do not beat your brains about it any more, for a dumb donkey will not go faster, even when beaten; and the next time you are asked this question, say, "A grave-maker." The houses he makes last until doomsday. Go to Yaughan and get me some liquor.*
      [Second Clown exits. First Clown digs and sings]
"In youth when I did love, did love, I thought it was very sweet, to spend, oh, my time, ah, as I pleased. Oh, I thought there was nothing better than that."

HAMLET: *Does this fellow not respect his business? He sings while he digs graves.*

HORATIO: *He is so used to it that he doesn't think about it.*

HAMLET: *This is true. A hand not hardened with work has more sensitivity.*

First Clown: *[Sings.]*
> But age with his stealing steps
> > Hath clawed me in his clutch,
> And hath shipped me intil the land,
> > As if I had never been such. *[Throws up a skull.]*

70

Hamlet: That skull had a tongue in it, and could sing once. How the
knave jowls it to the ground, as if were Cain's jawbone, that did
the first murder! This might be the pate of a politician,
which this ass now o'erreaches; one that would circumvent

75 God, might it not?

Horatio: It might, my lord.

Hamlet: Or of a courtier, which could say 'Good morrow, sweet lord!
How dost thou, sweet lord?' This might be my Lord Such-a-
one, that praised my Lord Such-a-one's horse when he meant

80 to beg it, might it not?

Horatio: Ay, my lord.

Hamlet: Why, e'en so! and now my Lady Worm's, chapless, and
knock'd about the mazard with a sexton's spade. Here's fine
revolution, and we had the trick to see't. Did these bones cost

85 no more the breeding, but to play at loggets with 'em? Mine
ache to think on't.

First Clown: *[Sings.]*
> A pickaxe and a spade, a spade,
> > For and a shrouding sheet;
> O, a Pit of clay for to be made

90
> > For such a guest is meet. *[Throws up another skull.]*

Hamlet: There's another. Why may not that be the skull of a lawyer?
Where be his quiddities now, his quillets, his cases, his ten-
ures, and his tricks? Why does he suffer this rude knave now

95 to knock him about the sconce with a dirty shovel, and will
not tell him of his action of battery? Hum! This fellow might

FIRST CLOWN: [Singing] *"But old age coming closer has taken hold of me, and it ships me into the ground, as if I had never been young."*

[Throwing up a skull]

HAMLET: *That skull had a tongue in it, and could sing once. How the fool flings it to the ground as if it were the jawbone of Cain, who committed the first murder! This might be the head of a politician, whom this fool now outranks, one who tried to bypass the laws of God, might it not?*

HORATIO: *It might, my lord.*

HAMLET: *Or it might be the head of a courtier who would say, "Good morning, sweet lord! How are you, sweet lord?" This might be my Lord so-and-so, who praised my Lord so-and-so's horse when he meant to borrow it—might it not be?*

HORATIO: *Yes, my lord.*

HAMLET: *Well, so it is. And now it belongs to my Lady Worm, missing a jawbone and knocked over the head with a sexton's spade. That's a fine change time has caused, and we were able to witness it. Were these bones brought into the world only to be thrown around as part of a game? My bones hurt just thinking about it.*

FIRST CLOWN: [Singing] *"A pickax and a spade, a spade. and also a shroud-like sheet. Oh, it is fitting to dig a hole of clay for a guest like this."*

[Throwing up another skull]

HAMLET: *There's another one. Could it be the skull of a lawyer? Where are his fine arguments now, his distinctions, his cases, his land titles, and his tricks? Why does he allow this mad fool now to knock him over the head with a dirty shovel, without accusing him of battery? Hmm! In his time, this fellow might have been a great*

be in's time a great buyer of land, with his statutes, his recog-
nizances, his fines, his double vouchers, his recoveries. Is this
the fine of his fines, and the recovery of his recoveries, to have
100   his fine pate full of fine dirt? Will his vouchers vouch him no
more of his purchases, and double ones too, than the length
and breadth of a pair of indentures? The very conveyances of
his lands will scarcely lie in this box; and must the inheritor
himself have no more, ha?

105   Horatio: Not a jot more, my lord.

Hamlet: Is not parchment made of sheepskins?

Horatio: Ay, my lord. And of calveskins too.

Hamlet: They are sheep and calves which seek out assurance in that.
    I will speak to this fellow. Whose grave's this, sirrah?

110   First Clown: Mine, sir.
     [Sings.]
      O, a pit of clay for to be made
        For such a guest is meet.

Hamlet: I think it be thine indeed, for thou liest in't.

First Clown: You lie out on't, sir, and therefore 'tis not yours. For my
115   part, I do not lie in't, yet it is mine.

Hamlet: Thou dost lie in't, to be in't and say it' 'tis thine. 'Tis for the
    dead, not for the quick; therefore thou liest.

First Clown: 'Tis a quick lie, sir; 'twill away again from me to you.

Hamlet: What man dost thou dig it for?

120   First Clown: For no man, sir.

Hamlet: What woman then?

*buyer of land, with his laws, his pleadges, his fines, his guaran-
tees, and his monies? Is this the finish of his fines, the recoup of
his recovered lands, to have his fine head full of fine dirt? Will his
witnesses not testify about his acquisitions and double acquisitions
of land, other than to the length and extent of a legal document?
The contracts of his lands will scarcely fit in this grave. Does the
owner himself have no more than this, ha?*

HORATIO: *Not a bit more, my lord.*

HAMLET: *Isn't parchment made of sheepskin?*

HORATIO: *Yes, my lord. And of calfskin, too.*

HAMLET: *People who find reassurance in this are sheep and calves. I will
speak to this fellow. Whose grave is this, sir?*

FIRST CLOWN: *Mine, sir.* [Singing]
"Oh, it's fitting to dig a hole for a guest like this."

HAMLET: *I think it is yours, indeed, because you're lying in it.*

FIRST CLOWN: *You lie outside of it, sir, and, therefore, it is not yours. As
for me, I do not lie in it, yet it is mine.*

HAMLET: *You are lying in it, if you are in it and say it is yours. It is for
the dead, not for the living. Therefore, you lie.*

FIRST CLOWN: *It is a lively lie, sir. It will move from me to you again.*

HAMLET: *What man are you digging it for?*

FIRST CLOWN: *For no man, sir.*

HAMLET: *For what woman, then?*

First Clown: For none, neither.

Hamlet: Who is to be buried in't?

First Clown: One that was a woman, sir; but, rest her soul, she's
125   dead.

Hamlet: How absolute the knave is! We must speak by the card, or
    equivocation will undo us. By the Lord, Horatio, this three
    years I have taken note of it: the age is grown so picked that
    the toe of the peasant comes so near the heel of the courtier he
130   galls his kibe. How long hast thou been a grave-maker?

First Clown: Of all the days i' the year, I came to't that day that our
    last king Hamlet overcame Fortinbras.

Hamlet: How long is that since?

First Clown: Cannot you tell that? Every fool can tell that. It was
135   the very day that young Hamlet was born—he that is mad, and
    sent into England.

Hamlet: Ay, marry, why was he sent into England?

First Clown: Why, because a was mad. A shall recover his wits there;
    or, if a do not, 'tis no great matter there.

140 Hamlet: Why?

First Clown: 'Twill not be seen in him there. There the men are as
    mad as he.

Hamlet: How came he mad?

First Clown: Very strangely, they say.

145 Hamlet: How 'strangely'?

FIRST CLOWN: *For no woman, neither.*

HAMLET: *Who is to be buried in it?*

FIRST CLOWN: *Someone who was a woman, sir; but, rest her soul, she's dead.*

HAMLET: *How precise the scoundrel is! We must speak carefully or ambiguity will ruin us. By God, Horatio, over the last three years, I have noticed that our times have become very refined. A peasant may follow the heel of a courtier so closely that he rubs sores into the courtier's heels. How long have you been a gravedigger?*

FIRST CLOWN: *Of all the days in the year, I began working as a gravedigger the same day that our last king, Hamlet, defeated Fortinbras.*

HAMLET: *How long ago was that?*

FIRST CLOWN: *Don't you know that? Every fool knows that. It was the very day that young Hamlet was born—the one who is mad and was sent away to England.*

HAMLET: *Oh, indeed, why was he sent to England?*

FIRST CLOWN: *Why, because he was mad. He is supposed to recover his mind there; or, if he doesn't, it doesn't matter much over there.*

HAMLET: *Why?*

FIRST CLOWN: *Nobody will notice it there. Over there, all men are as mad as he is.*

HAMLET: *How did he turn mad?*

FIRST CLOWN: *Under very strange circumstances, they say.*

HAMLET: *Why "strange?"*

FIRST CLOWN: Faith, e'en with losing his wits.

HAMLET: Upon what ground?

FIRST CLOWN: Why, here in Denmark. I have been sexton here, man and boy, thirty years.

150 HAMLET: How long will a man lie i' the earth ere he rot?

FIRST CLOWN: I' faith, if he be not rotten before he die—as we have many pocky corses nowadays that will scarce hold the laying in—he will last you some eight year or nine year. A tanner will last you nine year.

155 HAMLET: Why he more than another?

FIRST CLOWN: Why, sir, his hide is so tanned with his trade that a will keep out water a great while; and your water is a sore decayer of your whoreson dead body. Here's a skull, now. This skull hath lain in the earth three and twenty years.

160 HAMLET: Whose was it?

FIRST CLOWN: A whoreson, mad fellow's it was. Whose do you think it was?

HAMLET: Nay, I know not.

FIRST CLOWN: A pestilence on him for a mad rogue! A poured a flagon
165 of Rhenish on my head once. This same skull, sir, was Yorick's skull, the King's jester.

HAMLET: *[Takes the skull.]* This?

FIRST CLOWN: E'en that.

HAMLET: *[Takes the skull.]* Alas, poor Yorick! I knew him, Horatio: a
170 fellow of infinite jest, of most excellent fancy. He hath borne

FIRST CLOWN: *Indeed, he lost his mind.*

HAMLET: *On what grounds?*

FIRST CLOWN: *Why, here in Denmark. I have been a sexton here, man and boy, for thirty years.*

HAMLET: *How long does a man lie in the earth before he rots?*

FIRST CLOWN: *Well, if he is not rotten before he dies—and we have many corpses wasting away from venereal disease that will scarcely hold together until burial—he will last some eight years or nine years. A tanner will last nine years.*

HAMLET: *Why does he last longer than others?*

FIRST CLOWN: *Well, sir, his hide is so tanned from his trade that he will keep out water for a long time. Water is the great destroyer of a bastard's dead body. Here's a skull now that has lain in the earth for twenty-three years.*

HAMLET: *Whose was it?*

FIRST CLOWN: *A bastard madman's it was. Whose do you think it was?*

HAMLET: *No, I don't know.*

FIRST CLOWN: *A plague on him, the mad rogue! He poured a goblet of Rhine wine on my head one time. This same skull, sir, was Yorick's skull, the King's jester.*

HAMLET: *This?*

FIRST CLOWN: *That one.*

HAMLET: [Taking the skull] *Alas, poor Yorick! I knew him, Horatio. He was a fellow of boundless humor, with an excellent imagination.*

me on his back a thousand times. And now how abhorred in my imagination it is! My gorge rises at it. Here hung those lips that I have kissed I know not how oft. Where be your gibes now? your gambols? your songs? your flashes of merriment,
175   that were wont to set the table on a roar? Not one now to mock your own grinning? Quite chop-fallen? Now get you to my lady's chamber, and tell her, let her paint an inch thick, to this favour she must come. Make her laugh at that. Prithee, Horatio, tell me one thing.

180   HORATIO: What's that, my lord?

HAMLET: Dost thou think Alexander looked o' this fashion i' the earth?

HORATIO: E'en so.

HAMLET: And smelt so? Pah!   *[Puts down the skull.]*

185   HORATIO: E'en so, my lord.

HAMLET: To what base uses we may return, Horatio! Why may not imagination trace the noble dust of Alexander till he find it stopping a bung-hole?

HORATIO: 'Twere to consider too curiously, to consider so.

190   HAMLET: No, faith, not a jot; but to follow him thither with modesty enough, and likelihood to lead it; as thus: Alexander died, Alexander was buried, Alexander returneth into dust; the dust is earth; of earth we make loam; and why of that loam, whereto he was converted, might they not stop a beer barrel?
195   Imperious Caesar, dead and turn'd to clay,
Might stop a hole to keep the wind away.
O, that that earth, which kept the world in awe
Should patch a wall to expel the winter's flaw!
But soft! but soft awhile! Here comes the King,
200   The Queen, the courtiers.

He carried me on his back a thousand times. And now, how awful it is to remember it! My stomach turns over at the thought. I often kissed those lips that used to hang here. Where are your jokes now, your games, your songs, your brilliant humor that caused everyone at the table to laugh loudly? Not one left now to mock your own grinning! You have lost your jaw. Now go to my lady's chamber, and tell her that, even if she puts on make-up an inch thick, she will still end up looking like this. Make her laugh at that. Please, Horatio, tell me one thing.

HORATIO: *What's that, my lord?*

HAMLET: *Do you think Alexander looked like this in the ground?*

HORATIO: *Exactly like that.*

HAMLET: *And smelled like that? Pugh!* [Putting down the skull]

HORATIO: *Just like that, my lord.*

HAMLET: *To what primitive uses we return, Horatio! Isn't it possible to imagine that the noble dust of Alexander will end up plugging the hole in a beer barrel?*

HORATIO: *You are thinking about this too intensely!*

HAMLET: *No, indeed, not a bit. You can trace his steps, keeping in mind what is possible and likely: Alexander died; Alexander was buried; Alexander returned into dust. The dust is earth; out of earth, we make mud; and why could the mud he was turned into not end up plugging the hole in a beer barrel? Imperial Caesar, dead and turned to clay, might fill a hole to keep the wind away. Oh, that this earthly matter, which impressed the entire world, could now possibly patch up a wall to stop the wind in winter from entering! But quiet! Here comes the King, the Queen, the courtiers.*

[Enter priests with a coffin in funeral procession, King, Queen, Laertes,
with Lords attendant.]
> Who is this they follow?
> And with such maimed rites? This doth betoken
> The corse they follow did with desperate hand
> Fordo it own life. 'Twas of some estate.
205 Couch we awhile, and mark.
> *[Retires with Horatio.]*

LAERTES: What ceremony else?

HAMLET: That is Laertes, a very noble youth. Mark.

LAERTES: What ceremony else?

PRIEST: Her obsequies have been as far enlarged
210 As we have warranty. Her death was doubtful;
And, but that great command o'ersways the order,
She should in ground unsanctified have lodged
Till the last trumpet. For charitable prayers,
Shards, flints, and pebbles should be thrown on her.
215 Yet here she is allow'd her virgin crants,
Her maiden strewments and the bringing home
Of bell and burial.

LAERTES: Must there no more be done?

PRIEST: No more be done.
220 We should profane the service of the dead
To sing a requiem and such rest to her
As to peace-parted souls.

LAERTES: Lay her i' the earth;
And from her fair and unpolluted flesh
225 May violets spring! I tell thee, churlish priest,
A ministering angel shall my sister be
When thou liest howling.

[Priests and others enter in a funeral procession, carrying the corpse of Ophelia. Laertes and mourners follow. The King, Queen, and Attendants follow]

Who are they burying? And without any customary ceremony? This certainly looks as if the corpse they follow committed suicide. The person was of some rank. Let's hide ourselves and see what happens.

[Hiding with Horatio]

LAERTES: *What other rituals?*

HAMLET: *That is Laertes, a very noble young man. Watch!*

LAERTES: *What else for this ceremony?*

PRIEST: *Her funeral rites have been as extensive as possible. Her manner of death was a matter of debate. If the King's orders had not overruled the customary procedures, she would have been buried in unsanctified ground until Judgment Day. Instead of charitable prayers, fragments of pottery, flint, and pebbles would have been thrown onto her grave. Yet, she is allowed to receive her virgin's funeral garland, her flowers, and a burial with church bells.*

LAERTES: *Can there be no more done?*

PRIEST: *No more can be done. We would profane the service of the dead if we sang a requiem and gave her the same rest we give souls that departed in a natural manner.*

LAERTES: *Lay her in the earth! From her fair and virgin flesh may violets spring! I tell you, you rude priest, my sister will be a healing angel when you will lie screaming for mercy in hell.*

261

HAMLET: What, the fair Ophelia?

QUEEN: *[Scatters flowers.]* Sweets to the sweet! Farewell.
230   I hoped thou shouldst have been my Hamlet's wife;
         I thought thy bride-bed to have deck'd, sweet maid,
         And not have strew'd thy grave.

LAERTES: O, treble woe
         Fall ten times treble on that cursed head
235   Whose wicked deed thy most ingenious sense
         Deprived thee of! Hold off the earth awhile,
         Till I have caught her once more in mine arms.
                    [Leaps in the grave.]
         Now pile your dust upon the quick and dead
         Till of this flat a mountain you have made
240   To o'ertop old Pelion or the skyish head
         Of blue Olympus.

HAMLET: *[Comes forward.]* What is he whose grief
         Bears such an emphasis, whose phrase of sorrow
         Conjures the wandering stars and makes them stand
245   Like wonder-wounded hearers? This is I,
         Hamlet the Dane.   *[Leaps in after Laertes.]*

LAERTES: The devil take thy soul!   *[Grapples with him.]*

HAMLET: Thou pray'st not well.
         I prithee, take thy fingers from my throat;
250   For, though I am not splenitive and rash,
         Yet have I in me something dangerous,
         Which let thy wisdom fear. Hold off thy hand!

KING: Pluck them asunder.

QUEEN: Hamlet, Hamlet!

255 ALL: Gentlemen!

262

HAMLET: *What? Is it the fair Ophelia?*

QUEEN: [Scattering flowers] *Flowers to the sweet! Farewell. I hoped you would become my Hamlet's wife. I thought I would have decorated your bridal bed with flowers instead of your grave.*

LAERTES: *Oh, a triple sorrow, ten times over should fall upon the cursed head whose evil deed robbed you off your precious sanity! Don't cover her with dirt, until I have held her once more in my arms.*
[Leaping into the grave]
Now pile your dust upon the living and the dead until you have turned this plain into a mountain taller than old Pelion or even blue Olympus.

HAMLET: [Coming forward] *Who is this man, whose grief requires such inflated language, whose words of sorrow put spells on the planets and force them to stop and listen in amazement? This is I, Hamlet the Dane!*
[Leaping in after Laertes]

LAERTES: *May the devil take your soul!* [Grappling with him]

HAMLET: *You don't pray well. Please remove your fingers from my throat. Although I am not impulsive and rash, there is something dangerous in me that you would be wise to fear. Take away your hand!*

KING: *Separate them!*

QUEEN: *Hamlet, Hamlet!*

ALL: *Gentlemen!*

HORATIO: Good my lord, be quiet.

HAMLET: Why, I will fight with him upon this theme
    Until my eyelids will no longer wag.

QUEEN: O my son, what theme?

260   HAMLET: I loved Ophelia. Forty thousand brothers
    Could not, with all their quantity of love,
    Make up my sum. What wilt thou do for her?

KING: O, he is mad, Laertes.

QUEEN: For love of God, forbear him!

265   HAMLET: 'Swounds, show me what thou'lt do.
    Woo't weep, woo't fight, woo't fast, woo't tear thyself?
    Woo't drink up eisel, eat a crocodile?
    I'll do't. Dost thou come here to whine,
    To outface me with leaping in her grave?
270   Be buried quick with her, and so will I.
    And, if thou prate of mountains, let them throw
    Millions of acres on us, till our ground,
    Singeing his pate against the burning zone,
    Make Ossa like a wart! Nay, an thou'lt mouth,
275   I'll rant as well as thou.

QUEEN: This is mere madness;
    And thus awhile the fit will work on him.
    Anon, as patient as the female dove
    When that her golden couplets are disclosed,
280   His silence will sit drooping.

HAMLET: Hear you, sir!
    What is the reason that you use me thus?
    I loved you ever. But it is no matter.
    Let Hercules himself do what he may,
285   The cat will mew, and dog will have his day.   *[Exit.]*

HORATIO: *My good lord, calm down!*

HAMLET: *Well, I will fight with him over this manner until I close my eyelids in death.*

QUEEN: *Oh, my son, for what reason?*

HAMLET: *I loved Ophelia. Forty thousand brothers together could not have loved her as much as I did. What will you do for her?*

KING: *Oh, he is mad, Laertes.*

QUEEN: *For the love of God, leave him alone!*

HAMLET: *By God, show me what you will do! Will you weep? Will you fight? Will you fast? Will you hurt yourself? Will you drink vinegar or eat a crocodile? I'll do it! Do you come here to whine? To outdo me by leaping into her grave? Be buried alive with her, and so will I! And if you talk of mountains, let them throw millions of acres on us, until our grave touches the hot sun and makes the mountain Ossa appear like a mere wart! You rail well, but I can rage as well as you.*

QUEEN: *This is only madness. This fit will go on for a while. Eventually, he will sit silently, like a female dove whose baby birds are hatching.*

HAMLET: *Listen, sir! Why are you treating me this way? I have always loved you. But it doesn't make a difference now. Hercules himself could try, but he couldn't prevent a cat from meowing or a dog from achieving happiness.*

[He exits]

KING: I pray thee, good Horatio, wait upon him.

[Exit Horatio.]

[To Laertes.] Strengthen your patience in our last night's speech.
We'll put the matter to the present push.—
290   Good Gertrude, set some watch over your son.
This grave shall have a living monument.
An hour of quiet shortly shall we see;
Till then, in patience our proceeding be.

[Exeunt.]

Scene 2

Elsinore. A hall in the Castle.

[Enter Hamlet and Horatio.]

HAMLET: So much for this, sir; now shall you see the other.
    You do remember all the circumstance?

HORATIO: Remember it, my lord!

HAMLET: Sir, in my heart there was a kind of fighting
5   That would not let me sleep. Methought I lay
    Worse than the mutines in the bilboes. Rashly—
    And praised be rashness, for it let us know,
    Our indiscretion sometime serves us well
    When our deep plots do pall; and that should learn us
10   There's a divinity that shapes our ends,
    Rough-hew them how we will—

HORATIO: That is most certain.

HAMLET: Up from my cabin,
    My sea-gown scarf'd about me, in the dark

KING: *Please, good Horatio, look after him.*

[Horatio exits]

[To Laertes] *Be patient and recall our conversation last night. We'll put our plan to the test immediately. Good Gertrude, have someone watch over your son. This grave will have an enduring monument. We will have a quiet hour soon. Until then, everyone must be patient.*

[They exit]

Scene 2

A hall in the castle.

[Hamlet and Horatio enter]

HAMLET: *So much for this, sir. Now you will hear the other news. Do you remember all the circumstances?*

HORATIO: *Remember them, my lord?*

HAMLET: *Sir, in my heart there was a struggle that did not let me rest. I thought I was worse off than mutineers in shackles. On impulse—and impulsiveness must be praised—for it teaches us that our indiscretion sometimes serves us well when our plans fail. That should show us that God determines our fate, no matter how much we try to control it.*

HORATIO: *That's for sure.*

HAMLET: *I came up from my cabin, dressed in my sailor's outfit, and felt my way in the dark to find them. I succeeded, stole their papers,*

15   Groped I to find out them; had my desire,
Fingered their packet, and in fine withdrew
To mine own room again, making so bold
My fears forgetting manners, to unseal
Their grand commission; where I found, Horatio—
20   O royal knavery!—an exact command,
Larded with many several sorts of reasons,
Importing Denmark's health, and England's too,
With, ho! such bugs and goblins in my life,
That on the supervise, no leisure bated,
25   No, not to stay the grinding of the axe,
My head should be struck off.

HORATIO: Is't possible?

HAMLET: Here's the commission; read it at more leisure.
    But wilt thou hear me how I did proceed?

30   HORATIO: I beseech you.

HAMLET: Being thus benetted round with villainies—
    Or I could make a prologue to my brains,
    They had begun the play—I sat me down,
    Devised a new commission, wrote it fair.
35   I once did hold it, as our statists do,
    A baseness to write fair, and labour'd much
    How to forget that learning; but, sir, now
    It did me yeoman's service. Wilt thou know
    The effect of what I wrote?

40   HORATIO: Ay, good my lord.

HAMLET: An earnest conjuration from the King,
    As England was his faithful tributary,
    As love between them like the palm might flourish,
    As peace should still her wheaten garland wear
45   And stand a comma 'tween their amities,
    And many such like as's of great charge,

and finally returned to my own room. My fears overcame man-
ners, and I boldly unsealed their official orders. In these papers—
Horatio, ah, royal deceit!—I found concrete orders, containing a
number of reasons about the safety of the King of Denmark, as well
as to the King of England with such threats of my being dangerous
that, immediately after reading the letter, without any delay, not
even to sharpen the axe, my head should be cut off!

HORATIO: *Is this possible?*

HAMLET: *Here's the letter. Read it at your leisure. But do you want to*
know how I proceeded?

HORATIO: *Yes, please tell me.*

HAMLET: *Caught and surrounded by this evil scheme, I began to act before*
my mind had conceived of a plan. I sat down, devised a new letter,
and wrote it in properly. Like our public officials, I once considered
writing neatly to be a primitive skill and worked hard to discard
this talent. But, now, sir, it did me a great service. Do you want to
know what I wrote?

HORATIO: *Yes, my good lord.*

HAMLET: *A sincere request from the King— since the King of England is*
his faithful servant, since the love between them should flourish
like the palm tree, since peace should always crown their relation-
ship and connect them in friendship, and many more items of that
sort— that, after reading the contents of the letter, and without
further delay, he should put the messengers to death without a
chance for absolution.

That on the view and knowing of these contents,
Without debatement further, more or less,
He should the bearers put to sudden death,
50   Not shriving-time allow'd.

HORATIO: How was this seal'd?

HAMLET: Why, even in that was heaven ordinant.
I had my father's signet in my purse,
Which was the model of that Danish seal;
55   Folded the writ up in the form of the other,
Subscribed it, gave't the impression, placed it safely,
The changeling never known. Now, the next day
Was our sea-fight; and what to this was sequent
Thou know'st already.

60   HORATIO: So Guildenstern and Rosencrantz go to't.

HAMLET: Why, man, they did make love to this employment!
They are not near my conscience; their defeat
Does by their own insinuation grow.
'Tis dangerous when the baser nature comes
65   Between the pass and fell incensed points
Of mighty opposites.

HORATIO: Why, what a king is this!

HAMLET: Does it not, think thee, stand me now upon—
He that hath kill'd my king, and whored my mother;
70   Popp'd in between the election and my hopes;
Thrown out his angle for my proper life,
And with such cozenage—is't not perfect conscience
To quit him with this arm? And is't not to be damn'd
To let this canker of our nature come
75   In further evil?

HORATIO: It must be shortly known to him from England
What is the issue of the business there.

HORATIO: *How did you seal it?*

HAMLET: *Well, heaven guided me even in that. I had my father's signet in my bag, which resembles the Danish seal. I folded the letter up exactly like the original. I signed it, stamped the seal on it, and returned it safely so that the change was not suspected. The next day was our battle at sea, and you know the rest of the story already.*

HORATIO: *So Guildenstern and Rosencrantz are dead.*

HAMLET: *Well, they did enjoy their work. Their deaths do not weigh on my conscience. They brought their ruin upon themselves. It is dangerous when inferior beings are caught between the fierce swords of mighty opponents.*

HORATIO: *Well, what a king we have!*

HAMLET: *Don't you think it is now my duty? He has killed my father, defiled my mother, stood in the way of my rightful succession, and tried to take my own life. And he did it with such trickery. Wouldn't it be appropriate if I killed him myself? Wouldn't it be a shame to let this abomination of nature commit further evil?*

HORATIO: *He will soon learn from the King of England what has happened.*

HAMLET: It will be short; the interim is mine,
And a man's life's is no more than to say 'One.'
80 But I am very sorry, good Horatio,
That to Laertes I forgot myself,
For by the image of my cause I see
The portraiture of his. I'll court his favours.
But, sure, the bravery of his grief did put me
85 Into a towering passion.

HORATIO: Peace, who comes here?

[Enter young Osric, a courtier.]

OSRIC: Your lordship is right welcome back to Denmark.

HAMLET: I humbly thank you, sir. Dost know this water-fly?

HORATIO: [Aside to Hamlet.] No, my good lord.

90 HAMLET: [Aside to Horatio.] Thy state is the more gracious; for 'tis a
vice to know him. He hath much land, and fertile. Let a beast
be lord of beasts, and his crib shall stand at the king's mess. 'Tis
a chough; but, as I say, spacious in the possession of dirt.

OSRIC: Sweet lord, if your lordship were at leisure, I should impart a
95 thing to you from his Majesty.

HAMLET: I will receive it, sir, with all diligence of spirit. Put your bon-
net to his right use. 'Tis for the head.

OSRIC: I thank your lordship, it is very hot.

HAMLET: No, believe me, 'tis very cold; the wind is northerly.

100 OSRIC: It is indifferent cold, my lord, indeed.

HAMLET: But yet methinks it is very sultry and hot for my
complexion.

HAMLET: *It will be known shortly, but, in the meantime, I will take charge. A man's life can come to an end in an instant. But I am very sorry, good Horatio, that I lost control with Laertes. I recognize my own situation in him. I will seek his favor. The exaggerated expression of his grief made me lose my temper.*

HORATIO: *Quiet! Who comes there?*

[Osric, a courtier, enters]

OSRIC: *Your lordship is welcome back in Denmark.*

HAMLET: *I humbly thank you, sir. Do you know this petty insect?*
    [Aside]
HORATIO: *No, my good lord.*
    [Aside]
HAMLET: *You are better off that way. It's a vice to know him. He owns a lot of fertile land. If a beast owned as many beasts as Osric does, the King would invite him to dinner. He is a fool, but, as I said, he owns a huge area of dirt.*

OSRIC: *Sweet lord, if your lordship has the time, I will deliver a message from his Majesty.*

HAMLET: *I will pay attention to your message, sir. Put your hat to its rightful use. It belongs on your head.*

OSRIC: *I thank your lordship, but it is very hot.*

HAMLET: *No, believe me, it is very cold. The wind blows from the north.*

OSRIC: *It is rather cold, my lord, indeed.*

HAMLET: *But still, I think it is very sultry and hot for my constitution.*

OSRIC: Exceedingly, my lord; it is very sultry, as 'twere—I cannot tell
how. But, my lord, his Majesty bade me signify to you that he
105   has laid a great wager on your head. Sir, this is the matter—

HAMLET: I beseech you remember—
                    [Hamlet moves him to put on his hat.]

OSRIC: Nay, good my lord; for mine ease, in good faith. Sir, here is
newly come to court Laertes; believe me, an absolute gentleman, full of most excellent differences, of very soft society and
110   great showing. Indeed, to speak feelingly of him, he is the card
or calendar of gentry; for you shall find in him the continent of
what part a gentleman would see.

HAMLET: Sir, his definement suffers no perdition in you; though, I
know, to divide him inventorially would dizzy the arithmetic of
115   memory, and yet but yaw neither, in respect of his quick sail.
But, in the verity of extolment, I take him to be a soul of great
article, and his infusion of such dearth and rareness as, to make
true diction of him, his semblable is his mirror, and who else
would trace him, his umbrage, nothing more.

120   OSRIC: Your lordship speaks most infallibly of him.

HAMLET: The concernancy, sir? Why do we wrap the gentleman in
our more rawer breath?

OSRIC: Sir?

HORATIO: Is't not possible to understand in another
125   tongue? You will to't, sir, really.

HAMLET: What imports the nomination of this gentleman?

OSRIC: Of Laertes?

HORATIO: *[Aside.]* His purse is empty already. All's golden words are
spent.

OSRIC: *Indeed, my lord, it is oppresively hot, as if it were—I cannot tell how. My lord, his Majesty told me to communicate to you that he has put a great wager on your head. Sir, this is the situation—*

HAMLET: *Please remember—*
[Hamlet signals him to put on his hat]

OSRIC: *No, my good lord. I really don't want to, honestly. Sir, Laertes has recently returned to court. Believe me, he is a total gentleman. He possesses extraordinary qualities, agreeable manners, and a splendid appearance. Indeed, to be honest, he is the perfect example of courtesy. You will agree that he possesses every quality a gentleman should have.*

HAMLET: *Sir, you do him great justice, not disrespect. It would cause dizziness to divide and inventory all his qualities, and it would not catch any of them, as he changes so quickly. But in explaining the truth of him, I feel that he is a person to be greatly praised. His qualities are so distinct, that the only person quite like him is his own reflection in the mirror. Whoever tries to live up to him would be his shadow and nothing else.*

OSRIC: *Your lordship speaks very highly of him.*

HAMLET: *What is the significance, sir? Why do describe the gentleman with inadequate words?*

OSRIC: *Sir?*

HORATIO: *Is it not possible to understand it in more simple terms? You can do it, sir, really.*

HAMLET: *Why are we speaking about this gentleman?*

OSRIC: *About Laertes?*
[Aside]
HORATIO: *He has nothing more to say, already! All his fine words have been used up!*

130 HAMLET: Of him, sir.

OSRIC: I know you are not ignorant—

HAMLET: I would you did, sir; yet, in faith, if you did, it would not much approve me. Well, sir?

OSRIC: You are not ignorant of what excellence Laertes is—

135 HAMLET: I dare not confess that, lest I should compare with him in excellence; but to know a man well were to know himself.

OSRIC: I mean, sir, for his weapon; but in the imputation laid on him by them, in his meed he's unfellowed.

HAMLET: What's his weapon?

140 OSRIC: Rapier and dagger.

HAMLET: That's two of his weapons. But, well.

OSRIC: The King, sir, hath wager'd with him six Barbary horses; against the which he has impawned, as I take it, six French rapiers and poniards, with their assigns, as girdle, hanger, and 145 so. Three of the carriages, in faith, are very dear to fancy, very responsive to the hilts, most delicate carriages, and of very liberal conceit.

HAMLET: What call you the carriages?

HORATIO: *[Aside to Hamlet.]* I knew you must be edified by the mar-150 gent ere you had done.

OSRIC: The carriages, sir, are the hangers.

HAMLET: The phrase would be more german to the matter if we could carry a cannon by our sides. I would it might be hangers till then. But on! Six Barbary horses against six French swords,

HAMLET: *About him, sir.*

OSRIC: *I know you are not ignorant—*

HAMLET: *I wish you thought me ignorant, but, if you did, it would not compliment me very much. Well, sir?*

OSRIC: *You are not ignorant of Laertes' excellence—*

HAMLET: *I cannot confess that, or I would compare my excellence to his because to know a man is to know oneself.*

OSRIC: *I mean, sir, his ability to use the sword. According to the reputation he enjoys among his followers, his skills are unequalled.*

HAMLET: *What's his weapon?*

OSRIC: *Rapier and dagger.*

HAMLET: *These are two of his weapons. But, well.*

OSRIC: *The King, sir, has wagered six Barbary horses against Laertes' wager of six French rapiers and daggers, along with all their accessories, such as the belts, straps, and so on. Three of the carriages, in fact, are very tasteful, matching the hilts—very delicate carriages with an elegant design.*

HAMLET: *What do you mean by "carriages"?*
[Aside]
HORATIO: *I knew you would need an explanation before you had finished.*

OSRIC: *The "carriages," sir, are the sheaths.*

HAMLET: *The phrase would be more appropriate if we could bring a cannon on our sides. Until that's the case, we should refer to them as sheaths. But continue! Six Barbary horses against six French*

155   their assigns, and three liberal-conceited carriages—that's the French bet against the Danish. Why is this 'impawned,' as you call it?

OSRIC: The King, sir, hath laid, sir, that, in a dozen passes between yourself and him, he shall not exceed you three hits; he hath
160   laid on twelve for nine, and it would come to immediate trial, if your lordship would vouchsafe the answer.

HAMLET: How if I answer no?

OSRIC: I mean, my lord, the opposition of your person in trial.

HAMLET: Sir, I will walk here in the hall. If it please his Majesty, it is
165   the breathing time of day with me. Let the foils be brought, the gentleman willing, and the King hold his purpose, I will win for him an I can; if not, I will gain nothing but my shame and the odd hits.

OSRIC: Shall I redeliver you e'en so?

170   HAMLET: To this effect, sir, after what flourish your nature will.

OSRIC: I commend my duty to your lordship.

HAMLET: Yours, yours. *[Exit Osric.]* He does well to commend it himself; there are no tongues else for's turn.

HORATIO: This lapwing runs away with the shell on his head.

175   HAMLET: He did comply with his dug before he sucked it. Thus has he—and many more of the same bevy that I know the drossy age dotes on—only got the tune of the time and outward habit of encounter, a kind of yesty collection, which carries them through and through the most fanned and winnowed opinions;
180   and do but blow them to their trial, the bubbles are out.

[Enter a Lord.]

swords, their accessories, and three greatly embellished straps. That's the French bet against the Danish. What is this "wager," as you call it?

OSRIC: The King, sir, has wagered that, in a dozen bouts between yourself and Laertes, he will not beat you by more than three hits. He wagered twelve for nine. It could be determined immediately, if your lordship would answer to it.

HAMLET: What if I say no?

OSRIC: I mean, my lord, if you accept the challenge.

HAMLET: Sir, I will walk across the hall. If it pleases his Majesty, it is my exercise time. If the foils are ready, the gentleman willing, and the King hasn't changed his mind, I will win for him if I can. If not, I will gain nothing but my shame and the remaining strikes.

OSRIC: Is this the answer you want me to deliver?

HAMLET: The essence of what I said, whichever way you want to say it.

OSRIC: My duty is at your service, my lordship.

HAMLET: Likewise. [Osric exits] He does well to commend his own duty. Nobody else would speak for him.

HORATIO: This young bird runs away with the shell still on his head.

HAMLET: He acted formally to his mother's breast before he sucked it. Like many more of his kind that I know this worthless age favors, he merely talks fashionably in his social interactions. He uses a stylish collection of words and phrases which help him participate in profound conversations. If you put the words to the test, they turn out to be meaningless.

[A Lord enters]

LORD: My lord, his Majesty commended him to you by young Osric, who brings back to him that you attend him in the hall. He sends to know if your pleasure hold to play with Laertes, or that you will take longer time.

185 HAMLET: I am constant to my purposes; they follow the King's pleasure. If his fitness speaks, mine is ready; now or whensoever, provided I be so able as now.

LORD: The King and Queen and all are coming down.

HAMLET: In happy time.

190 LORD: The Queen desires you to use some gentle entertainment to Laertes before you fall to play.

HAMLET: She well instructs me. *[Exit Lord.]*

HORATIO: You will lose this wager, my lord.

HAMLET: I do not think so. Since he went into France I have been in
195 continual practice. I shall win at the odds. But thou wouldst not think how ill all's here about my heart. But it is no matter.

HORATIO: Nay, good my lord—

HAMLET: It is but foolery; but it is such a kind of gain-giving as would perhaps trouble a woman.

200 HORATIO: If your mind dislike anything, obey it. I will forestall their repair hither and say you are not fit.

HAMLET: Not a whit, we defy augury; there's a special providence in the fall of a sparrow. If it be now, 'tis not to come, if it be not to come, it will be now; if it be not now, yet it will come. The
205 readiness is all. Since no man has aught of what he leaves, what is't to leave betimes? Let be.

LORD: *My lord, his Majesty addressed you through young Osric, who has reported that you are waiting to meet his Majesty in the hall. He wants to know whether you are willing to compete with Laertes, or if you require some more time.*

HAMLET: *My intentions have not changed. I go along with the King's suggestions. If he is ready, I am ready, too. Now or whenever, as long as I'm as able as I am now.*

LORD: *The King and Queen and others are coming down.*

HAMLET: *At the right time.*

LORD: *The Queen wants you to greet Laertes politely before you begin the competition.*

HAMLET: *She teaches me well.*   [Lord exits]

HORATIO: *You will lose, my lord.*

HAMLET: *I do not think so. I have practiced continuously since he left for France. Given the odds, I will win. You wouldn't believe how uncomfortable I feel in my heart, but it doesn't make a difference.*

HORATIO: *No, my lord good—*

HAMLET: *It is only nervousness, but it is the same feeling of apprehension that would, perhaps, trouble a woman.*

HORATIO: *If your mind has any reservations, you should listen to it. I will stop them from coming here and tell them that you are unwell.*

HAMLET: *Not in the least. We must defy our premonitions. God has predetermined our fate. If our death comes now, it won't come later; if it is not meant to come later, it comes now. If it doesn't come now, it will come eventually. Preparedness is everything. No man knows when he leaves, there is no best time to leave. Let it be.*

[Enter King, Queen, Laertes, Osric, and Lords, with other Attendants with foils and gauntlets. A table and flagons of wine on it.]

KING: Come, Hamlet, come, and take this hand from me.
    [The King puts Laertes' hand into Hamlet's.]

HAMLET: Give me your pardon, sir. I have done you wrong;
    But pardon't, as you are a gentleman.
210   This presence knows,
    And you must needs have heard, how I am punish'd
    With sore distraction. What I have done
    That might your nature, honour, and exception
    Roughly awake, I here proclaim was madness.
215   Was't Hamlet wrong'd Laertes? Never Hamlet.
    If Hamlet from himself be taken away,
    And when he's not himself does wrong Laertes,
    Then Hamlet does it not, Hamlet denies it.
    Who does it, then? His madness. If't be so,
220   Hamlet is of the faction that is wrong'd;
    His madness is poor Hamlet's enemy.
    Sir, in this audience,
    Let my disclaiming from a purposed evil
    Free me so far in your most generous thoughts
225   That I have shot my arrow o'er the house
    And hurt my brother.

LAERTES: I am satisfied in nature,
    Whose motive in this case should stir me most
    To my revenge. But in my terms of honour
230   I stand aloof, and will no reconcilement
    Till by some elder masters of known honour
    I have a voice and precedent of peace
    To keep my name ungor'd. But till that time
    I do receive your offer'd love like love,
235   And will not wrong it.

HAMLET: I embrace it freely,
    And will this brother's wager frankly play.—
    Give us the foils. Come on.

[The King, Queen, Laertes, Lords, Osric, and other Attendants enter with foils and gauntlets. They bring a table and wine]

KING: *Come, Hamlet, come. Take this hand!*
[The King puts Laertes' hand into Hamlet'S]

HAMLET: *Forgive me, sir. I have done you wrong. Please pardon me since you are a gentleman. This assembly well knows, and you must have heard, that I have suffered from severe instability. Whatever I have done to provoke your natural feelings, your honor, and your disapproval, I now declare an act of madness. Was it Hamlet who wronged Laertes? Never Hamlet! If Hamlet has been alienated from himself, and, in this state, offends Laertes, then it is not Hamlet who does it. Hamlet denies it. Who does it, then? His madness. If that's the case, Hamlet, too, is wronged. His madness is poor Hamlet's enemy. Sir, in front of this assembly, let my declaration that I intended to do no harm earn your pardon and help you understand that I have hurt you only by accident.*

LAERTES: *I am satisfied as far as my personal feelings are concerned, which should force me to seek revenge more than anything. But, as a man of honor, I accept it, until, according to the authoritative and reliable judgment agreed upon by honorable and experienced men, I can reconcile with you without ruining my reputation. Until then, however, I will accept the love you have offered without reservations.*

HAMLET: *I am satisfied and will accept this brotherly challenge. Give us the swords. Come on.*

283

LAERTES: Come, one for me.

240 HAMLET: I'll be your foil, Laertes. In mine ignorance
Your skill shall, like a star i' the darkest night,
Stick fiery off indeed.

LAERTES: You mock me, sir.

HAMLET: No, by this hand.

245 KING: Give them the foils, young Osric. Cousin Hamlet,
You know the wager?

HAMLET: Very well, my lord.
Your Grace has laid the odds o' the weaker side.

KING: I do not fear it, I have seen you both;
250 But since he is better'd, we have therefore odds.

LAERTES: This is too heavy; let me see another.

HAMLET: This likes me well. These foils have all a length?
[*They prepare to play.*]

OSRIC: Ay, my good lord.

KING: Set me the stoups of wine upon that table.
255 If Hamlet give the first or second hit,
Or quit in answer of the third exchange,
Let all the battlements their ordnance fire;
The King shall drink to Hamlet's better breath,
And in the cup an union shall he throw
260 Richer than that which four successive kings
In Denmark's crown have worn. Give me the cups;
And let the kettle to the trumpet speak,
The trumpet to the cannoneer without,
The cannons to the heavens, the heaven to earth,
265 'Now the King drinks to Hamlet.' Come, begin.
And you the judges, bear a wary eye.

LAERTES: *Come, one for me.*

HAMLET: *I'll be your foil, Laertes. Against my ignorance, your skills will shine brightly.*

LAERTES: *You mock me, sir.*

HAMLET: *No. I swear.*

KING: *Give them the foils, young Osric. Cousin Hamlet, you are familiar with the wager?*

HAMLET: *Yes, my lord. Your Grace has placed his bets on the weaker contestant.*

KING: *I am not worried. I have seen you both, but, since Laertes is better, we have adjusted the odds.*

LAERTES: *This one's too heavy. Let me see another one.*

HAMLET: *This one suits me well. These foils all have the same length?*
[They are preparing to compete]

OSRIC: *Yes, my good lord.*

KING: *Set the wine on the table. If Hamlet gives the first or second hit or wins the third round, let all the castle walls fire their cannons. The King will drink to Hamlet's health, and he will throw a precious pearl into the cup, more valuable than that which four successive kings have worn in Denmark's crown! Give me the cups! And let the drums signal to the trumpet, the trumpet to the cannons outside, the cannons to heaven, and heaven to earth, proclaiming, "Now the King drinks to Hamlet!" Come, begin. And you, the judges, watch very closely.*

HAMLET: Come on, sir.

LAERTES: Come, my lord.   *[They play.]*

HAMLET: One.

270   LAERTES: No.

HAMLET: Judgment!

OSRIC: A hit, a very palpable hit.

LAERTES: Well, again!

KING: Stay, give me drink. Hamlet, this pearl is thine;
275   Here's to thy health.
        [Drum; trumpets sound; a piece goes off within.]
        Give him the cup.

HAMLET: I'll play this bout first; set it by awhile.
        Come. *[They play.]* Another hit. What say you?

LAERTES: A touch, a touch; I do confess.

280   KING: Our son shall win.

QUEEN: He's fat, and scant of breath.
        Here, Hamlet, take my napkin, rub thy brows.
        The Queen carouses to thy fortune, Hamlet.

HAMLET: Good madam!

285   KING: Gertrude, do not drink.

QUEEN: I will, my lord; I pray you pardon me.

KING: *[Aside.]* It is the poison'd cup; it is too late.

286

HAMLET: *Come on, sir.*

LAERTES: *Come, my lord.*   [They fence]

HAMLET: *One.*

LAERTES: *No.*

HAMLET: *Judgment!*

OSRIC: *A hit, a very obvious hit.*

LAERTES: *Well, let's do it again!*

KING: *Wait, give me a drink. Hamlet, this pearl is yours. Here's to your health.* [Trumpets sound. Cannons go off outside]
Give him the cup!

HAMLET: *I'll play this bout first. Set it aside for a few moments. Come!*
[They fence] *Another hit! What do you say?*

LAERTES: *A touch, a touch. I admit it.*

KING: *Our son will win.*

QUEEN: *He's fat and short of breath. Here, Hamlet, take my handkerchief and wipe your face. The Queen drinks to your good fortune, Hamlet!*

HAMLET: *Thanks, madam!*

KING: *Gertrude, do not drink.*

QUEEN: *I will, my lord. Please, pardon me.*

KING: [Aside] *It is the poisoned cup. It is too late!*

HAMLET: I dare not drink yet, madam—by-and-by.

QUEEN: Come, let me wipe thy face.

290 LAERTES: My lord, I'll hit him now.

KING: I do not think't.

LAERTES: *[Aside]* And yet it is almost against my conscience.

HAMLET: Come for the third, Laertes! You but dally.
    I pray you, pass with your best violence;
295   I am afeard you make a wanton of me.

LAERTES: Say you so? Come on. Play.

OSRIC: Nothing, neither way.

LAERTES: Have at you now!
    [Laertes wounds Hamlet; then, in scuffling, they
    change rapiers, and Hamlet wounds Laertes.]

KING: Part them! They are incensed.

300 HAMLET: Nay come! again!   *[The Queen falls.]*

OSRIC: Look to the Queen there, ho!

HORATIO: They bleed on both sides. How is it, my lord?

OSRIC: How is't, Laertes?

LAERTES: Why, as a woodcock to mine own springe, Osric.
305   I am justly kill'd with mine own treachery.

HAMLET: How does the Queen?

KING: She swoons to see them bleed.

HAMLET: *I dare not drink yet, madam. Soon I'll drink.*

QUEEN: *Come, let me wipe your face.*

LAERTES: *My lord, I'll hit him now.*

KING: *I don't think so.*

LAERTES: [Aside] *And yet it almost goes against my conscience.*

HAMLET: *Come for the third round, Laertes! You're wasting time. Thrust violently! I am afraid you treat me like a child.*

LAERTES: *You think so? Come on.* [They fence]

OSRIC: *Nothing, either way.*

LAERTES: *Here's a blow for you!*
    [Laertes wounds Hamlet. In scuffling, they change rapiers, and   Hamlet wounds Laertes]

KING: *Separate them! They are incensed!*

HAMLET: *No, do it again!*[The Queen falls]

OSRIC: *Look after the Queen over there!*

HORATIO: *They are both bleeding. How are you, my lord?*

OSRIC: *How are you, Laertes?*

LAERTES: *Well, I feel like a bird caught in its own trap, Osric. I am being justly killed by my own treachery.*

HAMLET: *How is the Queen doing?*

KING: *She fainted when she saw them both bleed.*

QUEEN: No, no! the drink, the drink!—O my dear Hamlet!—
    The drink, the drink! I am poison'd.   *[Dies.]*

310   HAMLET: O villainy! Ho! let the door be lock'd.
    Treachery! Seek it out.   *[Laertes falls.]*

LAERTES: It is here, Hamlet. Hamlet, thou art slain;
    No medicine in the world can do thee good.
    In thee there is not half an hour of life.
315   The treacherous instrument is in thy hand,
    Unbated and envenom'd. The foul practice
    Hath turn'd itself on me. Lo, here I lie,
    Never to rise again. Thy mother's poison'd.
    I can no more. The King, the King's to blame.

320   HAMLET: The point envenom'd too! Then, venom, to thy work.
    [Stabs the King.]

ALL: Treason! treason!

KING: O, yet defend me, friends! I am but hurt.

HAMLET: Here, thou incestuous, murderous, damned Dane,
    Drink off this potion! Is thy union here?
325   Follow my mother.   *[King dies.]*

LAERTES: He is justly served.
    It is a poison temper'd by himself.
    Exchange forgiveness with me, noble Hamlet.
    Mine and my father's death come not upon thee,
330   Nor thine on me!   *[Dies.]*

HAMLET: Heaven make thee free of it! I follow thee.
    I am dead, Horatio. Wretched Queen, adieu!
    You that look pale and tremble at this chance,
    That are but mutes or audience to this act,
335   Had I but time—as this fell sergeant, Death,
    Is strict in his arrest—O, I could tell you—

QUEEN: *No, no! The drink, the drink! Oh, my dear Hamlet! The drink, the drink! I have been poisoned!*   [The Queen dies]

HAMLET: *Oh, villainy! Quick, lock the door! Treachery! Uncover it!*
        [Osric exits. Laertes falls]

LAERTES: *It is here, Hamlet. Hamlet, you are dying! No medicine in the world can save you. You don't have half an hour left to live. The murder weapon is in your hand, unprotected and poisoned. The evil plot has turned itself on me. Behold, here I lie, never to rise again. Your mother's poisoned. I can speak no more. The King, the King's to blame!*

HAMLET: *The dagger's point poisoned, too! Then, poison, do your work!*
[Stabbing the King]

ALL: *Treason! Treason!*

KING: *Oh, defend me, friends! I am just wounded.*

HAMLET: *Here, you incestuous, murderous, damned Dane, drink this potion! Is this your marriage? Follow my mother!* [The King dies]

LAERTES: *He receives what he deserves. He mixed the poison himself. Exchange forgiveness with me, noble Hamlet. My death and my father's death will not be held against you, nor will your death be held against me.*   [Laertes dies]

HAMLET: *May God forgive you! I follow you. I am dying, Horatio! Unhappy queen, adieu! You who watch this scene, pale and trembling, you silent spectators, if I only had time—oh, this cruel officer, death, is strict in his arrest—oh, I could explain everything to you, but I must let it be. Horatio, I am dying, but you live. To those who want to know more, explain me and my reasons to them.*

But let it be. Horatio, I am dead;
Thou livest; report me and my cause aright
To the unsatisfied.

340 HORATIO: Never believe it.
I am more an antique Roman than a Dane.
Here's yet some liquor left.

HAMLET: As th'art a man,
Give me the cup. Let go! By heaven, I'll have't.
345 O God, Horatio, what a wounded name,
Things standing thus unknown, shall live behind me!
If thou didst ever hold me in thy heart,
Absent thee from felicity awhile,
And in this harsh world draw thy breath in pain,
350 To tell my story.
                [March afar off, and shot within.]
What warlike noise is this?

OSRIC: Young Fortinbras, with conquest come from Poland,
To the ambassadors of England gives
This warlike volley.

355 HAMLET: O, I die, Horatio!
The potent poison quite o'er-crows my spirit.
I cannot live to hear the news from England,
But I do prophesy the election lights
On Fortinbras. He has my dying voice.
360 So tell him, with the occurrents, more and less,
Which have solicited—The rest is silence.   [Dies.]

HORATIO: Now cracks a noble heart. Good night, sweet prince,
And flights of angels sing thee to thy rest!
           [March within.]
Why does the drum come hither?

[Enter Fortinbras and English Ambassadors, with Drum, Colours, and
Attendants.]

HORATIO: *Don't believe it. I'd rather commit suicide like the ancient Romans than lose my honor like the Danes. Here's still some liquor left.*

HAMLET: *You are a man; give me the cup! Let go! By heaven, I'll have it! Oh, God, Horatio, what a bad reputation would I leave behind if the truth was never explained! If you ever loved me, suffer for a while, and endure this harsh world to tell my story.*
[Marching can be heard in the distance. Shots are heard]
What warlike noise is this?

OSRIC: *Young Fortinbras has victoriously returned from Poland and fired his cannons to welcome the English ambassadors.*

HAMLET: *Oh, I'm dying, Horatio. The potent poison triumphs over my spirit. I will not live long enough to hear the news from England, but I do prophesy that Fortinbras will become the new King. He has my dying vote. So, tell him what you can about what has happened, more or less. The rest is silence.* [He dies]

HORATIO: *There breaks a noble heart. Good night, sweet prince. May flights of angels sing you to your rest!*
[The sound of marching is heard]
Why does the drum come this way?

[Fortinbras and the English ambassadors enter drums, flags, and Attendants]

365   FORTINBRAS: Where is this sight?

HORATIO: What is it you will see?
       If aught of woe or wonder, cease your search.

FORTINBRAS: This quarry cries on havoc. O proud Death,
       What feast is toward in thine eternal cell
370   That thou so many princes at a shot
       So bloodily hast struck?

AMBASSADOR: The sight is dismal;
       And our affairs from England come too late.
       The ears are senseless that should give us hearing
375   To tell him his commandment is fulfill'd
       That Rosencrantz and Guildenstern are dead.
       Where should we have our thanks?

HORATIO: Not from his mouth,
       Had it the ability of life to thank you.
380   He never gave commandment for their death.
       But since, so jump upon this bloody question,
       You from the Polack wars, and you from England,
       Are here arrived, give order that these bodies
       High on a stage be placed to the view;
385   And let me speak to the yet unknowing world
       How these things came about. So shall you hear
       Of carnal, bloody and unnatural acts;
       Of accidental judgments, casual slaughters;
       Of deaths put on by cunning and forced cause;
390   And, in this upshot, purposes mistook
       Fall'n on the inventors' heads. All this can I
       Truly deliver.

FORTINBRAS: Let us haste to hear it,
       And call the noblest to the audience.
395   For me, with sorrow I embrace my fortune.
       I have some rights of memory in this kingdom,
       Which now, to claim my vantage doth invite me.

FORTINBRAS: *What is this sight?*

HORATIO: *What do you want to see? If you're looking to see suffering and destruction, you have found it.*

FORTINBRAS: *This pile of corpses proclaims senseless slaughter. Oh, proud Death, what kind of feast are you preparing in your hall of eternity that caused you to kill so many nobleman brutally at once?*

AMBASSADOR: *This sight is dreadful, and our news from England has come too late. The ears that should hear how we have fulfilled our orders and killed Guildenstern and Rosencrantz are lifeless. How will we receive thanks?*

HORATIO: *Not from the King, even if he had the ability to thank you. He never ordered them to be killed. But since you have arrived just in time for this bloody spectacle—you from the war on Poland, and you from the King of England—please give orders that these bodies will be placed on a high stage for everyone to see. And allow me to explain to the ignorant public how these events came about. Then, you will hear about incestuous, murderous, and unnatural acts, about retribution and accidental killings, about deaths caused by treachery and violent schemes, and, to this effect, about faulty plots that backfired. All this, I can truthfully relate.*

FORTINBRAS: *Let us hear it immediately. Call the nobles together. As for me, with sorrow I embrace my good fortune. I have a right to the Danish crown that has not been forgotten, which I am now claiming.*

HORATIO: Of that I shall have also cause to speak,
And from his mouth whose voice will draw on more.
400 But let this same be presently perform'd,
Even while men's minds are wild, lest more mischance
On plots and errors happen.

FORTINBRAS: Let four captains
Bear Hamlet like a soldier to the stage;
405 For he was likely, had he been put on,
To have proved most royal; and, for his passage,
The soldiers' music and the rites of war
Speak loudly for him.
Take up the bodies. Such a sight as this
410 Becomes the field, but here shows much amiss.
Go, bid the soldiers shoot.
[Exeunt marching; after the which a peal of ordnance is shot off.]

THE END

HORATIO: *I will also address this issue, and I will speak on behalf of someone whose vote will recruit others for your support. But let the rituals be performed at once, even while confusion exists among our men, to make sure no more disasters and mistakes occur.*

FORTINBRAS: *Let four captains carry Hamlet like a soldier to the platform. If he had lived to become King, he would haven proven to be truly royal. Let military music and war honors praise him loudly in his passing. Take up the bodies. A sight like this belongs on the battle-field. It is inappropriate here. Go, tell the soldiers to shoot!*

[A march for the dead sounds. All exit, carrying off the bodies. A salute is fired]

STUDY GUIDE

Act I, Scene I

1. What background information is provided in this scene? Include an explanation of the quarrel with Norway.

2. What atmosphere is created by this scene? How?

3. Why has Horatio been asked to join the soldiers on the midnight watch? What has he decided to do?

4. How does the reader know this ghost is not a hallucination?

5. How could this ghost be explained as a warning of coming evil?

6. Describe each of the following characters and explain their relationship to one another:

   Old Hamlet -

   Horatio -

   Fortinbras -

Act I, Scene II

1. Why is Hamlet upset?

2. What is your opinion of the marriage of Gertrude and Claudius? Consider the customs of the time.

3. Why didn't Hamlet become king when his father died?

4. Describe Claudius' personality and attitude.

5. How does Hamlet describe his father?

6. What are Hamlet's feelings about his mother and his new father, Claudius? Consider the quotation, "frailty, thy name is woman!"

7. Explain Hamlet's state of mind. Consider the following quote: "O that this too, too solid flesh would melt, thaw, and resolve itself into a dew."

8. What does the king want Hamlet to do? Why does Hamlet give up his plan to return to Wittenburg so easily?

Act I, Scene III
1. Describe the personalities, attitudes, and values of Laertes and Polonius.

2. Explain the reasons that Laertes and Polonius give Ophelia to convince her not to trust Hamlet's love.

3. Evaluate Polonius' advice to his son.

4. What is comical about Polonius?

Act I, Scene IV
1. What are the points of Hamlet's long speech?

2. Why do Hamlet's friends fear for his safety?

Act I, Scene V
1. According to the ghost, what has happened? What does the ghost want Hamlet to do?

2. Describe Hamlet's reaction to the ghost.

3. Discuss the nature of the ghost; is it a devil or an angel in the form of King Hamlet, who is in purgatory?

4. In your opinion, is Hamlet mad?

Act II, Scene I

1. List what has occurred between Act I and Act II.

2. What do Ophelia and Polonius decide about Hamlet's odd behavior?

3. How do you think Ophelia treated Hamlet? Imagine you are Ophelia. How would you treat Hamlet? Or, imagine that you are Hamlet. How would you like Ophelia to treat you?

4. Do you think Polonius follows the advice he give to Laertes, "to thy own self be true," regarding the instructions he gives to Reynaldo?

Act II, Scene II

1. How does this scene prepare the reader for future scenes?

2. Compare and contrast Hamlet and Fortinbras. Why has Fortinbras changed his plan to attack Denmark?

3. Why does Claudius hire Rosencrantz and Guildenstern as spies?

4. How does Hamlet feel about Rosencrantz and Guildenstern? Why?

5. What is the story of Hecuba and Priam? Explain the story's significance. What is Hamlet's reaction to the story? Explain.

6. Explain Hamlet's state of mind as revealed by his soliloquy. What do Hamlet's remarks to Polonius tell about Hamlet's thoughts? In his dialogue with Rosencrantz and Guildenstern, Hamlet reveals a change he has undergone. What is it?

7. What idea does Hamlet get from having the players in the court?

Act III, Scene I

1. What is Claudius' opinion of Hamlet's madness? What action does Claudius decide to take? Why?

2. To what idea of Hamlet's madness does Polonius cling? Why?

3. Describe and explain Hamlet's treatment of Ophelia. Is Hamlet aware that he's being watched?

4. What is your opinion of Ophelia's reactions to her father's ideas?

5. What does Ophelia reveal about Hamlet?

6. What ideas are suggested in Hamlet's speech "To be, or not to be . . ."?

7. What gives a universal quality to this speech?

Act III, Scene II

1. Why does Hamlet trust and admire Horatio?

2. When Hamlet speaks to Ophelia, what shows that he has lost faith in her?

3. What does the play-within-a-play reveal?

4. What is Hamlet's attitude toward Rosencrantz and Guildenstern?

5. What is Hamlet's state of mind at this point in the play?

Act III, Scene III

1. How does Claudius feel about himself? What has changed?

2. Why doesn't Hamlet kill Claudius when he has the opportunity?

Act III, Scene IV
1. How does Hamlet behave towards his mother? What changes after the ghost?

2. What happens to Polonius?

3. Describe Gertrude's reactions. Do you think she is guilty in any way? Explain.

4. Do you believe Hamlet when he says he is only pretending to be mad?

Act IV, Scene I
1. After learning of Polonius' death, what is the king's reaction? Why?

2. Is Gertrude loyal to Claudius?

Act IV, Scene II
1. How does Hamlet treat Rosencrantz and Guildenstern? Why?

Act IV, Scene III
1. What does the king's opening soliloquy reveal? What contradiction between his surface behavior and his real feelings is apparent?

2. How does Hamlet react to being sent to England?

Act IV, Scene IV
1. What effect does meeting Fortinbras have on Hamlet?

2. What does Hamlet's soliloquy reveal about his present idea of himself?

Act IV, Scene V

1. Describe Ophelia's behavior. How does Claudius react to Ophelia?

2. Describe Laertes' response to his father's death. How is he a foil for Hamlet?

3. What happens to Ophelia?

Act IV, Scene VI

1. What news is revealed in Hamlet's letter to Horatio? What does this reveal about Hamlet?

2. What will happen to Rosencrantz and Guildenstern?

Act IV, Scene VII

1. Explain the plan between Laertes and Claudius. How is Claudius taking advantage of Laertes?

Act V, Scene I

1. Who is Yorick? How has Hamlet's attitude toward death changed?

2. What dramatic function do the gravediggers have, and what theme do they express?

3. Explain Hamlet's reaction to Laertes' behavior at Ophelia's funeral?

Act V, Scene II

1. Explain Hamlet's remarks to Horatio about fate.

2. Describe Hamlet's state of mind before he fences with Laertes. How has Hamlet changed?

3. Why does Hamlet apologize to Laertes?

4. Explain who dies in the end and how each person dies.

    Hamlet -

    Laertes -

    The queen -

    The king -

5. Why does the play have to end this way?

6. Who does Hamlet appoint to tell his story to the world? Why?

7. Who will be the next King of Denmark?